T0305067

Governments, Competition and Utility Regulation

Governments, Competition and Utility Regulation

Edited by

Colin Robinson

Emeritus Professor of Economics, University of Surrey, UK

In Association with the Institute of Economic Affairs and the London Business School

Edward Elgar

Cheltenham, UK • Northampton, MA, USA

Published by
Edward Elgar Publishing Limited
Glensanda House
Montpellier Parade
Cheltenham
Glos GL50 1UA
UK

Edward Elgar Publishing, Inc.
136 West Street
Suite 202
Northampton
Massachusetts 01060
USA

A catalogue record for this book
is available from the British Library

ISBN 1 84542 209 0

Printed and bound in Great Britain by MPG Books Ltd, Bodmin, Cornwall

Contents

Figures and tables

FIGURES

TABLES

Notes on the authors

David Arculus has been Chairman of the Better Regulation Task Force since 2002. He is also Chairman of O2, a non-executive director of Barclays plc, a delegate of the Finance Committee at Oxford University Press, a member of the Council of the Confederation of British Industry and an advisory board member, Veronis Suhler Stevenson International Limited.

Chris Bolt was appointed by the Secretary of State for Transport as the statutory arbiter for the London Underground PPP Agreements from 31 December 2002 for four years. He was appointed as the Chairman of the Office of Rail Regulation from 5 July 2004, for a five-year term.

An economist by training, his career has included senior roles in both the public and private sector. From 1988 to 1989, he was part of the DoE team responsible for privatizing the water industry and establishing its initial regulatory regime. He then joined Ofwat, on its establishment, as Head of Economic Regulation. He moved to ORR in a similar role in 1994 and was appointed as Rail Regulator in December 1998.

In July 1999, he joined Transco plc, and became Regulation and Corporate Affairs Director. He was appointed to a new role of Group Director, Regulation and Public Policy in Transco's parent company, Lattice Group plc, in November 2001. He left Lattice in October 2002 on completion of its merger with National Grid Group plc.

Robert W. Crandall is a Senior Fellow in the Economic Studies Program of the Brookings Institution. His research has focused on telecommunications regulation, cable television regulation, the effects of trade policy in the steel and automobile industries, environmental policy, and the changing regional structure of the US economy. His current research focuses on competition in the telecommunications sector and the development of broadband services. His book on universal service, *Who Pays for 'Universal Service'?* (written with Leonard Waverman of the London Business School), was published by Brookings in 2000. He was also a contributor, with Professor Jerry Hausman of MIT, to the recently published Brookings book, *Deregulation of Network Industries: What's Next?* (edited by Sam Peltzman and Clifford Winston).

Crandall was a Johnson Research Fellow at the Brookings Institution and has taught economics at Northwestern University, MIT, the University of Maryland, the George Washington University, and the Stanford in Washington program. Before assuming his current position at Brookings, he served as assistant, acting, and deputy director for the Council on Wage and Price Stability.

Crandall is the author of *Talk is Cheap: The Promise of Regulatory Reform in North American Telecommunications* (with Leonard Waverman) (Brookings Institution, 1996); *Cable TV: Regulation or Competition?* (with Harold Furchtgott-Roth) (Brookings Institution, 1996); *The Extra Mile: Rethinking Energy Policy for Automotive Transportation* (with Pietro Nivola) (Brookings Institution, 1995); *After the Breakup: The U.S. Telecommunications Sector in a More Competitive Era; Manufacturing on the Move; Changing the Rules: Technological Change. International Competition, and Regulation in Communications* (with Kenneth Flamm) (Brookings Institution, 1991), and numerous journal articles.

He holds an MS and a Ph.D. in economics from Northwestern University.

Philip Fletcher was appointed for a renewable five-year term as Director General of Water Services on 1 August 2000.

His previous career was based mainly in central government public service, with an emphasis on financial issues.

Born in 1946, Philip's immediate previous post was as Receiver for the Metropolitan Police District from 1996. The Receiver had statutory responsibility for the administration of the Metropolitan Police Fund. He was a full member of the Commissioner's management team but was separately accountable to the Home Secretary. He was in charge of finance, procurement, internal audit and property services, and the legal owner of all Metropolitan Police property. In that role, he managed projects to improve financial management and review and outsource support services.

Earlier, he was a founder member of the Department of the Environment from 1970. His work there covered such issues as planning and land use, urban regeneration, rural issues, local government, finance and private housing. As Director of Central Finance there, he took part in the issues leading up to the privatization of the water industry in England and Wales in 1989.

Fletcher was appointed Chief Executive of PSA Services (the former Property Services Agency) in 1993. When he had completed its privatization, he transferred to head the Cities and Countryside Group in DoE in 1994.

Educated at Marlborough College and Oxford University, Philip Fletcher is married with one daughter. He is a lay reader in the Church of England and his hobbies include walking and bird-watching.

Annegret Groebel was born in 1960 in Hanau (Main), Germany. From 1981 to 1986 she was a student at the University of Heidelberg (MA in economics) and at the University Paris IX (Dauphine), France. Her Ph.D. in economics was at the University of Mannheim. She joined the BMPT (Federal Ministry of Posts and Telecommunications) in 1997 as a junior representative in the Special Network Access incl. Interconnection section. From 1998 to 2001 she was Vice-Chair of Ruling Chamber 4 – Special Network Access incl. Interconnection of the Regulatory Authority for Telecommunications and Posts (RegTP). She was Research Fellow at the Global Communications Consortium (Director: Prof. Len Waverman) of London Business School from October to December 2000. Since May 2001 she has been Head of the Co-ordination of RegTP's International Activities/Bodies section and since July 2002 she has been a member of the IRG Secretariat and Chair of the IRG Fixed-Network Working Group.

Frédéric Jenny is a Professor in the Economics Department and Director of International Relations at ESSEC. He has doctorates from Université de Paris II and Harvard. Since 1994 he has been Chairman of the Committee on Competition Law and Policy of the Organization for Economic Co-operation and Development; he is a Judge on the French Supreme Court and the former Vice Chairman of the Competition Council; and he chaired the World Trade Organization's Task Force on the Interaction between Commerce and Competition Policy until 2003. His principal research interests are in the relationship between structure and performance in France and other European countries and in European antitrust legislation. He has published numerous books and papers on microeconomic theory, competition policy, mergers and regulation.

Stephen Littlechild was UK Director General of Electricity Supply (DGES) for nearly ten years. He was in charge of the Office of Electricity Regulation (Offer), from its foundation in September 1989, to December 1998. Previously he advised ministers on the regulatory regime for British Telecom and the water industry. In 1983, he proposed the RPI–X approach to price controls, which has since been widely adopted for regulating utilities in the UK and overseas. He was a member of the Monopolies and Mergers Commission for six years. Before 1989, he acted as a consultant to public and private sector organizations including HM Treasury, several UK government departments.

NZ Treasury, the World Bank, AT & T, Bell Telephone Laboratories and General Motors.

Professor Littlechild graduated as Bachelor of Commerce from the University of Birmingham in 1964. He did postgraduate work at Stanford University (Operations Research program) 1965–67, Northwestern University (Engineering faculty) 1967–68, and the University of Texas at Austin (Graduate School of Business) 1968–69, obtaining his Ph.D. there in 1969. He did postdoctoral research at UCLA and Northwestern. From 1972 to 1975 he was Professor of Applied Economics and Head of the Economics, Econometrics, Statistics and Marketing Subject Group at Aston Management Centre. He was Professor of Commerce and Head of the Department of Industrial Economics and Business Studies at the University of Birmingham from 1975 to 1989. During 1979–80 he was a visiting professor or research fellow at Stanford University, New York University, University of Chicago and Virginia Polytechnic and Institute. Since 1994, he has been an honorary professor in the University of Birmingham Business School.

Professor Littlechild's publications include *Operational Research for Managers* (Philip Allan, 1976), *The Fallacy of the Mixed Economy* (IEA, 1978), *Elements of Telecommunications Economics* (Institute of Electrical Engineers, 1979), *Energy Strategies for the UK* (with K.G. Vaidya) (Allen and Unwin, 1982), *Regulation of British Telecommunications' Profitability* (Department of Industry, 1983), *Economic Regulation of Privatized Water Authorities* (HMSO, 1986), and over 60 articles.

Since stepping down as DGES at the end of 1998, Professor Littlechild has engaged in lecturing and consulting for government departments, regulatory bodies, universities, research institutes, regulated companies and international organizations including the World Bank. He has been involved since January 1999 in policy discussions in the USA, Mexico, India, Brazil, Australia, New Zealand, Poland, Thailand, the Philippines, Spain, Germany, Argentina and Italy, as well as in the UK. In May 1999, Stanford University conferred on him the Zale Award for Scholarship and Public Service. He was awarded an Honorary D.Sc. by the University of Birmingham in 2001.

Eileen Marshall worked as a stockbroker in the City of London before becoming a university lecturer, then senior lecturer, in industrial economics. Her research specialism was in energy economics and she acted as consultant to many companies and bodies.

Dr Marshall took up the position of Director of Regulation and Business Affairs with the Office of Electricity Regulation (Offer) in October 1989. In April 1994, she was appointed Chief Economic Adviser and Director of Regulation and Business Affairs at the Office of Gas Supply (Ofgas). Her responsibilities covered the full range of Ofgas policy issues, including the setting of price controls and the introduction of domestic competition. In January 1997, while retaining her previous responsibilities at Ofgas, Dr Marshall became a part-time economic adviser to Offer, and from autumn 1997 led the Review of Electricity Trading Arrangements. In January 1998, she was awarded the CBE for services to regulatory policy. In June 1999, the former regulatory offices, Ofgas and Offer, were merged and renamed the Office of Gas and Electricity Markets (Ofgem). Dr Marshall took up the new position of Deputy Director General, with particular responsibility for competition and trading arrangements.

Colin Mayer is Peter Moores Professor of Management Studies at the Saïd Business School, University of Oxford, Professorial Fellow at Wadham College, Oxford and Director of the Oxford Financial Research Centre. He was a Harkness Fellow at Harvard University (1979/80), a Houblon–Norman Fellow at the Bank of England (1989) and the first Leo Goldschmidt Visiting Professor in Corporate Governance at the Solvay Business School, Université Libre de Bruxelles (2000 and 2001). He is a member of the Executive Committee of the Royal Economic Society, and an Inaugural Fellow and Board Member of the European Corporate Governance Institute (ECGI) in Brussels. He is a director of OXERA Holdings Ltd, a delegate and Chairman of the Audit Committee of the Oxford University Press, an Honorary Fellow of St Anne's College, Oxford, a governor of St Paul's School, London and is on the editorial board of numerous economics and finance journals.

He researches in the fields of corporate finance, governance, regulation and taxation. He has worked on international comparisons of financial systems and corporate governance and their effects on the financing and control of corporations. He also researches financial aspects of the regulation of utilities and the regulation of financial institutions.

Recent publications include 'Financing the New Economy: Financial Institutions and Corporate Governance', *Information Economics and Policy*, 2002, *Asset Management and Investor Protection*, with Julian Franks and Luis Correia da Silva, Oxford University Press, 2002, and 'Finance, Investment and Growth', with Wendy Carlin, *Journal of Financial Economics*, 2003.

Sir Derek Morris is Provost of Oriel College, Oxford. He was previously Chairman of the Competition Commission (formerly the Monopolies and Mergers Commission). He first joined the MMC in 1991 as a member, becoming a deputy chairman in 1995 and chairman in 1998. Having studied Politics, Philosophy and Economics at Oxford from 1964 to 1967, and then for a D.Phil. in economics at Nuffield College, he took up a Research Fellowship at the Centre for Business and Industrial Studies at Warwick University. Then, from 1970 until 1998, he was fellow and tutor in economics at Oriel College, Oxford.

During this time he wrote numerous books and articles, primarily in the field of industrial economics. Books included *The Economic System in the UK* (third edition, Oxford University Press, 1985); *Unquoted Companies* (Macmillan, 1984); *Industrial Economics and Organisation* (Oxford University Press, 1979, second edition, 1991); and *Chinese State Owned Enterprises and Economic Reform* (the last three co-written by D. Hay). Other academic activities included chairmanship of the Economics sub-faculty and then Social Studies faculty at Oxford and editorial board responsibilities for the *Journal of Industrial Economics*, the *Oxford Review of Economic Policy*, *Oxford Economic Papers*, among others.

Other activities have included three years on secondment as Economic Director of the National Economic Development Council, and Chairman of Oxford Economic and Social Research. He has also been involved for over 20 years in various types of advisory and consultancy work, initially in the field of competition policy but more recently for the Asian Development Bank, in helping to design and implement economic reform measures in China and Central Asia.

Derek Morris was knighted in the 2002 New Year Honours List.

Jrissy Motis is a Ph.D. student at the Universite des Sciences Sociales de Toulouse.

Damien Neven is Professor of International Economics at the Graduate Institute of International Studies, Geneva. Previous appointments include Professeur Ordinaire, Universite de Lausanne, Professor, Universite de Liege and Associate Professor of Economics, INSEAD. His principal research interests are in industrial organization and international integration. Current research is focussed on the co-ordination of antitrust policies across jurisdictions, merger control and the antitrust analysis of sports competitions. He has been a member of the Economic Advisory Committee to the Directorate General for Competition of the EU since 1996.

Sir Charles Nicholson has, in a 35-year career with BP plc, held a variety of posts. In 1975 he became involved with the development of BP's position in the USA and in 1979 moved to New York as Vice-President of Government and Public Affairs. He was later appointed Head of Corporate Communications in London and currently holds the position of Group Senior Advisor. He has been closely involved with the development of BP's position on the environment and sustainable development. He chairs the Climate & Energy Groups of the World Business Council for Sustainable Development and the European Round Table.

He is a graduate of Oxford University and the Sloan Fellowship Programme.

Sir Geoffrey Owen is senior fellow at the Inter-Disciplinary Institute for Management, London School of Economics, where he specializes in issues relating to corporate strategy, corporate performance and industry evolution. Before joining the LSE in 1991, Sir Geoffrey spent most of his earlier career as a journalist on the _Financial Times_, where he held several posts, including US Correspondent and Industrial Editor, before being appointed Editor in 1980. He served as Editor for ten years. Between 1967 and 1972 he worked first as an executive in the Industrial Reorganisation Corporation and then in the international division of British Leyland Motor Corporation. His most recent book is _From Empire to Europe: the decline and revival of British industry since the second world war_ (HarperCollins, 1999).

Colin Robinson was educated at the University of Manchester, and then worked for 11 years as a business economist before being appointed, in 1968, to the Chair of Economics at the University of Surrey where he founded the Department of Economics and is now Emeritus Professor.

He is a Fellow of the Royal Statistical Society, Fellow of the Society of Business Economists and Fellow of the Institute of Energy. He is a past member of the Monopolies and Mergers Commission and of the Secretary of State for Energy's Advisory Council on Research and Development (ACORD). He was named British Institute of Energy Economics 'Energy Economist of the Year' in 1992 and in 1998 received the award of 'Outstanding Contribution to the Profession and its Literature' from the International Association of Energy Economics.

Robinson is sole or joint author of 23 books and monographs and over 150 papers, including studies of North Sea oil and gas, the British coal industry, energy policy, nuclear power, energy privatization programmes and the international oil, gas and coal markets. He has appeared as expert witness in numerous legal proceedings in Britain and abroad.

He was Editorial Director of the Institute of Economic Affairs from 1992 to 2002 and is a member of the Institute's Academic Advisory Council and a Trustee of the Wincott Foundation.

Paul Seabright is Professor of Economics at the Universite des Sciences Sociales de Toulouse, having previously been Reader in Economics at the University of Cambridge, 1999–2001, Lecturer in Economics at the College of Europe, Bruges, 1998–99 and Assistant Director of Research, University of Cambridge, 1988–99. His main research interests are in microeconomic theory, industrial and competition policy, development economics, industrial policy in transition economies, state aids to industry, economic geography and European integration. He is Managing Editor, *Economic Policy*, a member of the European Commission's Academic Advisory Panel on Competition Policy Questions, and a Commissioner on the Independent Commission on UK membership of the euro appointed by the Britain in Europe group.

Jacques Steenbergen is a partner in the European Union practice group in Brussels. He practises competition and European law. He teaches competition law at the University of Louvain (KUL), has been a regular visiting professor at the University of Amsterdam and is chairman of the Board of Editors of the Belgian–Dutch law review *SEW*. He is an active member of various professional and scientific organizations. He has published extensively on European Community and economic law and lectures at seminars and universities in Europe, the USA and China. Jacques Steenbergen received his first degrees in law, philosophy and economics from the University of Antwerp (UFSIA), and his Master's and Doctoral degrees in law from the University of Louvain (KUL).

Sir John Vickers became Director General of Fair Trading on 1 October 2000 and OFT Chairman on 1 April 2003. Previously he spent two and a half years as Chief Economist at the Bank of England, and was a member of the Monetary Policy Committee. Most of his career has been spent teaching economics at Oxford University, where he was made the Drummond Professor of Political Economy in 1991. He has published widely on privatization, regulation and competition. He is a fellow of the British Academy, the Econometric Society and All Souls College, Oxford. He was knighted in 2005.

Leonard Waverman is Professor and Chair of Economics as well as Director of the Centre for the Network Economy at the London Business School. He has recently been appointed Director of the Economic and Social Research Council's E-Society Research Programme and has been awarded a four-year £1.1 million research grant from the Leverhulme Trust to examine 'the social/economic impact of information and communication technology' – why don't we see the 'New Economy' in Europe?

He received his B.Comm. and MA from the University of Toronto, and his Ph.D. from MIT. His teaching specialities are in telecommunications, antitrust and energy economics. A recent paper is 'Telecommunications

Infrastructure and Economic Development: A Simultaneous Approach'
with H. Roeller, *American Economic Review*, September 2001.

Professor Waverman is a non-executive board member of GEMA
– the UK's electricity and gas market authority. He is a member of the
Scientific Advisory Board of the German Institute for Economic Research
in Berlin (DIW). He is a Fellow of Columbia University's Centre for Tele-
Information. He was on the Advisory Committee introducing Competition
in Ontario's Electricity system (1995–96), a part-time board member of
the Ontario Energy Board, as well as of the Ontario Telephone Service
Commission, and a member of the National Association of Regulatory
Utility Commissioners (NARUC) for six years.

Professor Waverman advises several European governments on
competition, communications and innovation policies. He has consulted
extensively in North America, Europe and Australia and has appeared
before regulatory authorities, competition tribunals, agencies and courts.
Recently, he represented Schneider Electric at the European Commission
and at the Court of First Instance in Luxemburg in their attempt to purchase
Legrand.

Professor Waverman has received the honour of Chevalier dans l'Ordre
des Palmes Academiques of the government of France.

Tom Winsor was appointed Rail Regulator and International Rail Regulator
for five years with effect from 5 July 1999.

He was born in 1957 and brought up in Broughty Ferry, Dundee. He was
educated at Grove Academy, Broughty Ferry and then at the University of
Edinburgh, where he graduated with an LL.B. (Scots Law) in 1979. As a
solicitor, he qualified first in Scotland, where he is a Writer to the Signet, and
subsequently in England and Wales. After general practice in Dundee, he
took a postgraduate qualification in oil and gas law at the Centre for Energy,
Petroleum and Mineral Law and Policy of the University of Dundee.

In the course of his legal career, Tom Winsor specialized first in UK and
international oil and gas law, later adding electricity, regulation, railways
and public law. He joined Denton Hall as a partner in 1991, where he
was responsible for the design of the regulatory regime for the electricity
industry in Northern Ireland. In 1993 he was seconded to the Office of the
Rail Regulator as Chief Legal Adviser and later as General Counsel. He
returned to his partnership at Denton Hall in 1995 as head of the railways
department, part of the firm's energy and infrastructure practice.

Tom Winsor is an honorary lecturer at the Centre for Energy, Petroleum
and Mineral Law and Policy of the University of Dundee, where he directed
the UK Oil and Gas Law summer course from 1993 to 1997. He is married,

with one daughter, and lives in Kent, travelling daily to his office in London by train.

Clifford Winston, a Senior Fellow in the Economic Studies programme, has been with the Brookings Institution since 1984. He specializes in analysis of industrial organization, regulation and transportation.

Winston has also been co-editor of the annual microeconomic edition of *Brookings Papers on Economic Activity*. Before his fellowship at Brookings, he was Associate Professor at the Transportation Systems Division of Massachusetts Institute of Technology's Department of Civil Engineering.

The author of numerous books and articles, Winston has published *Deregulation of Network Industries: What's Next?*, with Sam Peltzman (AEI–Brookings, 2000); *Essays in Transportation Economics and Policy: A Handbook in Honor of John R. Meyer*, with Jose A. Gomez-Ibanez and William B. Tye (1999); *Alternate Route: Toward Efficient Urban Transportation*, with Chad Shirley (1998); *The Evolution of the Airline Industry*, with Steven A. Morrison (1995); *The Economic Effects of Surface Freight Deregulation*, with Thomas M. Corsi, Curtis M. Grimm and Carol A. Evans (1990); *Road Work: A New Highway Pricing and Investment Policy*, with Kenneth A. Small and Carol Evans (1989); *Liability: Perspectives and Policy*, with Robert E. Litan (1988); *Blind Intersection? Policy and the Automobile Industry*, co-author (1987); and *The Economic Effects of Airline Deregulation*, with Steven Morrison (1986). His articles have appeared in such journals as *American Economic Review*, *Econometrica*, *Review of Economics and Statistics*, *Journal of Economic Literature*, *Bell Journal of Economics* and the *Rand Journal of Economics*.

Dr Winston received his A.B. in economics from the University of California at Berkeley in 1974, his M.Sc. from the London School of Economics in 1975, and his Ph.D. in economics from U.C. Berkeley in 1979.

Introduction

Colin Robinson

The thirteenth series of the Beesley Lectures on Regulation was held in the autumn of 2003. The Lectures, arranged by the London Business School and the Institute of Economic Affairs, are named after the late Professor Michael Beesley, who originated the series in 1991 and was the main organizer until his death in September 1999. Lectures given in the 2003 series are reprinted in this volume: all have been revised by their authors for publication. Also included in this volume are the comments on the lectures made by the chairman of each session, acting in his or her capacity as discussant.

Analysis of regulation of the privatized utilities in Britain – gas, electricity, water, telecommunications and the railways – constitutes the core of the series, as it has done from the beginning. But the emphasis on experience in other countries and on international issues has increased, as was Michael Beesley's intention. In the 2003 series, in addition to papers on the British utilities, there were lectures on competition policy and trade, on US experience of deregulation, on emissions trading and on European merger control.

Chapter 1 is by Professor Frédéric Jenny, of the Conseil de la Concurrence in Paris, who has studied in great detail the debate within the World Trade Organization (WTO) on whether international trade rules should be complemented by competition rules. Jenny argues that transnational anticompetitive practices, in particular 'hardcore cartels', impose significant costs on developing countries and undermine attempts to liberalize trade. However, because there is a public good aspect to the elimination of these practices, countries negotiating in a WTO round may be unwilling to make concessions on other issues to secure the benefits of increased competition. Jenny claims that the competition agreement suggested by the European Union under the Cancun negotiations imposed too high costs on small developing countries for it to be acceptable. Nevertheless, says Jenny, although the Cancun Ministerial conference failed to deal with these issues, compromises would be possible. For example, there could be a non-binding agreement, or an agreement under which WTO members could join when they were prepared to do so, or an agreement that allowed 'members to choose their level of commitment to the competition issue'.

Sir Geoffrey Owen, of the London School of Economics, commenting on Jenny's paper, describes transnational cartels as a 'blight on the world trading system'. Bilateral agreements among national competition authorities will not do, says Owen, because they will be confined to advanced countries with well-developed competition laws. A multilateral solution is therefore essential. Rather than trying to rush developing countries into agreements, the more developed countries should try to foster a greater understanding of the benefits from action against cartels. Furthermore, multinational companies should look into their own activities to ensure they do not 'run counter to their rhetorical commitments' to benefit the world.

In Chapter 2, Robert Crandall and Clifford Winston, of the Brookings Institution, consider whether antitrust policy enhances consumer welfare. The paper, which was presented in the lecture series by Winston, was first published in the *Journal of Economic Perspectives*, volume 17, no. 4 and is reproduced here by permission. The authors point out that economic theory, which is very fertile in demonstrating that various actions by firms can be interpreted as either procompetitive or anticompetitive, offers little policy guidance. The empirical evidence is therefore crucial. Crandall and Winston review that evidence and conclude that US antitrust policy appears to have been ineffective: among the reasons are the excessive duration of monopolization cases, which means that issues change while cases are being pursued, and the power of the market in curbing anticompetitive practices, which leaves little for antitrust to do. In the short term, the competition authorities should concentrate on 'the most significant and egregious violations'. More research is required into why some policies have succeeded and other have failed.

David Arculus, Chairman of the UK's Better Regulation Task Force (BRTF), looks at some of the lessons of the failures of US antitrust policies for government departments and regulatory bodies that wish to impose regulations in Britain. He sets out the principles of good regulation and the procedures the BRTF has put in place, and stresses the importance of thinking about alternatives to regulation: the Task Force has deliberately tried to make it more difficult for government to introduce new regulations. Government should concentrate on outcomes and leave the market to find the way to achieve the desired results.

Chapter 3, about efficiencies in merger control, is written by Jrissy Motis (IDEI), Damien Neven (GIIS, Geneva) and Paul Seabright (University of Toulouse). It was presented in the Beesley Lecture series by Neven. The authors argue that a better understanding and treatment of efficiencies is essential if EU merger control is to be improved: the present EU approach is likely to lead to significant type II errors (allowing anticompetitive mergers) as well as type I errors (prohibiting or imposing conditions on procompetitive mergers). In particular, the evaluation of synergies in mergers needs to be improved. For instance, the competition authorities could ask firms why they propose to undertake a merger rather than carrying out some alternative form of corporate reorganization. The reallocation of intangible assets may be an important source of synergies but, regardless of whether or not it is, it would be advantageous for the authorities to enquire directly into management's view of the sources of gains to shareholders and then to judge to what extent those gains can be achieved without significant costs to consumers.

Sir John Vickers, of the Office of Fair Trading (OFT), comments on the paper from the OFT's viewpoint. He argues that efficiency assessments enter into the OFT's work both when it determines whether there is likely to be a substantial lessening of competition (SLC) and also when it assesses whether, even if there is an adverse SLC verdict, there are likely to be sufficient customer benefits to offset it: the OFT must necessarily be demanding when investigating claims about prospective efficiency gains. It already asks for the business case for a merger. According to Vickers, efficiency considerations fit more easily into an SLC-based regime than if the test is based on dominance.

Chapter 4 is a description and analysis of the UK and EU emissions trading regimes by Sir Charles Nicholson of BP plc. Nicholson explains the two main types of trading systems (allowance trading and baseline and credit trading) and points out that such markets are in their infancy as means of reducing carbon dioxide emissions. The UK's system, a voluntary regime starting in 2002, in Nicholson's view had a successful first year. The EU scheme, which begins in 2005, will be far-reaching and mandatory: about 95 per cent of allowances to emit carbon dioxide will be allocated free of charge. The trend towards trading systems applies not just to the developed world – seven regions of China are adopting market-based emissions trading schemes. Nicholson points out some of the uncertainties in how the EU scheme will work – for example, whether some accession states will opt out and whether allocations will be challenged in the courts. But, he says, it offers a chance to meet Kyoto targets.

Colin Robinson (University of Surrey) comments on some of the implicit assumptions underlying emissions trading schemes. For example, it is assumed that a global warming trend has been established, whereas the evidence is unclear. Second, the assumption that any warming is due to carbon emissions is open to question. Third, the assumption that collective action is required has not been established. Fourth, the option to let people adapt receives little consideration. Emissions trading schemes are better than centralized interventionist measures, says Robinson, but people should be sceptical of the argument that there is a 'massive and looming global problem' that requires urgent action.

Chapter 5 is an analysis by Annegret Groebel, of the German Regulatory Authority for Telecommunications and Post, of 'convergence' in telecommunications and broadcasting markets and its impact on regulation. In Britain, a decision was made to create one 'converged' regulator (Ofcom) from five existing regulators, to regulate all electronic communications markets. The British regime is different from that in the rest of the EU in that Ofcom is a content regulator, possibly leading, Groebel argues, to diseconomies of scope. Groebel contrasts Ofcom with its German counterpart, RegTP, in terms of both scope and organizational structures, noting that RegTP (responsible for energy as well as telecoms) has three times the staff of Ofcom even though it does not deal with content regulation. Groebel concludes that, while there may be benefits in having content and conduit regulation in one organization, there may also be conflicts of interest because conduit regulation is market-driven whereas content regulation has a significant 'public interest' aspect.

Colin Robinson, commenting on Groebel's paper, agrees with her that it is uncertain whether the merging of previously separate regulators in Ofcom will be successful: the outcome might be managerial diseconomies. Content regulation is a difficult issue, especially when it is centralized. There might be advantages in decentralizing it, as in Germany where it is a responsibility of the states. Other aspects of the German system seem less worth emulating: for example, the very wide scope of RegTP, which includes energy and post as well as electronic communications, may well lead to diseconomies. Nevertheless, inter-country comparisons of the kind used by Groebel are fruitful sources of ideas about how to improve regulatory systems.

Eileen Marshall, formerly of Ofgem, considers energy regulation in Chapter 6. A White Paper of February 2003 gave priority to two policy goals – control of carbon dioxide emissions and maintenance of security of energy supply – but the way the government is pursuing these goals is likely to lead to serious problems, she argues. The government's method of setting many different targets and using many policy instruments will politicize environmental policy, leaving it open to lobbying by pressure groups. Moreover, by specifying the amount of energy saving which should occur and the quantities of some energy sources (such as renewables) which should be used, the government is likely to dampen competition, creating a managed market. There may also be an adverse impact on security of supply as government intervention on both the supply and demand sides restricts the ability of markets to provide security. A change in the government's approach to policy is required, says Marshall, to avoid compromising independent economic regulation and competition. Instead of targeting particular fuels and activities, the government should leave it to a carbon trading scheme to achieve its environmental goals.

Stephen Littlechild, University of Cambridge and former electricity regulator, is in general agreement with Marshall's view. In particular, he agrees that adoption of a carbon trading scheme would be the most efficient way to achieve the government's environmental objectives, though he has doubts whether market participants would regard commitments to these objectives as credible. He is sceptical also about the underlying issue of climate change, asking whether it is rational 'to impose high costs on customers today to deal with a possible eventuality a century or two in the future, of which we presently know very little?' He concludes by asking whether it is prudent to commit to carbon dioxide reduction goals at present.

Chris Bolt, at the time of the lecture the PPP (Public–Private Partnership) Arbiter but now the Rail Regulator, considers the supervisory regime for London Underground Limited (LUL) in Chapter 7. The PPP arrangements for LUL are different from those in other infrastructure sectors, he says, and the role of the Arbiter is different from those of the utility regulators. The Arbiter has a restricted remit, compared with traditional regulators, not covering specification and enforcement of delivery; he is reactive, giving guidance or directions only when requested by the parties; and he can be given 'narrow' terms of reference even at the time of a Periodic Review. According to Bolt, compared with the national rail network, there are some favourable aspects of the PPP arrangements for LUL – for example the smaller number of direct contractual relationships and the clear customer focus. He is optimistic about the prospects for the PPP and the Arbiter, principally because the structure of the PPP arrangements seems more robust than that for the national rail network and the system for modifying contracts offers some useful alternatives to the licensing approach.

Tom Winsor, at the time of the lecture the Rail Regulator, comments that the PPP Arbiter's hands are rather closely tied compared with the Rail Regulator's. Furthermore, Winsor argues that a licence, as in the utility regulation regimes, is different from a regulatory contract under the PPP. A change mechanism is inherent in a licence, so the regulator can modify a licence at any time, whereas under the PPP arrangements the main contract change mechanism is only every seven-and-a-half years. Winsor also criticizes the idea of 'partnership' or 'public interest' directors (the 'spy on the board'). In the case of the national rail network, the appointment of a Public Interest Director to Railtrack at the behest of government scared the markets because it looked like political intervention in the affairs of a private company and in a regulatory settlement.

In Chapter 8, Colin Mayer of the Saïd Business School, University of Oxford, argues that water has been one of the most successful British privatizations. A sound regulatory regime for assessing the cost of capital, valuing assets and making efficiency comparisons has been established and there has been a big increase in investment. In recent times, however, water firms have become more highly leveraged than at the time of privatization, partly because of the financing requirements of large investment programmes but partly also because of the tightening of the regulatory contract at the time of the last price review. The creation of low-cost corporate vehicles, argues Mayer, has caused an increasing divergence between private and social costs and changed the nature of the regulatory relation. Ideally, long-term commitments by both firms and regulators are required for the regime to move forward, though better control systems by regulators may also be required. In the long run, the equity model is a more suitable basis for firm–regulator relations so the regulator should try to sustain rates of return consistent with that model.

Philip Fletcher, the water regulator, commenting on Mayer's paper, points to the 'continuing appetite for new investment' in the water industry. He disagrees with Mayer in that he believes there is already a high degree of commitment in the industry: the regulator is committed to enabling the companies to finance their activities and to having a clear, consistent and objective regulatory system. Moreover, though regulators cannot 'commit' by binding their successors, they create precedents which are difficult to overturn. Fletcher does not see his ability to regulate constrained by high levels of gearing and indeed welcomes the operation of the market, which has led to the mergers, acquisitions and restructuring that have characterized the water industry.

The final chapter is by Jacques Steenbergen of Allen and Overy and Leonard Waverman of London Business School. They consider how well European merger control has worked, whether it might be replaced by *ex post* action to control any abuse that occurs as a result of a merger, and whether control could be exercised by national governments alone. Steenbergen and Waverman point out that, both in the USA and the EU, merger law became part of competition policy long after laws that prevent anti-competitive agreements and abuse of a dominant position. Fundamental differences among these various parts of competition policy are that anticompetitive agreements or monopoly abuses cannot be welfare-increasing activities so there is a clear case for laws to ban them; however, merger law concerns mergers, which *could* increase dominance. According to Steenbergen and Waverman, recent studies cast great doubt on the ability of competition authorities to ban only those mergers that are anticompetitive. They argue, therefore, that in general the European competition authorities should only prohibit mergers where *ex post* remedies would clearly be ineffective. Otherwise, they should wait until evidence of welfare losses appears.

Sir Derek Morris, at the time of the lecture the Chairman of the UK Competition Commission, disagrees with Steenbergen and Waverman about the advantages of *ex post* actions. In his view, most of the potential dangers of a merger could never be addressed *ex post* by an Article 82 case. The purpose of a merger regime is to prevent a substantial lessening of competition. Acquisition of a new entrant, for instance, may lessen competition because it reduces the flow of new ideas and threatens diversity, neither of which would provide the basis for an Article 82 case. So there is a good case for a powerful merger policy separate from the use of Article 82. Morris also urges caution in using financial data to determine whether or not competition authorities have made the right decisions in merger cases.

It is clear that there are now sufficient differences among countries in their approaches to competition policy, utility regulation and market liberalization for analysis of those differences to be fruitful. Sometimes there may be good reasons for differences because they are rooted in local circumstances, but international comparisons can be helpful in challenging assumptions about existing practices.

There are also now a number of issues that cut across international boundaries and that will undoubtedly be discussed further in future Beesley series. One, for example, is to what extent the trend towards liberalizing utility markets will continue. In Britain, except for the railways and water, there has been a significant injection of competition in recent years, principally because of procompetitive actions by utility regulators and the competition authorities. Other countries have tended to follow the same path, if less wholeheartedly. Now, however, in the energy utilities, where liberalization has gone furthest, governments are once more introducing specific measures to promote particular energy sources and to reduce energy demand, even though an EU carbon trading scheme is about to come into operation. These measures are, it is claimed, necessary because markets will fail to protect against climate change. It will be some time before it becomes clear to what extent competitive markets will survive this new interventionism that relies mainly on environmental arguments.

Another issue that emerges from this book and that will be prominent in economic policy debate in the next few years is the effectiveness of anti-monopoly policies. Attempts to promote and sustain competition are inevitably difficult, for instance because of the problem of distinguishing between entrepreneurial activity and attempts to stifle competition. Governments and competition authorities, faced with academic research that shows apparently poor results from antitrust action and, in particular, from attempts to control mergers, may need to reappraise existing laws that attempt to promote competition and to outlaw anticompetitive practices.

1. Competition policy and trade: the WTO after the Cancun Meeting

Frédéric Jenny

The question whether international trade rules should be complemented by competition rules has been hotly debated in the World Trade Organization (WTO) since the end of the Uruguay Round when the European Union (EU) obtained the creation of working groups on four 'new' issues: trade facilitation, transparency on procurement markets, investment and competition.

Several questions were examined by the WTO Working Group on the Interaction between Trade and Competition Policy: what is the relationship between competition and international trade? Would a competition agreement benefit developing countries? What is the EU proposal on competition?

At the Cancun Ministerial the Singapore issues figured prominently in the discussions but, as is well known, no agreement was reached on any issue. It is thus important to ask what positions were expressed on the issue of competition at Cancun and under what conditions the negotiating process on this issue could go forward in the near future.

This chapter is divided into six sections. The first gives examples of transnational anticompetitive practices which restrain trade to illustrate the problem of governance of international markets. Section 2 examines the economic consequences for developing countries of some transnational anticompetitive practices. Section 3 discusses the differences of approach between trade and competition officials. Section 4 offers possible solutions to the problem of trade and competition interaction. Section 5 describes the state of play before Cancun and section 6 gives an account of the failed Cancun negotiations. Finally, the conclusion provides some views on how the negotiating process could proceed.

1.   CASES OF INTERNATIONAL CARTELS

Cement in Egypt

Cement is important in Egypt because of the rapid expansion of tourism infrastructure along the Red Sea and the Mediterranean Coast and because of the boom in residential construction around Greater Cairo. Thus the availability of cement at a competitive price is crucial both for the welfare of consumers (cement represents roughly 50 per cent of the total cost of low-cost housing) and for the development of the tourist industry, which is a major source of foreign exchange.

The Egyptian cement industry was privatized and deregulated in 1999. Customers can now order directly from producers (previously they had to go through licensed distributors who were alleged to hoard cement to increase prices artificially); prices are free from controls and foreign investors have invested heavily in the sector both by buying formerly state-owned cement plants and by increasing capacity and modernizing equipment.

As a result of privatization and the mergers that followed (both in and outside Egypt), the industry is now dominated by a small number of powerful groups. Suez Cement Company now accounts for 31 per cent of Egyptian cement production; Lafarge (a French company) which merged with Blue Circle (a British company) and is now the world's second largest cement manufacturer, produces 25 per cent of Egyptian cement and Cemex (a Mexican company), which is the world's third largest cement manufacturer, accounts for 14 per cent of production. Together these three cement producers account for 70 per cent of Egyptian cement production. Because prospects for the industry seemed attractive, a few Egyptian firms entered the industry, including one called Egyptian Cement Company.

As capacity increased (by 7.5 million tons between 1999 and 2002) and as demand slowed in 2001, producers started looking for new markets. The Egyptian Cement Company in particular started exporting to the Canary Islands at a very competitive price.

Cemex (the Mexican manufacturer) and the other foreign suppliers of the Egyptian market who are also major suppliers of the Canary Islands cement market allegedly 'retaliated by pushing local prices to their lowest levels to prevent local companies from exporting by burdening them with losses'.[1] The National Cement Company marketing department head stated that 'We cannot control the practices of foreign companies; being the affiliates of international cement heavyweights, they can afford losses for one or two years till they achieve their aim in the market.'

Anonymous sources in Egypt (quoted by *Al Ahram*) allege that as a result of this retaliation, the Egyptian Cement Company retreated by 'lowering its shipments to the Canary islands by 75% as a reaction to the local price war'.

What is public knowledge is the fact that once the export problem was under control for the major cement manufacturers, they decided to end the price war and fix the price of Egyptian cement at a profitable level through collusion. Thus almost all cement producers met in the middle of December 2002 and decided to increase the price of cement from LE 125 per ton to roughly LE 170 per ton. From press reports we know that cement manufacturers also considered the possibility of entering a market-sharing agreement (based on the distribution of production capacity between firms) in case the price-fixing agreement did not hold.

What do we learn from this example? First, in spite of the desire of governments to facilitate international trade through multilateral or bilateral trade agreements, Egyptian cement producers are prevented from exporting to an area of the European Union (the Canary Islands) by private firms trying to protect their market shares and their profits there. Second, although the European Union has a domestic antitrust law which prohibits price fixing and market sharing or the erection of artificial barriers to entry to limit competition on its territory, it would have difficulty in enforcing this law against cement manufacturers because the evidence needed is likely to be found in Egypt, a country which does not have a domestic competition law yet and does not have a cooperation agreement with the EU.

Thus the absence of a competition law in Egypt directly hurt Egyptian consumers (the increase in the price of cement decided by the cartel multiplied by the consumption of cement in Egypt amounts to US$250 000 000 per year) and the absence of a cooperation agreement between Egypt and the EU hurts Canary Islands consumers.

The Aluminium Cartel

Let us now move to the second case, the case of the aluminium cartel reported by J. Stiglitz in *Globalization and Its Discontents* and for which additional material is available from the *Wall Street Journal*.[2]

When the Soviet Union collapsed, the demand for aluminium from the former Soviet 'military complex' decreased considerably. The price of aluminium per pound dropped from 93 US cents in September 1990 to 58 US cents in September 1993. During the same period inventories went up from 58 000 metric tons at the end of 1989 to 25 million metric tons at the end of 1993.

The aluminium glut led to losses for the main producers: Alcan lost US$112 million in 1992 while Pechiney lost US$36 million the same year.

Alcoa's profits were diminished by 50 per cent during the first quarter of 1993.

A debate started in the industry as to what remedies should be adopted to face the situation. Whereas Alcoa chief executive Paul O'Neill advocated the creation of 'a global industry cartel', the US Aluminum Association called for antidumping measures against Russia.

The US State Department was reluctant to impose antidumping duties against Russia for a variety of reasons. For example, Russia badly needed hard currency to be able to repay the huge debt contracted with European and North American banks. Antidumping duties would limit Russian exports to the USA and therefore Russia's ability to earn hard currency. Furthermore, the price of aluminium in the rest of the world would remain depressed, which would be detrimental to the major aluminium manufacturers both in the West and in Russia. An industry cartel, however, would restore the profitability of all manufacturers.

The major Western producers could agree among themselves to cut their production by 1.5 million tons in order to increase prices. Under this scheme, North American producers would cut their production by 20 per cent and European producers by 25 per cent. However, before proceeding with this cartel arrangement Western producers needed the help of the US government to make sure that the Russian industry would not use this opportunity to flood the international market with their surpluses and would themselves cut their production by 500000 tons. According to J. Stiglitz, in return for a 500000 ton production cut by Russia, Deputy Secretary of State Strobe Talbott promised Moscow a US$250 million equity investment guaranteed by the Overseas Private Investment Corporation to modernize its industry and develop its domestic demand. The agreement also provided that participants would meet to monitor world aluminium supplies and prices. Alcoa's chief executive made clear that Alcoa would initiate antidumping proceedings if the cartel agreement was not respected.

J. Stiglitz (who, as head of the council of Economic Advisors, opposed the formation of the cartel but lost) states:

> At least for a while the cartel did work. Prices were raised. The profits of Alcoa and other producers were enhanced. The American consumers – and consumers throughout the world – lost, and indeed the basic principles of economics which teach the value of competitive markets, show that the losses to consumers outweigh the gains to producers.

The *Wall Street Journal* reported on these events and described the result of its own reporting as 'a fascinating study in international brinkmanship, Washington clubbiness, the limits of free trade, political expediency rules ...'.

Ann Bingaman, US Assistant Attorney General in charge of the Antitrust Division, who attended some of the aluminium cartel negotiation meetings in 1992 and was 'livid' according to Stiglitz, declared to the *Wall Street Journal*: 'The guts of this in our view is that to date, from all we know, these are individual decisions by producers .... No one has brought any evidence to us of any coordinated agreement. If somebody has something to tell us to the contrary we're open for business'.

What can we learn from this case? First, an international cartel (in this instance created with the help of the US government) can defeat trade liberalization. Second, this international cartel has been detrimental to consumers the world over. Stiglitz suggests that between November 1993 and June 1994 prices rose by 30 per cent, helped among other things by improved economic conditions. If one assumes that only half of the price increase was due to the cartel, it remains the case that the cost imposed by the cartel, particularly on developing countries which rely on aluminium imports for a variety of uses, is significant. For example, the imports of aluminium into Egypt in 1995 amounted to US$29 million, which suggests that the amount overpaid by Egypt (on a yearly basis) due to the cartel may have been between US$4 and 5 million. The South African Customs Union (which includes South Africa, Botswana, Lesotho, Namibia and Swaziland) imported US$135 million dollars worth of aluminium in 1995 (a fairly stable level of annual imports). Thus its import cost increased by roughly US$15 million due to the cartel. That same year, Indonesian aluminium imports represented US$431 million, and the import costs of Indonesia were increased by US$65 million because of the cartel. The value of Chinese aluminium imports in 1995 amounted to US$1 billion; thus the import cost of China increased by US$150 million and so on.

Third, US antitrust authorities chose not to prosecute this cartel and even denied its existence while being perfectly aware of it and having all the evidence of its existence (the Justice Department was so worried about the negotiations with the Russians that it had sent two of its attorneys to Europe where the negotiations were being held to make sure that no smoking gun could be found that would implicate the US government). The victims of the cartel were left with practically no recourse.

The Heavy Electrical Equipment Cartel

Lack of space precludes us from giving other examples, but one additional case is worth mentioning – the heavy electrical equipment cartel. What is of particular interest about this cartel is, first, that even though it was publicly documented, it was never prosecuted and, second, that unlike the aluminium cartel it applied worldwide except in the USA and in the EU (which is probably why it was never prosecuted in these jurisdictions). In addition, we know that Egypt was a victim of the heavy electrical equipment cartel. We do not know whether it was still in operation in the 1990s but this is a distinct possibility since it has never been prosecuted. In 1995 Egyptian imports of heavy electrical equipment amounted to US$281 million.

How can Egypt Deal with these Cases?

Can Egypt rely on the USA and the EU to prosecute international cartels?

In spite of the great experience of the US antitrust enforcement agencies, they cannot be counted on to fight international hardcore cartels that either they do not choose to pursue (such as the aluminium cartel) or are unable to pursue because they do not affect US territory (the heavy electrical equipment cartel or the cement cartel). Second, if the US authorities cannot handle such cartels, can we count on the EU Commission to prosecute them? Again the answer is negative. The heavy electrical equipment cartel does not (or did not) apply in Europe. The European Commission was fully aware of the existence of the aluminium cartel (since negotiations with the Russians took place partly in Brussels and with the help of the EU Commission) but chose not to prosecute it. Finally the European Commission has neither the evidence necessary to investigate the cement situation in the Canary Islands nor a cooperation agreement in the area of competition with Egypt.

Could Egypt fight these cartels if it had a competition law? In that case the Egyptian authorities would at least be able to prosecute the cement cartel but would not be able to prosecute the heavy electrical equipment cartel or the aluminium cartel (assuming of course that these cartels continued to operate). To prosecute either of these cartels, Egyptian antitrust authorities would need to have a cooperation agreement with the EU and the US authorities. The EU would be able to prosecute the cement cartel in the Canary Islands only if it had a cooperation agreement with the Egyptian antitrust authority.

However, it is somewhat unlikely that the EU or the USA would have a bilateral cooperation agreement with the Egyptian competition authority. There are very few cases of cooperation agreements between developed and developing countries. The obvious reason for this is that the risk that firms from developed nations might engage in anticompetitive practices in developing countries is higher than the risk that firms from developing countries might restrict competition in developed countries.

Even if Egypt had a voluntary bilateral agreement with the EU or the USA, the question is how much cooperation it would have obtained from the European and the US competition authorities if it had asked for cooperation in prosecuting the heavy electrical equipment or the aluminium cartel. Indeed bilateral cooperation agreements always permit the parties to decline to cooperate on particular cases if they feel that it is in their best interest not to do so.[3] The enthusiasm of the US government to assist a prosecution of the aluminium cartel would probably have been limited if one considers the comments of Ann Bingaman and the role of the US government in making the cartel effective. The enthusiasm of the EU to help Egyptian authorities prosecute the heavy electrical equipment cartel in which European firms were heavily involved and which did not apply (at least directly) to the European market may be similarly limited.

2.   THE IMPORTANCE OF TRANSNATIONAL ANTICOMPETITIVE PRACTICES FOR DEVELOPING COUNTRIES

The next question I would like to consider is whether the externality problem we have just mentioned is important enough to worry about. One of the consequences of the creation of a WTO working group on trade and competition has been that research on international cartels has been revived.

One of the most important studies in this area was undertaken by Margaret Levenstein and Valerie Suslow from the University of Michigan for the World Bank's *World Development Report* of 2001. In this document they state:

> In 1997, the latest year for which we have trade data, developing countries imported $81.1 billion of goods from industries which had seen a price-fixing conspiracy during the 1990s. These imports represented 6.7% of imports and 1.2% of GDP in developing countries. They represented an even larger fraction of trade for the poorest developing countries, for whom these sixteen products represent 8.8% of imports. The consumption impact appears to be the largest for upper middle income countries, for whom these imports represent 1.5% of GDP. (Four of these conspiracies are still under investigation by anti-trust authorities: if these four are excluded from our analysis, the total value of imports drop to $42.8 billion and 3.5% of imports and 0.64% of GDP).[4]

These figures are clearly underestimates, as various international cartels active during the 1990s and mentioned previously are not taken into account. Furthermore cartel activity is generally secret, so often remains unknown.

If one assumes, on the basis of available evidence for prosecuted cartels, that the monopoly mark-up is frequently between 25 per cent and 30 per cent of the final price of cartelized goods, a rough estimate suggests that the order of magnitude of the annual monopoly rent extracted by members of these international cartels on developing countries is in the US$20–25 billion range.

These figures should be related to two other figures. First, the order of magnitude of international aid to development is about US$50 billion per year. Thus, at a minimum, the existence of anticompetitive transnational cartels implies transfers (in the form of overcharge) from developing countries to cartel members (mostly firms from developed countries) which represent at least half the value of the development aid given by the governments of developed countries to developing countries. Another cost of international cartels is the deadweight loss to consumer surplus in developing countries due to artificial increase in prices. To estimate this deadweight loss, one would need to have data on price elasticities of demand for the cartelized products in developing countries. Unfortunately these data are unavailable.

Second, a recent UNCTAD study[5] estimates the welfare impact of various hypothetical trade liberalization measures and states:

> In the first experiment, a worldwide reduction of 50 per cent in all agricultural tariffs brings about an aggregate welfare gain of $21.5 billion. This estimate is in line with those recently produced using the GTAP5 database. All the world regions appear to gain, but gains differ widely both in absolute and relative terms. The largest absolute gains are captured by Japan, North America, the NICs, North Africa and the Middle East, and Oceania. In percentage terms, those regions that appear to gain most are Oceania, the Asian NICs and North Africa. The estimated percentage gain for sub-Saharan Africa and Latin America is lower than in other studies conducted under similar assumptions. This is likely because of the inclusion of tariff preferences in the protection database used by UNCTAD. Since Africa and Latin America are among the major beneficiaries of preferential schemes, it seems likely that gains from liberalization for these countries in other studies could be overstated when full account is not taken of tariff preferences as has been done here.

A further analysis using the UNCTAD figures shows that the net welfare benefit for developing countries from such an agreement would be equal to US$13.4 billion.[6]

Thus the net annual welfare benefit for developing countries from a drastic multilateral reduction in agricultural tariffs (US$13.4 billion) is only about half the minimum estimate of the direct benefit they would get if a multilateral agreement on competition enabled the elimination of international cartels and therefore the supracompetitive margin they have to pay to cartel members when they import (US$20–25 billion).

3. TWO APPROACHES TO THE PROBLEM OF EXTERNALITIES BECAUSE OF INTER- NATIONAL ANTICOMPETITIVE PRACTICES

The internationalization of markets due to the combination of trade liberalization, deregulation and communications development creates two interrelated sets of problems for market governance. These problems have a well-known common origin: while the geographical boundaries of relevant markets expand and while firms increasingly operate in many national markets, competition law enforcement remains territorially limited by national boundaries (except in the EU).

As the examples we started with show, the internationalization of markets allows firms operating in several national markets to implement anticompetitive practices in one country which have an effect in another country. They are thus sheltered from the rigours of competition law enforcement. On the one hand, the competition authority of the affected country (if such an authority exists) cannot use its power of investigation in another country to gather the evidence it would need to prosecute the authors of the anticompetitive practice affecting its domestic market. On the other hand, the competition authority of the country in which the firms are located does not have jurisdiction if the practice does not affect its domestic market. Thus some mechanism needs to be invented to deal with the externality problem created by transnational anticompetitive practices. If this is not done violators will go unpunished and national competition authorities will be less and less able to exercise their operational sovereignty.

Another problem is due to a second type of externality arising because when firms engage in domestic or transnational anticompetitive practices they may render trade liberalization commitments entered into by governments ineffective (for example, an import cartel or the predatory behaviour of a local monopoly may prevent importers from selling in a country even if there are no tariff barriers). Alternatively, they may defeat the purpose of these commitments (for example an export cartel or an international cartel does not prevent international trade from taking place but may result in a situation where monopoly rent is extracted from the importers and may thus defeat the purpose of international trade). Thus what is at stake here is the externality between the governance of international markets from the point of view of competition and international trade policy.[7]

These two sets of problems overlap partially but not completely. They overlap partially to the extent that some transnational practices (such as an international cartel) clearly restrict trade and competition and may escape being detected and punished because of the limitation on the territorial jurisdiction of the competition authorities of the affected countries. But some domestic anticompetitive practices, such as an import cartel or a domestic abuse of dominance, over which the competition authority of the country in which the practice is implemented clearly has jurisdiction, may also have the effect of preventing international trade and clash with the trade commitments of that country.

Seen from the standpoint of competition law enforcement against transnational practices, the main problem raised by globalization is to develop protocols of cooperation through which a competition authority of a country wanting to prosecute a practice which has a detrimental effect on its domestic market can obtain the help of the competition authority of another country even if the domestic market of this other country is not affected. Seen from the standpoint of the interface between trade and competition, the problem is not limited to securing the necessary international cooperation between national competition authorities to ensure that they can enforce their own domestic legislation against international practices which restrict trade. The problem is also to make sure that domestic competition laws are consistent with the principles of international trade and that national competition enforcement agencies act in a way that is consistent with the trade commitments of their country and allow those commitments to be met.

Hence the trade perspective on the issue of the competitive governance of markets is more limited than the competition perspective because there is only one particular type of anticompetitive practice which is of interest to international trade policy makers (i.e. practices that may affect international trade) but it is also wider because international trade policy makers are equally concerned with the design of domestic laws and the quality of domestic enforcement to the extent that they may have an effect on the ability of foreign firms to gain market access.

Thus it is understandable that competition enforcers (for example in the context of the ICN – International Competition Network) focus primarily on cooperation on transnational mergers. Indeed, this type of transaction raises the most crucial problems for competition authorities in terms of operational sovereignty since there is a risk that, when several competition authorities examine the same transaction, they will arrive at contradictory decisions for entirely legitimate reasons (for example, because market conditions are not the same in different countries). In such cases, some of these decisions (for example to allow a merger) may become irrelevant because of contradictory decisions taken by competition agencies in other countries (such as to prohibit a merger). Competition officials are also extremely interested in convergence of national laws (particularly in the merger area) as a way to reduce the frequency of possible conflicts when several national authorities examine the same transaction. They are also focusing their efforts on the exchange of information between authorities because such exchanges allow competition authorities which have jurisdiction but not the means to investigate a practice to enforce their own laws. Finally, competition officials tend to be quite concerned about government restrictive regulations or policies. Such regulations or policies often limit both competition and the scope of intervention of competition authorities themselves and are perceived as a threat by competition officials. Therefore competition advocacy is one of the important activities of competition authorities.

By contrast, when trade policy makers address the issue of competition, they are less interested in international mergers because such mergers rarely create an international trade problem. They tend to focus more on international cartels because such cartels nearly always do create such a problem. They are less interested in promoting the convergence of the substantive provisions of competition laws (and possibly more pragmatic in recognizing that there is no one-size-fits-all competition law that could be applied to all countries), but more interested in ensuring that such laws and their enforcement are non-discriminatory. When considering cooperation protocols between national competition agencies, trade policy makers are mainly concerned with the conditions under which an authority requested to investigate an alleged anticompetitive practice by another country whose trade interests are presumably hurt by the practice would respond (or would have to respond). They are less concerned with the problems about information a competition authority investigating a case could obtain from a sister agency to successfully complete its investigation of a practice implemented outside its territory but having a domestic effect. Finally, just as competition enforcers are interested in using their advocacy powers to try to limit the scope of government restrictive regulations or policies, international trade policy makers are interested in limiting the scope of private practices which may contradict the trade commitments they negotiate or the policies of the governments they represent.

4. POSSIBLE REMEDIES

Having outlined the differences of approach to the issue of the competitive governance of international markets between trade and competition specialists, let me focus briefly on some possible solutions.

Whether one looks at the problem from the standpoint of competition or from the standpoint of trade and competition, the possible solutions to externality problems raised by the gap between the limited geographical area of jurisdiction of national competition authorities and the internationalization of markets are: (1) reliance on the US and EU systems to police international anticompetitive practices; (2) voluntary bilateral (or regional) cooperation between competition authorities; (3) the creation of a supranational body of law and a supranational enforcement authority; and (4) a multilateral agreement on competition.

As mentioned earlier, the first solution is the preferred option of Harry First, who states:[8]

> How might our evolving system of international antitrust enforcement deal with this problem? One approach is a unilateral one. The United States, as the network enforcer with the most expertise in private litigation, should use its forum to greatest advantage. There is no inherent jurisdictional limitation on US courts giving damages for non-US sales of products whose prices are fixed in international markets, nor is there any constitutional limitation on including worldwide harm in estimating criminal fine.

However, such a solution is at best partial for a number of reasons. The first is that probably a large number of international anticompetitive practices which affect other countries do not affect the USA or the EU precisely because the firms engaging in these practices are wary of implementing them in jurisdictions where there is strict enforcement of competition or antitrust laws.[9] The second reason is that even for international cartels which operate in the USA, Harry First admits

> suits for damages occurring outside the United States must allege a causal connection between the conduct within the United States and the injuries sustained outside the United States. ... it is not enough to prove that an international cartel existed, which fixed prices both inside and outside the United States and that the market is an international one.

Thus relying on US (or EU) enforcement of antitrust laws is likely to lead to significant underenforcement of international cartels.

As already suggested when discussing the Egyptian cement cartel, the second solution (voluntary cooperation between competition authorities) is also unsatisfactory for two reasons. First, it is nearly impossible for developing countries to enter into a cooperation agreement on competition with developed countries. In the world today there are only a handful of such agreements (for example, one between Australia and Papua New Guinea, one between Canada and Chile, and one between Canada and Costa Rica) because governments of developed countries do not care to enter into cooperation agreements on competition with other countries unless their level of economic development (and their size) is fairly similar. Developing countries have entered into cooperation agreements on competition with other developing countries (in the context, for instance, of Mercosur, the Andean community, Caricom, Comesa), particularly at the regional level, but these agreements have so far led to very few tangible results and do not address adequately the issue of transnational anticompetitive practices undertaken by firms from developed countries.

Furthermore, such bilateral or regional cooperation agreements always provide that the competition authorities involved will cooperate on specific cases only when it is in their mutual interest to do so. This makes such agreements particularly unsatisfactory to solve the problem of anticompetitive practices which restrict international trade because typically in such cases the trading interests of one country do not coincide with the trading interests of the other.[10]

The third solution, the adoption of a supranational law and the creation of an enforcement agency with supranational powers, has worked well in the context of the EU. However, it is politically unrealistic at the multilateral level both because of the importance of the differences in levels of economic development of countries around the world and because of the importance of the abandonment of national sovereignty by each country that it implies. This solution has not been proposed or considered in the current debate at the WTO.

The fourth and last solution, a multilateral agreement on competition in the context of the Doha Round of trade negotiations, a solution aimed at addressing the issue of the externality of anticompetitive practices on trade liberalization, has been under consideration in the WTO since the Singapore conference.[11]

Misconceptions abound (even in learned journals) regarding the nature and likely scope of a possible WTO agreement on competition policy. For example, a recent article in *Foreign Affairs* reiterates the concern that WTO rules on competition policy 'could be administered through a supranational agency',[12] notwithstanding that this possibility figures nowhere in any of the current or earlier proposals that have been made in the context of the WTO and has been explicitly disavowed by the proponents of WTO negotiations on various occasions.[13] References also continue to be made to the possibility of a WTO antitrust 'code'[14] – implying a comprehensive set of substantive rules – notwithstanding that the current proposals embody a distinctly more modest and gradual approach.

Such misconceptions may, in some cases, reflect a confusion between the proposals that have been put forward in the WTO and the considerably more far-reaching proposal that was put forward by the Munich Group in the early 1990s.[15] They may also find their origin in the difference of perspective between competition enforcers and trade policy makers mentioned earlier.

Led by the EU, a number of WTO member governments have put
forward a proposal for the development, in the context of the new Round
of multilateral trade negotiations launched at Doha, of a 'multilateral
framework on competition policy'.[16] Such an agreement would have five
main elements:[17]

- A commitment by WTO members to a set of core principles relating to
  the application of competition law and policy, including transparency,
  non-discrimination and procedural fairness in the application of
  competition law and/or policy.
- A parallel commitment by member governments to the taking of
  measures against hardcore cartels.
- The development of modalities for cooperation between member
  states on competition policy issues. These would be of a voluntary
  nature, and could encompass cooperation on national legislation,
  the exchange of national experience by competition authorities and
  aspects of enforcement.
- A commitment to ongoing support for the introduction/strengthening
  of competition institutions in developing countries, in the framework
  of the WTO but in cooperation with other interested organizations
  and national governments.
- The establishment of a standing WTO Committee on Competition
  Policy which would administer the proposed agreement and act as a
  forum for ongoing exchange of national experience, the identification
  of technical assistance needs and sources for such assistance, and
  so on.

First, as already noted, this proposal has very little in common with calls
for development of a detailed multilateral 'code' on competition policy
proposed some time ago by the Munich Group or related calls for the
establishment of an international competition law enforcement agency.[18] The
proposal does not aim at a comprehensive 'harmonization' of competition
law.[19] Rather, it is framed in terms of adherence to certain core principles
and other elements that embody fundamental values of both competition
policy and the multilateral trading system (non-discrimination, transparency
and the proposed commitment to action against hardcore cartels).

Second, the approach to hardcore cartels and modalities for cooperation
that is called for under the current proposals is extensively informed by
cooperative approaches favoured in other fora, for example the OECD
Recommendations on Hardcore Cartels and Cooperation, and is less
ambitious than elements that were proposed in the past. For example, an
early proposal for the introduction of 'compulsory positive comity' was

dropped some time ago. The proponents of negotiations have also made it clear that, as they envision it, a WTO framework would *not* require the exchange of confidential information[20] – though it also would not preclude individual countries from exchanging such information to the extent that it is provided for in relevant bilateral arrangements. Much emphasis would be placed on voluntary cooperation in the development of national legislation and the exchange of national experience, in addition to the enforcement process as such.

Third, the EU proposal (and the Doha Declaration) places much emphasis on support for technical assistance and capacity building in this area, responding to a key concern of developing countries. This represents a clear recognition that simply mandating the adoption of relevant laws without long-term support for institution building is unlikely to yield satisfactory or appropriate results. Moreover, the clear expectation is that the required capacity-building activities would be undertaken not principally by the WTO itself; rather, it would be a cooperative effort in which the support and cooperation of other relevant organizations would be essential (although the WTO would play a catalytic role).[21]

Fourth, by relying on broad principles, measures to strengthen cooperation and support for institution building rather than on detailed legal prescriptions, the EU proposal sought to avoid additional potential problems. For the most part, individual countries would be free to define the details of their national legislation. Moreover, and perhaps in response to concerns expressed previously by various commentators, the proposal of the EU did not appear to place excessive weight on market access objectives.[22] Rather, the focus of the EU proposal appeared to be on promoting the development of effective national competition institutions and expanded international cooperation to address the various types of anticompetitive practices identified by the competition policy community. As noted, the value of competition advocacy activities was also stressed. This approach was expected ultimately to yield significant benefits for market access, in that robust competition policies and institutions are supportive of market access objectives in various ways (including through their advocacy functions). However, arguably, it avoided the risk of distorting the principles of competition policy in favour of market access imperatives which was highlighted by past commentators.

A key remaining issue concerned the role of the WTO Dispute Settlement Mechanism (DSM) in a possible multilateral framework for competition policy.[23] A range of views had been expressed on this question. Whereas the European Community and its member states favoured at least some application of the WTO DSM in this area, other delegations favouring negotiations had suggested that a system of voluntary peer reviews might provide a more appropriate (non-confrontational) compliance mechanism in this area.[24] It is noteworthy, though, that in the course of discussions in the Working Group, it became clear that none of the proponents (including the European Community and its member states) called for more than a limited application of the WTO dispute settlement machinery in this field. In particular, the Community suggested that dispute settlement would apply only in respect to *de jure* (as opposed to *de facto*) violations of non-discrimination and other core principles and that dispute settlement should not, in any case, apply to individual decisions of national competition authorities.[25]

5.   THE STATE OF PLAY BEFORE CANCUN

As the Cancun Ministerial Conference was approaching, discussions of the EU proposal on competition intensified. Roughly speaking, at the beginning of the summer of 2003,WTO members were divided into four groups.

First a number of countries (including all the Eastern European countries, Switzerland, Canada, Australia, Korea, Japan, Chinese Taipei, Morocco, Costa Rica) supported the EU proposal on competition.

Second, a number of countries (including Hong Kong China, the USA, Malaysia, India, Indonesia and so on) objected to the EU proposal, either because they did not have a competition law and did not want to be pushed into adopting one or because they did not want the Dispute Settlement Mechanism (DSM) to apply to the issue of competition.

Third, a number of small developing countries (including the African group and most of the Caribbean countries) opposed the EU proposal, arguing that they could not afford a competition law, either because they were too small or because they were at a level of underdevelopment which required a strong industrial policy rather than the promotion of competition.

Finally, most of the South American countries (including Brazil, Argentina and Chile) reserved their position on the EU proposal and stated that they could accept it if, but only if, the ' balance of negotiations' was sufficiently in their favour. This meant that their position would depend on what was offered to them on other issues such as agriculture.

None of the opponents objected to the principal goal of the EU (to contribute to the fight against transnational anticompetitive cartels which restrict trade). However, they objected to the specific proposal of the EU because they considered that, as it applied to them, its cost would outweigh its benefits. Most notably, they worried about the possibility that their commitment to having a non-discriminatory competition law would in fact prevent them from pursuing the developmental policies they judged necessary or desirable for their economies. When considering the possible benefits of cooperation, developing countries were generally sceptical of the possibility that 'voluntary' cooperation would be forthcoming if they were the victims of transnational anticompetitive practices. Some also objected to the fact that such an agreement would not apply to export cartels engaged in by firms from developed countries which they considered to be a particular problem for their economies.

The EU explained that the dispute settlement mechanism would play a very limited role since it would apply only *de jure*. It also pointed out that countries party to the agreement could exempt certain sectors or actors or practices from the ambit of their domestic competition law as long as these exemptions were not discriminatory and were transparent. However, on the whole, the EU failed to convince its opponents that they had nothing to fear from the DSM. In fact, the EU was caught in a contradiction: the more it explained that the DSM would play a very limited role, the more opponents felt justified in criticizing the EU proposal which included a binding commitment subject to review through the DSM.

This discussion led a number of countries that could not accept the EU proposal but recognized that there was some merit to the competition issue (such as Hong Kong China, the USA and Malaysia) to suggest that, even though they were not proponents, they could (possibly) go along with a 'soft agreement' which would not require any commitment on the part of WTO members. Building on the suggestions of these WTO members, the chair of the Working Group then put forward an intermediate proposal which simply called for the creation of a WTO competition committee in which members would explore general issues relating to the interface between trade and competition, conduct peer reviews, study cooperative mechanisms and oversee a technical assistance programme.

This intermediate proposal attracted the attention of a number of delegates. Among them were opponents of the EU proposal because they found it more acceptable than the EU proposal since it did not impose any obligation on them, as well as supporters of the EU proposal who saw the 'soft agreement' proposal as a possible and useful second best in view of significant opposition to the EU proposal.

In the weeks preceding the Cancun Ministerial Conference, the EU Commission became quite alarmed, fearing that the 'soft agreement' approach was gaining momentum. It thus decided to focus its energy on discrediting this option. The reasons for which it chose this line of conduct are somewhat unclear. However, three hypotheses can be put forward.

First, for trade negotiators, the idea that a WTO agreement would not result in rules that would be subject to the DSM was difficult to imagine. They point out, with some justification, that the strength of the WTO rests precisely on its dispute settlement mechanism. Thus there may have been some fears among the EU negotiators that allowing an agreement on competition to be outside the scope of the DSM could set a dangerous precedent (even if the scope for actual use of the DSM in the case of competition was limited). However, such an approach overlooked the fact that the creation of a committee could have been a way to further educate the membership of the WTO on competition issues and to disseminate a competition culture, thereby playing a useful role in preparing the ground for moving toward a 'hard agreement' (that is, an agreement including commitments subject to the DSM) in the next round of negotiations.

Second, rumour suggests that the EU Commission inflexibility was partly due to persistent bureaucratic infighting between the EU Competition Directorate and the EU Trade Directorate. The former (like the US Department of Justice) did not approve of the discussions taking place in the WTO on anticompetitive practices, principally because they feared that trade officials would interfere in their 'territory'. In particular, they considered that voluntary cooperation agreements were traditionally initiated, negotiated and enforced by competition authorities and that any interference from trade officials in these mechanisms was unacceptable. Thus, previously the EU Competition Commissioner had given little support to the EU Commission initiative in the WTO and had preferred to promote the International Competition Network (an international network of competition authorities) whenever he was asked to comment on the WTO discussion on competition. An uneasy truce between the Competition Directorate and the Trade Directorate was achieved in the first part of 2003 after several high-level meetings. The Competition Directorate agreed that it would not try to undermine the efforts of the Trade Directorate on condition that the latter would support the view that competition enforcers or experts could (or should) participate in WTO dispute settlement proceedings resulting from an agreement on the EU proposal on competition.[26] If, then, the EC Commission supported the 'soft agreement' at the WTO, there would be no dispute settlement panels (since the soft agreement did not include obligations for the members) and the EC Directorate for Competition would consider that the agreement with the EC Trade Directorate was void, which would lead to renewed infighting within the European Commission.

According to a third hypothesis, the EU was counting on the fact that most developing countries would not easily accept an agreement on the Singapore issues when it put those issues on the agenda at the end of the Singapore Ministerial Conference. However, the EU reasoned that a conflict with developing countries on those issues would make it more difficult to finish the round, thereby alleviating the pressure on the EU to reform its agricultural policy and to make its agricultural markets more open. According to this scenario, the goal of the EU was not to find a compromise solution on the Singapore issues but rather to stick as long as possible to its initial proposals.

Whichever hypothesis was correct, the Commission was successful in preventing the 'soft agreement' option from being presented as one of the possible options in the Draft Ministerial Declaration prepared for the Trade Ministers by the Chair of the General Council at the end of August 2003. The ministers were told that two options were possible: either to continue the Working Group for further clarification on the issue or to open negotiations on the EU proposal.

6. THE CANCUN MINISTERIAL CONFERENCE

This WTO Ministerial Conference was a gathering of 148 delegations led by trade ministers of the Member countries during which it was hoped that they would come to an agreement on the progress of negotiations on 20 to 30 different topics (agriculture, industrial tariffs, services, special and differential treatment, investment, competition, trade facilitation and so on). During a round of negotiation, such ministerial conferences are organized every two years. The ministers register the progresses of the previous two years and give direction for the next two. The failure of a conference during a round means that ministers do not agree that there has been progress and also usually implies that the round will take longer than had been anticipated. Decisions are by consensus and nothing is agreed until everything is agreed (that is, until every delegation agrees on the outcome for every topic).

The success of a ministerial conference depends on a number of elements, three of which deserve mention. The first is the importance (or lack of importance) member states attribute to progress in the negotiations. The second is the quality of the preparatory work in Geneva which has preceded the ministerial conference. The third is the quality of the conference leadership.

There are some indications that, in the case of Cancun, several major countries did not care if the conference failed. One of the most significant issues was agriculture, with developing countries stridently arguing for the elimination of export subsidies, a decline in production subsidies, and the elimination of custom duties on agricultural products exported to the EU and the USA. Furthermore, the USA was in the spotlight because of the very vocal demand by a small number of African countries that it phase out the huge subsidies it offers to its cotton producers (resulting in increased production and exports, a fall in the international price of cotton and severe economic difficulties for African producers). Because of the upcoming presidential election, the US administration did not seem eager to make important concessions which would have important domestic political repercussions and probably did not mind if the conference was a failure. Similarly the EU could not go very far in its concessions on agriculture since the internal debate on the reform of its agricultural policy was proceeding only slowly.

India was concerned about the recent entry of China into the WTO and the end of the textile quota system. Given the forthcoming difficulties India would face due to these two factors, it was not keen to make new trade concessions and was therefore determined to defend a tough uncompromising line (particularly on the investment issue), even if this meant failure of the conference and a setback for the round of negotiations.

China had paid a high price for its entry into the WTO. It was still adjusting to the conditions thereby imposed and was not looking forward to additional commitments at this point.

Finally, some observers suggest that because the EU gives preferential access (with little or no customs duties) to its domestic agricultural markets to a number of African countries, these countries were not particularly interested in seeing EU customs duties reduced for other developing countries since they would then have to compete with them on the European market. This would explain why the African countries also took a very rigid approach to negotiations in Cancun.

If we now turn to the preparatory process, one observation is important. During a ministerial conference, negotiating time is very short, given the large number of highly technical issues involved. Much of this time was taken at the beginning of the conference, because countries do not want to reveal their fallback positions too early and tend to spend the first few days of the conference restating their demands rather than negotiating. As a result, the prepared draft ministerial declaration is crucial because ministers will have neither the time nor the ability to devise new solutions for the problems that they must negotiate. They will simply choose between the alternatives presented to them on each issue. Hence, if a solution on which a consensus could possibly be reached (such as, for example, the 'soft agreement' option for the competition issue) is not in the draft ministerial declaration, it will not be examined.

The third determinant of success or failure of a conference is the quality of the leadership of the conference itself. The chair of the conference, that is, the trade minister of the country in which the conference is held, is not bound by any prior rule on how to organize it. He/she decides how to organize discussions (for example in which order the issues will be taken when negotiations have started in earnest) and when to end the conference.

In Cancun, the chair of the conference appointed facilitators for each of the main issues. The Trade Minister of Canada was appointed facilitator for the Singapore issues. The method he chose for his consultations was the following. First, he did not hold specific consultations on each Singapore issue, but global consultations on all four. Second, he called in the proponents (the EU and major countries supporting the EU) and asked them which of the four issues were most important to them. He also asked the opponents which issues were most acceptable to them. The proponents answered that investment and government procurement were more important to them than competition. The opponents chose not to answer the facilitator's question and stated that they opposed all issues. On the basis of his consultations, the facilitator then proposed to start negotiations immediately on trade facilitation and government procurement, to start negotiations on investment soon, and to continue the clarificatory process in the working group on competition.

From the preparatory process in Geneva, it was widely known that investment was much more controversial than competition because a few countries (for example India and Malaysia) could not accept a binding commitment on investment. However, the facilitator did not factor in this information in his recommendation to the conference chair. Similarly, at no point did the facilitator try to determine if there was a possibility to propose a middle ground for each of the issues or for some of them.

The facilitator's proposal for the Singapore issues was integrated into a revised draft ministerial declaration established by the conference chair on the night before the last day of the conference.

On the last day the chair gathered about thirty of the most important delegations to try to move the negotiations forward. He decided to start with the Singapore issues. The EU Commissioner insisted that negotiations on all four should be launched at Cancun. However, after a while, it became evident that there was no agreement to start negotiations on all four Singapore issues. The EU Commissioner then asked for a recess so that he could get permission from the European Council to separate the Singapore issues (that is, to accept that some would move forward whereas others would not).

When the EU Commissioner returned, he offered to drop competition and investment from the agenda as a concession to get an agreement to start negotiations on the EU proposals for the other two issues (trade facilitation and transparency in government procurement). (Interestingly, Mr Lamy is reported to have said before making his concession that, at a personal level, he thought that competition should not be dropped from the agenda because this was a most important question for the future of the multilateral trading system.)

However, this offer from the EU Commissioner was rejected by other countries either because they could not accept transparency on government procurement (for example, Malaysia stated that it could not accept government procurement but that it could live with competition) or trade facilitation (speaking for the African group, Botswana explained that it could not accept negotiations on any of the Singapore issues) or because they could not accept dropping competition from the agenda (Korea). At this stage, and somewhat to the surprise of the negotiators, the conference chair decided to declare that the conference had failed, rather than try to create a consensus on other issues and come back to the Singapore issues later, or try to consider intermediate solutions between the positions of the proponents and of the opponents of the Singapore issues.

Thus, on the last day of the conference, the crucial issue of agriculture was not even discussed. There is ample evidence to suggest that the reason the African group in particular took an uncompromising stand on the Singapore issues (which ultimately lead to the chair to declare the conference a failure) was partly due to the disappointment of African countries regarding the issue of agriculture in general and the issue of cotton in particular. At the beginning of the conference, eight African cotton-producing countries (including Benin, Mali, Chad, Cameroon and Burkina Faso), heavily dependent on the revenues of cotton exports, had, in a dramatic press conference, denounced US subsidies to the 25 000 US cotton growers. In 2001/2002 the amount of these subsidies was US$3.9 billion for a production whose value at world prices was US$3 billion. These subsidies were considered to have resulted in an increase in US cotton production (+ 42 per cent between 1998 and 2001), an increase in US cotton exports (US cotton exports represent 30 per cent of total cotton exports) and a significant decrease in world cotton prices (with a decline in price from 72 cents per pound in 1997 to 42 cents in 2001/2002), thereby creating a very serious economic problem for two million African cotton growers and their families (about ten million persons in all). These African countries were in effect asking for a phasing out of US cotton production subsidies and a compensation for the harm caused to them by these subsidies.

The cotton issue rapidly became symbolic of everything that was unfair about international trade liberalization. Early on in the ministerial conference, the Director General of the WTO had indicated that he would himself participate in negotiations to try to come up with an acceptable compromise on the cotton problem.

The day before the end of the conference, when the revised draft ministerial was presented to the delegates, a number of them could not help feeling that the African countries had been slapped in the face because the paragraph on cotton merely instructed the Director General of the WTO 'to consult with the relevant international organizations including the Bretton Woods Institution, the Food and Agricultural Organization and the International Trade Center to effectively direct existing programmes and resources toward diversification of the economies where cotton accounts for the major share of their GDP'. There was no mention of a decrease of US subsidies or of any compensation to the African countries whose economies were badly hurt by these subsidies. It was simply suggested that they should diversify their agricultural production!

One should not minimize the far-reaching impact of this incident or the influence that it had on the failure of the conference. Some commentators have even suggested that the fact that the USA was in an embarrassing position over this issue was precisely the reason why, on the last day of the conference, the chairman (the Trade and Foreign Minister of Mexico) chose to start the negotiations with the Singapore issues and to declare the conference a failure without even considering the other issues. In this way, it is argued, the Mexican government was saving the face of the US administration since it would appear that the negotiations failed on the Singapore issues (pushed by the EU) rather than on the cotton issue (an issue on which the refusal of the USA to compromise because of domestic political pressure was bitterly resented).

Some other observers have also hypothesized that the eight African countries which had raised the issue of cotton at the beginning of the ministerial conference had been manipulated by the EU (and possibly by the French), which knew full well that in a presidential election year the USA could not offer to eliminate or even compensate for cotton subsidies. Thus having (French-speaking) African countries raise the cotton issue would deflect attention from grievances against EU agricultural policy and ensure that the conference would fail, thereby reducing pressure on the EU to further reform its agricultural policy in the immediate future.[27]

7. CONCLUSION

The consequences of the failure of the Cancun Ministerial Conference for the Singapore issues are unclear and it will take some time before it is known whether or not these issues will remain on the agenda of the round of negotiations. In the meantime, a number of observations are in order on the basis of the previous discussion.

First, the Cancun negotiations did not fail because of a disagreement on the Singapore issues. The reasons for the failure are far more complex.

Second, the liberalization of international trade creates a governance issue for global markets. If left unchecked, transnational anticompetitive practices in general, and hardcore cartels in particular, impose significant costs on trading partners, especially on developing countries, and undermine the goals of trade liberalization. It is worth mentioning that nearly all bilateral or regional trade agreements negotiated in the recent past (such as the Canada–Chile and the Canada–Costa-Rica agreements) or which are in the process of being negotiated (such as the FTAA) include a competition chapter or competition provisions. This is a relatively new development which reflects the understanding on the part of the trade community that trade liberalization will deliver its expected benefits only if some form of market governance ensures that anticompetitive practices do not defeat the purpose of negotiated trade concessions. Thus the complementarity between trade and competition policy, which was first recognized in the Havana Charter, but which was subsequently forgotten for nearly half a century, is making a comeback. At a time when the legitimacy of the multilateral trading system is called into question by anti-globalization non-governmental organizations (NGOs), it may be useful for the WTO to focus its attention on ways to ensure that the global markets it creates do not simply allow powerful firms to abuse their market power internationally and that trade liberalization is development friendly.

Third, the competition issue is different from most of the other issues being negotiated in this trade round. If it were easier to eliminate transnational anticompetitive practices, the world trading system would be more efficient and global welfare would increase. Furthermore, the global trading system would presumably be less criticized for being biased in favour of the interests of large multinational firms. Thus, besides the possible private benefits that victims of anticompetitive practices which negatively affect trade can hope to derive from a competition agreement, there is also an important 'public good' aspect to the competition issue in the WTO. This public good aspect of competition does not lend itself easily to the type of negotiations that take place in a WTO round where countries exchange concessions and commitments having primarily domestic implications. Indeed, even if a large number of both developed and developing countries recognize that they can be the victims of transnational anticompetitive practices and that the goal of preventing market power abuses in international trade is a legitimate one, they are not necessarily ready to make concessions on other issues to get such an agreement on competition because they feel that a large part of the benefits will accrue to other members. This is why the EU argues that 'it will not pay' to have this issue on the agenda by making concessions elsewhere (for example on agriculture) and why proponents tend to give a higher priority to issues likely to bring them more 'private' benefits.

Fourth, a competition agreement along the lines suggested by the EU would have more implications (and would therefore imply a higher private cost) for small developing countries than for larger and more developed countries because most of the latter already have a competition or antitrust law that meets the standards of non-discrimination, transparency and due process, whereas in developing countries that do not yet have a competition law a legal apparatus (and an enforcement system) would have to be created and the possible conflict between industrial policy and competition law would have to be addressed. At the same time, in the EU proposal, the potential private benefits of a competition agreement (that is, cooperation between national competition authorities) for developing countries depends on the goodwill of developed countries (since cooperation would only be on a voluntary basis). Additionally, some developing countries point out that they are victims of export cartels originating in developed countries but that such cartels would be exempted from the agreement. This explains why a number of WTO members, either small (for example a number of Caribbean islands, Hong Kong China and so on) or developing countries (in particular in Africa) have opposed the EU because they consider that the balance of benefits and costs in its proposal is not in their favour.

The refusal of the EU Commission to acknowledge this point and its reticence to consider a 'softer agreement' is somewhat mystifying. Although the EU rightly claims that the strength of the WTO is that it is a rule-based organization, it does not seek a binding rule on cooperation between national authorities to eliminate anticompetitive practices that impair trade even though one of the important reasons for having a competition agreement in the WTO would be to fight transnational hardcore cartels. Presumably, pragmatic reasons have prevented the EU from proposing an agreement on competition that would include a binding commitment to cooperate. Some developed countries (the USA in particular) have expressed the fear that they would be swamped with requests for cooperation emanating from developing countries and that any obligation to cooperate would necessarily interfere with their prosecutorial discretion. However, for reasons that are not explicitly stated, the EU Commission does not follow the same pragmatic approach when it proposes that all member countries should adopt a domestic competition law meeting international trade standards.

Two different goals can be assigned to an agreement on competition in the WTO: to allow the elimination of anticompetitive practices that restrict trade or to develop a culture of competition and an awareness of competition issues which might in a future round lead to negotiations for a rule allowing the elimination of anticompetitive practices. The EU proposal does not truly fit either goal. On the one hand, it is too modest to ensure cooperation between competition authorities and, on the other hand, it is too ambitious to be merely a pedagogical tool to increase the awareness of the WTO members regarding the merits of the competition issue.

However, some compromise solutions could be considered. The solution of a non-binding agreement, which was discussed in Geneva before the Cancun Ministerial, is a possible solution if the goal is to raise the awareness of the WTO members during this round so as to lay the groundwork for the possible negotiation of a binding agreement in a future round. Another solution would be a binding agreement at a plurilateral level, with an option for WTO members to join the agreement when they feel that they are prepared to do so. A third option could be based on the model of the GATS (General Agreement on Trade and Services) agreements, including a schedule of commitments allowing members to choose their level of commitment to the competition issue. Presumably such options would have to be studied carefully in order to achieve a consensus on competition in the WTO.

Fifth, treating the Singapore issues globally rather than individually increases the difficulty of the negotiation. Yet this is precisely what was done during the Cancun Ministerial. Contrary to what some 'proponents' (and the 'facilitator') seem to have believed, attempting to trade some of the Singapore issues for others is not helpful for developing countries. Indeed, all the EU proposals for these 'new' issues require the adoption of rules and an expansion of the scope of the DSM. This is precisely what developing countries object to, rightly or wrongly, because they consider that they have not yet been able to implement their commitments from the Uruguay Round. Therefore it comes as no surprise that the opponents of the EU proposals on the Singapore issues refused to answer when the facilitator asked them to indicate which were the issues they least objected to, saying that they objected to all proposals. This means that, as became obvious during the last part of the negotiation in Cancun, 'abandoning' competition or investment was not going to make transparency in government procurement more palatable for developing countries.

Developing countries have stated that they will accept resumed discussions on the Singapore issues only if they are satisfied that these discussions will not require them to negotiate binding agreements during this round. The real questions to ask about each Singapore issue are then: would it make sense to consider non-binding agreements as a possibility? Or, if all agreements must be binding, what kind of flexibility can be offered to developing countries on each issue that would allow countries to join the binding agreement only when they feel ready to do so? The answers may well differ from issue to issue.

NOTES

1. Declaration of the head of the marketing department of National Cement and of the head of Suez Cement sales department to *Al Ahram*, 19 December 2002.
2. Joseph E. Stiglitz, *Globalization and Its Discontents*, W.W. Norton and Company, Inc., New York, 2002. See, for example, E. Norton and M. du Bois, 'Foiled competition: Don't call it a cartel but world aluminum has forged new order', *Wall Street Journal*, June 1994.
3. On the limits of bilateral cooperation see Frédéric Jenny, 'International cooperation on competition: Myth, reality and perspective', presented at the University of Minnesota Law School Conference on Global Antitrust Law and Policy, Minneapolis September 2002, forthcoming in *'The Antitrust Bulletin'*.
4. Margaret Levenstein and Valerie Suslow, 'Private international cartels and their effects on developing countries', background paper for the World bank's *World Development Report*, 2001.
5. 'Back to Basics: Market Access Issues in the Doha Agenda, Chapter V: Estimated gains from multilateral trade liberalization', United Nations, Feb. 2003.
6. Developing countries in this calculation include the Asian NICs, China, South Asia, transition economies, sub-Saharan Africa, North Africa and the Middle East, and Latin America. If one eliminates the Asian NICs from the list, the benefit to developing countries of the tariff reduction amounts to US$9.55 billion.
7. For a typology of anticompetitive practices that affect trade see Frédéric Jenny, 'Globalization, competition and trade policy: convergence, divergence and cooperation', in *EC Law Facing the New Millennium Challenges, XIV Congress of the European Lawyers Union*, Brussels, 2001.
8. Harry First, 'Evolving toward what? The development of international antitrust', Harry First, Spring 2003, Globalization and Its Discontents (Colloquium, New York University School of Law, New York, p. 24.
9. For an example see *International Electrical Association: A Continuing Cartel*, Report for the Committee on Interstate and Foreign Commerce, US House of Representatives, June 1980.
10. See Jenny, 'International cooperation on competition'.
11. The following is based on Robert Anderson and Frédéric Jenny, 'The current proposals for WTO negotiations on competition policy: background and overview', March 2003 Conference on Antitrust Issues in Today's Economy, The Conference Board.
12. David S. Evans, 'The new trustbusters', *Foreign Affairs*, vol. 81, no. 1, January–February 2002, pp. 1–19, at 19.
13. Ignacio Garcia-Bercero and Stefan Amarasinha, 'Moving the trade and competition debate forward', *Journal of International Economic Law*, 2001, pp. 481–506.
14. See Daniel K. Tarullo, 'Norms and institutions in global competition policy', *American Journal of International Law*, vol. 94, no. 3, July 2000, pp. 478–504.
15. See 'Draft International Antitrust Code (DIAC)', *World Trade Materials*, vol. 5, September 1993, pp. 126–96. The draft code was a detailed, ambitious proposal for a binding international agreement on competition law that was put forward by a private group of academics and practitioners in July 1993.
16. See, for example, Communication from the European Community and its Member States (WT/WGTCP/W/152, 25 September 2000) and Communication from Japan (WT/WGTCP/W/156, 19 December 2000).
17. See also Anderson and Jenny, 'Current proposals'.
18. 'Draft International Antitrust Code (DIAC)'.
19. See also Garcia-Bercero and Amarasinha, 'Moving the trade and competition debate forward'.
20. Report (2002) of the Working Group on the Interaction between Trade and Competition Policy to the General Council, paragraph 76.

21. In a related vein, paragraph 24 of the Doha Ministerial Declaration specifies that assistance mandated by the Declaration will be provided 'in cooperation with other relevant intergovernmental organisations, including UNCTAD, and through appropriate regional and bilateral channels'. Ministerial Declaration (WT/MIN(01)/DEC/1, 9–14 November 2001), paragraph 24.

22. Robert D. Anderson and Peter Holmes, 'Competition policy and the future of the multilateral trading system', *Journal of International Economic Law*, vol. 5, no. 2, 2002, pp. 531–63.

23. For an interesting academic perspective on this question, see C.D. Ehlermann and L. Ehring, *WTO Dispute Settlement and Competition Law*, European University Institute Florence, Policy Paper 02/12 (2002).

24. See Contribution of Canada (WT/WGTCP/W/226).

25. See Report (2001) of the WTO Working Group on the Interaction between Trade and Competition Policy to the General Council (WT/WGTCP/5), paragraph 87 and, for related discussion, Garcia-Bercero and Amarasinha, 'Moving the trade and competition debate forward', pp. 504–6.

26. As a result of this intra-EU agreement, during the last meeting of the WTO Working Group on Competition, the EU delegate stated that competition experts would participate in WTO panels dealing with the competition agreement; this led the Hong Kong delegate to ask why this should be so since the EU had maintained that only *de jure* violations would be submitted to the panel. The question to the panel would then be whether or not the laws or regulations of a country met the WTO standard of non-discrimination and transparency; answering such questions would not require any particular expertise in competition law enforcement.

27. The fact that early on in the conference the EU put out a communiqué expressing sympathy for the African cotton growers and implicitly urging the USA to find a solution lends some credibility to this hypothesis.

CHAIRMAN'S COMMENTS

Geoffrey Owen

Professor Jenny's admirable account of the issues raised by transnational cartels, and the links between cartelization and trade policy, prompts three questions. How serious is the problem? What is the most effective means of dealing with it? Why are large, multinational companies, supposedly committed to high standards of corporate governance, apparently willing to condone price-fixing or market-sharing activities within their organizations?

On the first, most observers, especially those sympathetic to globalization, have assumed that the opening up of markets which has taken place over the last 20 years has increased competition, encouraged new entrants and reduced the market power of incumbents. This is certainly true in some sectors, such as automobiles, but, as Professor Jenny has reminded us, there are numerous cases where companies have sought in various ways to keep competition within bounds. This is particularly true of commodity-type, capital-intensive, price-sensitive industries such as aluminium, cement, pulp and paper, steel and bulk chemicals. Horizontal mergers have been frequent in these industries, leading to an oligopolistic structure which facilitates market-sharing arrangements.

This is an aspect of globalization which gets little publicity, perhaps because supporters of globalization and free markets, like myself, have been preoccupied with defending multinational companies against what seem to be unjustified attacks – that they exacerbate poverty in the developing world, that they trample on human rights, that they despoil the environment and so on. In rebutting these criticisms, we must be careful not to paint multinational companies in too rosy a colour. Like other businesses, they will be tempted to engage in anticompetitive practices if the opportunity and incentive to do so are there.

Evidence cited by Professor Jenny shows that transnational cartels are persistent and costly, especially to consumers in developing countries. Some researchers have even suggested that this type of activity is more extensive than at any time since the heyday of international cartels in the decades preceding the First World War. It is a blight on the world trading system which urgently needs to be addressed.

On the second question – how to curb and if possible eliminate transnational cartels – Professor Jenny has outlined a number of possible approaches, ranging from the minimalist to the highly ambitious. The easiest route is to promote the extension of bilateral agreements between national competition authorities. The problem is that these agreements are almost wholly confined to the advanced industrial countries which have well-developed competition laws and established competition authorities. These authorities have no jurisdiction over what happens in countries with which they do not have cooperation agreements, and no strong incentive to pursue anticompetitive practices which do not directly affect their domestic markets. Many developing countries, for their part, have no competition authorities, or are only just beginning to set them up. Under present arrangements, transnational cartels can too easily bypass national regulation.

Some form of multilateral solution is essential, and the World Trade Organization seems the obvious forum within which to develop a workable approach. This was the thinking that led to the inclusion of the so-called Singapore issues, one of which was competition, as topics to be dealt with in the current Doha Round of trade negotiations. Although there were dangers in this decision – particularly the risk of overloading the Doha Round with a set of tricky issues that might distract attention from dealing with the contentious subject of agriculture – it was entirely logical. Trade and competition policy are intimately linked, if only because, as Professor Jenny has shown in his paper, the gains from market-opening measures can all too easily be negated by anticompetitive behaviour.

Moreover, there is, at least in principle, a clear commonality of interest between developing and developed countries on transnational cartels. The developed world is committed to a liberal trading system. Developing countries want to import at competitive prices, and want their national companies to be free to trade fairly in world markets. In addition, as Professor Jenny has remarked, there is a public relations advantage in giving the WTO – so often portrayed by its critics as a tool of multinational companies – a central role in policing the anticompetitive behaviour of those firms. This might offset some of the damage caused by the inclusion within the WTO of TRIPS (trade-related intellectual property rights). This topic has been the subject of acrimonious argument between Western pharmaceutical companies and developing countries; although the argument has now been resolved, the whole affair put the pharmaceutical companies in a bad light.

In practice, reaching agreement on cartels and related competition questions has proved extraordinarily difficult. The ministerial meeting at Cancun made no progress on any of the Singapore issues, although the reasons for the failure may have had more to do with poor tactics on the part of the negotiators than with fundamental disagreements between them. Perhaps inevitably, the issue of cartels and competition became entwined with a range of other topics, all of which demanded flexibility on the part of the negotiating governments, and a willingness to make trade-offs. There were not enough of these qualities on display at Cancun.

The battle is by no means lost, and the principal lesson from Cancun is that progress towards an international agreement on cartels needs to take place gradually and incrementally, without any attempt by the developed countries to rush developing countries into commitments which they are not equipped to fulfil. It is a matter of fostering a competition culture, a greater understanding of the benefits that can come from national and international action against cartels – benefits that far exceed the costs of setting up and running a national competition authority. In this way the momentum towards a liberal, procompetitive trading system can be maintained.

The third question – why do multinational companies engage in international cartels – might be said to have been answered a long time ago by Adam Smith. If the incentive is there, and punishment is likely to be light or non-existent, companies will be inclined to fix prices and allocate markets. But this is entirely at odds with the strenuous efforts that multinational companies have been making in the last few years to burnish their reputation with elaborate commitments to high standards of corporate governance and corporate social responsibility. Some companies have established new board-level posts and new departments to deal with these topics; the vogue for 'triple-bottom-line' reporting (embracing social and environmental as well as financial issues) is spreading. Competition, and competition rules, tend to be given much less prominence at board level, except when the company finds itself embroiled in an investigation. Indeed, one has the impression that many boards of directors are largely unaware of whether or not codes of conduct on anticompetitive practices are in force throughout the company.

In the UK this is beginning to change as a result of recent legislation – the prospect of jail sentences for miscreants should concentrate the mind – but the focus of attention has been largely on domestic cartels, not transnational ones. Yet it is the latter that can cause serious damage to developing countries. Multinational companies are wont to claim that their operations, bringing investment and technology to countries which need them, are good for the world and help to reduce poverty, and for the most part these claims are justified. But some of these companies – an unknown number, since so few transnational cartels see the light of day – are engaged in activities that run counter to their rhetorical commitments. While international action to curb these practices is necessary, there also needs to be a much greater awareness of the issue among multinational companies themselves.

2. Does antitrust policy improve consumer welfare? Assessing the evidence*

Robert W. Crandall and Clifford Winston

Should the United Stales pursue a vigorous antitrust policy? Soon after the passage of the Sherman Antitrust Act of 1890, economists led by John Bates Clark (1901) argued that the enforcement of such laws should be informed by the prevailing economic theory on the merits of competition and the extent to which firms' conduct can enhance or weaken competition. However, economic theory since then has proven remarkably fertile in pointing out how various actions by firms may be interpreted as either procompetitive or anticompetitive. For example, when prices decline sufficiently so that no firm in an industry is earning economic profits and some firms exit, this outcome may reflect a highly competitive market adjusting to a condition of temporary oversupply, or it could indicate that a large competitor is employing a strategy of predatory pricing to drive out its rivals. Similarly, when a firm builds a large factory, it may be engaged in vigorous competition and new entry, or it may be creating excess capacity as an implicit threat to potential competitors that it may raise output and cut price quickly if circumstances warrant. Although economic theory can help organize analysis of the economic variables affected by antitrust policy, it often offers little policy guidance because almost any action by a firm short of outright price fixing can turn out to have procompetitive or anticompetit ive consequences.

Given this range of theoretical possibilities, the case for a tough and broad antitrust policy must rest on empirical evidence that shows that such policies have worked in the broad social interest. In this paper, we argue that the current empirical record of antitrust enforcement is weak. We start with an overview of the budgets and actions of the federal government's antitrust authorities. We then synthesize the available research regarding the economic effects of three major areas of antitrust policy and enforcement: changing the structure or behavior of monopolies; prosecuting firms that engage in anticompetitive practices, namely, price fixing and other forms of collusion; and reviewing proposed mergers. We find little empirical evidence that past interventions have provided much direct benefit to consumers or significantly deterred anticompetitive behavior.[1] We acknowledge that the literature has not been able to utilize all potentially fruitful sources of data and has rarely implemented recent empirical advances in industrial organization to analyze the effects of specific antitrust cases. Thus, the state of knowledge is not at a point where we are ready to make sweeping policy recommendations. Nonetheless, the economics profession should conclude that until it can provide some hard evidence that identifies where the antitrust authorities are significantly improving consumer welfare and can explain why some enforcement actions and remedies are helpful and others are not, those authorities would be well advised to prosecute only the most egregious anticompetitive violations.

THE SCOPE OF ANTITRUST ACTIVITY

US antitrust enforcement is primarily the responsibility of the Department of Justice (DOJ) and the Federal Trade Commission (FTC). (There are also state antitrust laws that are enforced by state attorneys general, but the federal activity is far more pervasive.) The DOJ enforces Section 1 of the Sherman Act prohibiting contracts, combinations and conspiracies in restraint of trade and also enforces Section 2 of the Sherman Act prohibiting actions to monopolize or attempts to monopolize markets. The DOJ and the FTC enforce Section 7 of the Clayton Antitrust Act of 1914 prohibiting mergers between firms that threaten to reduce competition substantially in any line of commerce. The Clayton Act also prohibits anticompetitive practices like tying arrangements (where consumers are forced to purchase from a firm a product like razor blades when they buy the firm's razors) and disallows competing firms from having overlapping boards of directors. The FTC may also initiate cases under Section 5 of the Federal Trade Commission Act for 'unfair methods of competition,' thereby providing it with the ability to combat abuses that DOJ attacks under Sections 1 and 2 of the Sherman Act. For example, the FTC initially investigated Microsoft for possible anticompetitive practices. The DOJ subsequently brought its Section 2 case after the FTC did not bring a complaint.

Data on investigations and budgets for the DOJ and the FTC, publicly available for only the past 20 years, are summarized in Table 2.1. Monopolization cases constitute a small share of antitrust investigations in a given year, but they still absorb a moderate fraction of the DOJ antitrust budget. The DOJ investigated a declining number of price-fixing

allegations and other potentially collusive arrangements such as vertical
market restraints during this period, but still spent at least one-third of
its budget on this activity. Investigations of proposed mergers currently
account for the largest share of antitrust activity, with the FTC handling
slightly more mergers than the DOJ. Until recently, the FTC's budget for
mergers was equal to the budget of the Antitrust Division of the DOJ for
all investigations.

*Table 2.1   DOJ Antitrust Division and FTC investigations and budgets:
1981, 1991, 2000 (in millions of year 2000 inflation-adjusted
dollars)*

Agency	Conduct	Investigations		
		1981	1991	2000
Antitrust Division	Monopolies	8	5	8
	Mergers	66	92	177
	Price fixing	145	77	82
FTC	Mergers	104	136	189
Total		323	310	456

Agency	Conduct	Budgets		
		1981	1991	2000
Antitrust Division[a]	Monopolies and mergers	$31.1	$23.3	$57.2
	Price fixing	$22.2	$24.6	$30.7
FTC[b]	Mergers	$54.4	$45.5	$59.0
Total		$107.7	$93.4	$146.9

Notes:
[a] Antitrust Division budgetary information does not distinguish between expenditures on
monopoly and merger cases.
[b] Although its primary antitrust responsibility concerns mergers, the FTC also occasionally
brings cases related to tying arrangements, price discrimination and unfair methods of
competition under provisions of the Clayton Act and the Federal Trade Commission Act.

Sources: US Budget, 1982, 1992, 2002; DOJ Budget. FY 1981, 1991, 2000: Antitrust Division
Workload Statistics 1981–1990, 1991–2000; 5th, 14th and 23rd Annual Hart–Scott–Rodino
Report (FY 1981, 1991 and 2000).

Total resources consumed by antitrust enforcement, however, amount to
much more than government antitrust agency expenditures shown in Table
2.1. Firms involved in antitrust cases must pay for legal advice, particularly
in obtaining approvals for mergers and acquisitions. Fisher and Lande
(1983) estimate that a merger case cost a firm as much as $1.5 million during

the 1980s. Firms that face a lawsuit must pay for their defense, which could involve a lengthy trial and subsequent appeals. Antitrust cases also require the time and resources of management and critical staff to address issues of firm conduct, to provide financial information and so on. We are not aware of estimates of the costs to firms caused by antitrust investigations and court proceedings, but they undoubtedly run into billions of dollars per year. Finally, the largest cost of antitrust enforcement may be that firms are discouraged from pursuing potentially efficient mergers, taking competitive pricing actions, developing new products or making new investments for fear of being embroiled in an antitrust action, especially if competitors use the antitrust authorities to block one another. Of course, the gains to consumers from curbing anticompetitive offenses could potentially outweigh these enforcement costs.

The ideal way to determine whether consumers have benefited from antitrust policy and enforcement in the areas of monopolization, collusion and mergers would be to compare consumer welfare with and without antitrust policy, all else constant.[2] However, twentieth-century US history has offered only one example of this counterfactual. During the Great Depression, antitrust laws were suspended for designated industries for a time as a byproduct of the 1933 National Industrial Recovery Act. Bittlingmayer (1995) studied this episode and found that prices did not rise, an intriguing finding, but dated and perhaps relevant only to the anomalous experience of the Great Depression. Other evidence is available from cases that compare prices before and after antitrust interventions or across industries subject to varying levels of antitrust enforcement.

MONOPOLIZATION

The Department of Justice typically investigates fewer than ten potential monopolization violations per year. To prove monopolization, the government must demonstrate that a firm has power over price and output in a market *and* that this power derives from business decisions whose principal intent and effect was to exclude competition (Areeda, 1988). Remedies in monopolization cases may be characterized as structural, behavioral or a reduction in the control of intellectual property. Structural remedies involve court-ordered changes in a firm's or industry's structure, such as horizontal divestiture, in which two or more directly competing companies are created from the assets of the defendant, and vertical divestiture, where separate companies are created at different production stages. Behavioral remedies address some aspect of the firm's behavior that the government identified as anticompetitive, such as tying arrangements, collusive agreements to exclude competitors, predatory pricing and so on. An enforcement agency must monitor those prohibitions, and the courts are inevitably required to resolve issues that arise between the agency and the firm. Finally, relief may involve forcing the firm to give up or to license key intellectual property that is the source of the alleged monopoly power.

Monopolization cases are impossible to analyze *en masse,* because they involve different market conditions and alleged misconduct over time. We therefore investigate the efficacy of antitrust policy in curbing monopolization by focusing on some landmark cases during the past century, including Standard Oil, American Tobacco, Alcoa, Paramount, United Shoe Machinery and AT&T. A detailed discussion of these and other cases and their effects on consumer welfare can be found in Crandall (2001). These cases are of particular interest here because the government prevailed in each of them and obtained substantial changes, leading to the expectation of consumer benefits. To be sure, these cases are decades old, but current law and attitudes toward monopolization are based on precedents established by such cases. We sketch each case and draw on the available empirical evidence to assess whether the remedy improved consumer welfare.

Standard Oil

During the late 1800s and early 1900s, the Standard Oil Company refined and marketed crude oil produced in Pennsylvania, Ohio, Indiana and several surrounding states and developed transportation and production facilities. Complaints about its business practices took various forms. Standard Oil was alleged to have used ruthless tactics in negotiating contracts with railroads and in denying independent oil companies access to its pipelines and transportation facilities. It was also alleged to have engaged in predatory pricing to drive rivals from the market, a claim disputed by McGee (1958). Public authorities feared that the Standard Oil 'Trust,' which pooled the company's profits, was a source of market power and facilitated price fixing. In 1911, the US Supreme Court upheld a 1909 lower court decision that Standard Oil had violated Sections 1 and 2 of the Sherman Act by attempting to monopolize the country's petroleum industry and using its New Jersey Trust to restrain trade (*Standard Oil Company of New Jersey v. United States*, 221 US 1 [1911]). The court's decree required that the Trust be dissolved, resulting in 38 separate and independent companies that were prohibited from being controlled by a single entity.

The government presumably expected the breakup of Standard Oil to reduce US refined petroleum product prices and perhaps also to reduce monopsony power over crude oil prices. Because of new oil discoveries, real crude oil prices were falling even before Standard Oil was brought to trial and actually rose somewhat after the breakup, as shown in Figure 2.1. Kerosene and gasoline prices fluctuated after the decree was entered. As a simple formal analysis, we collected annual time series data from 1889–1917, and we regressed real US crude oil prices on GNP, total automobile registrations and total electricity production (which control for major influences on petroleum demand), a time trend from 1889 to 1900 that controls for the opening up of new western US fields that increased petroleum supply, and a dissolution dummy (defined as 1 for 1912–17, 0 otherwise). The coefficient for the dissolution dummy was actually positive, 0.50, but statistically insignificant with a t-statistic of 0.88. (The dummy's sign and significance were not affected when we deleted some of the explanatory variables.)

Earlier commentators have also concluded that the breakup of Standard Oil had little effect on either consumers or on profits, because Standard's alleged market power had already declined substantially from its heyday.

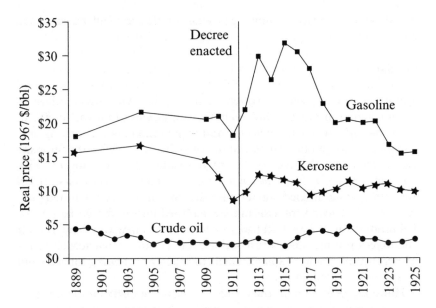

Notes: Gasoline and kerosene prices are deflated by the Consumer Price Index for all urban consumers. Crude oil prices are deflated by the GNP deflator.

Sources: Williamson et al. (1963); US Bureau of the Census, *Historical Statistics of the United States, Colonial Times to 1970, Bicentennial Edition* 224, 593–594 (US Department of Commerce, 1975); Bureau of Labor Statistics Internet.

Figure 2.1   Real petroleum product prices, 1899–1925

For example. Standard Oil's market share of refinery capacity in the United States had fallen before the decree from 82 percent in 1899 to 64 percent in 1911 as oil-producing regions in the mid-Continent, Gulf of Mexico and western regions developed, and well-capitalized independents such as Gulf Oil, Union Oil, the Texas Company, Sun Oil, Phillips and Cities Service provided competition. By 1920, Standard's share of refined petroleum products had fallen to 50 percent, but this decline was simply an extension of an earlier trend (Comanor and Scherer, 1995; Williamson et al., 1963). In addition, the breakup of Standard into a large number of separate companies did not dilute the Rockefeller family's control over the new entities. Thus, Burns (1977) concludes that the stock market interpreted the Standard Oil decree as 'benign.' The decree might have promoted competition had it been imposed before 1900, but by 1911, the oil industry was much more competitive and the decree had little effect.

American Tobacco

The American Tobacco Company produced little and regular cigars, plug and smoking tobacco, snuff and cigarettes. By 1910, it accounted for at least 75 percent of US sales of each product, except for its smaller share of regular cigars. Organized as a trust, it obtained its market position by acquiring firms such as Union Tobacco Company and the Continental Tobacco Company and by aggressive pricing behavior, which allegedly often resulted in prices below manufacturing costs (Tennant, 1950). In 1908, the federal government filed and won a Sherman Act case against American Tobacco that sought to dissolve the Trust. After the Supreme Court found that the trial court's initial dissolution remedy was extreme, the court entered a decree in *United States v. American Tobacco* (221 US 106 [1911]) that divided cigarette production into three separate parts: American Tobacco kept assets that accounted for roughly 37 percent of US production, P. Lorillard had 15 percent and a new company, Liggett and Myers, was provided with assets to produce brands that accounted for 28 percent of output. Assets devoted to plug and smoking tobacco and cigars were divided similarly.

However, the effect of restructuring the tobacco industry into a three-firm oligopoly was to unleash a battle for market share through advertising, not price (Tennant, 1950). Real cigarette prices were essentially stable in the few years preceding and following the decree, and they rose several years later in response to increases in tobacco excise taxes. The breakup of American Tobacco also did not affect the price paid to farmers for tobacco. Absent price competition, the three-firm oligopoly was highly profitable, essentially earning the same profit rate during 1912–49 as the Trust earned during

1898–1908. The stability of the industry's profit rate and the absence of any clear decline in prices after 1911 suggest that the American Tobacco case did little to spur meaningful competition in this industry.

Alcoa

The Aluminum Company of America ('Alcoa'), formerly the Pittsburgh Reduction Company, took its name in 1907 and by 1909 was integrated backward into mining ore and forward into fabricating products. Alcoa also controlled Aluminum Limited of Canada, the largest source of aluminum imports into the United States at the time. The production of aluminum consists of mining aluminum ore (usually bauxite), refining the ore to extract alumina, reducing alumina into aluminum ingot and fabricating the ingot into mill products like sheet, tube and wire. In 1912, the Department of Justice charged Alcoa with restraining trade and monopolizing the aluminum industry. Alcoa signed a consent decree that required it to give up its interest in its Canadian subsidiary, to terminate a contract with two chemical firms whose bauxite it had purchased, not to participate in any collusive agreements or mergers and not to discriminate against any competing fabricator in the sale of ingot.

But the decree did not reduce Alcoa's dominance of a very small market that, with economies of scale, could probably support only one supplier. By the late 1930s, Alcoa's primary production and imports still constituted 90 percent of the supply of aluminum in the United States. In 1937, the Department of Justice filed a Sherman Act civil suit, again charging Alcoa with monopolizing the aluminum market and restraining trade. The government appealed the District Court's 'not guilty' verdict to the Supreme Court, which could not muster a quorum because many justices had previously worked on the case. Legislation was enacted to allow the three senior judges of the Circuit Court of Appeals with territorial jurisdiction to serve as the ultimate appellate court. In *United States v. Aluminum Company of America,* 148 F.2d 416 (2d Cir. 1945), Judge Learned Hand reversed the lower court's decision, concluding that Alcoa had monopolized the market for primary aluminum and had engaged in a price squeeze from 1925 to 1932 by selling some aluminum sheet at prices that were too close to the price of primary aluminum ingot to allow independent fabricators to achieve adequate margins on their sales of aluminum sheet. Judge Hand did not rest his opinion on this violation, but identified it as a major problem to be dealt with in designing a remedy.

The final decree was postponed until after the Second World War, during which the government had constructed plants for alumina reduction, aluminum smelting and fabrication. Crandall (2001) provides empirical evidence that the decree had no effect on real aluminum prices and little effect on the margin between fabricated aluminum products and primary aluminum. After the war, virtually all of the government's aluminum properties were assigned to Reynolds Metals and Kaiser (then Permanente Metals Corporation), thus creating two viable competitors. In 1950, the District Court ruled against Alcoa's divestiture, but the court retained jurisdiction over the case for five years in the event that the two new competitors did not provide sufficient competition. Three additional companies entered the primary aluminum market between 1950 and 1955, again with government assistance, and in 1956 District Judge Cashin found sufficient evidence of competition and ruled against another five-year test.[3]

The failure of the first decree in 1912 to erode Alcoa's monopoly position derived from the small and even declining market for aluminum that by the early and mid-1980s amounted to fewer than 150 000 tons per year. In contrast, the second decree in 1945 required little of Alcoa because government programs dispersed production facilities to new entrants. When annual demand for aluminum grew in the 1940s and 1950s to more than 1.25 million tons, it is quite likely that more firms would have entered the market even without government assistance. Given that Alcoa could not control the supply of the two most important inputs to aluminum production, bauxite and electricity, it is difficult to conclude that it could have blocked entry after the Second World War. Moreover, the market was sufficiently large that Alcoa did not exhibit the characteristics of a natural monopoly. By 1955, Alcoa's market share was less than half of what it was when the government filed its 1937 lawsuit, yet its output was more than four times greater.

Paramount

The motion picture industry is composed of movie studios, film distributors and theatres. During the 1930s, some distributors owned theatre chains. The defendants in the Paramount case, initially brought in 1938, were five major distributors that owned theatres and three 'minor' distributors, which together controlled 95 percent of total film rentals in the early 1940s (Conant, 1960). In 1946, a US District Court found that the distributors had engaged in several practices that violated the Sherman Act, including fixing admission prices and restricting output to competing theatres through tying arrangements and 'formula deals.' The District Court's decree did not order divestiture, but prohibited agreements to maintain uniform prices and required a system of competitive bidding among theatres for each run of a feature film. The US Supreme Court, however, found the bidding system unworkable and in *United States v. Paramount Pictures* (334 US 131 [1948]) it ordered the lower court to reconsider divestiture. By the early 1950s, the five major distributors had completely divested their theatre chains.

The primary objective of the decree was to force distributors to compete for theatre space by offering attractive terms for renting their films. Independent distributors would presumably have better access to theatres, and new distributors might even enter. Under this scenario, admission prices would fall and the number of film distributors and annual film releases would increase. In fact, the average real price of a movie ticket rose in the two decades following the *Paramount* decision; specifically, the Consumer Price Index for indoor theatres rose 36.4 percent between 1948 and 1958, while the overall CPI rose just 20.1 percent. The trend continued during 1958–67, with the CPI for indoor theatres rising 68.9 percent, while the overall CPI rose just 15.5 percent. In addition, little entry occurred into motion picture distribution. Twenty years after the *Paramount* litigation, seven of the original eight defendants accounted for nearly three-fourths of all US theatrical rentals (Crandall, 1975).

Two interpretations are possible. Either the defendants' original actions were not raising ticket prices and restricting output, in which case the antitrust suit should not have been filed, or the decree failed to end collusive behavior. A fundamental problem in analyzing the postdecree market is evaluating how the introduction of television affected theatrical admissions, which declined dramatically. New entrants and independents may have fared poorly under these market conditions, and after decades of agreeing on clearances and lengths of runs, the *Paramount* defendants may have been able to coordinate a cartel agreement by reporting their weekly revenues from each theatre to the trade press. Distributors' share of theatrical admission receipts rose from 30.4 percent in 1948 to 45.8 percent in 1967. Thus, distributors captured approximately two-thirds of the 66 percent increase in real ticket prices during this period.

United Shoe Machinery

United Shoe Machinery manufactured a full line of machines used to produce shoes. By the 1940s, USM offered more than 300 types of machines, of which a shoe manufacturer might need as many as 100 to produce a shoe (Masten and Snyder, 1993). USM sold and leased its machines and provided repair and advisory services. In 1949, its market share of major machines was 91 percent, and its share of minor machines was 64 percent (Kaysen, 1956). The government claimed that USM had monopolized the shoe machinery market through leases that impeded the purchase or lease of its competitors' machines and prevented the development of a secondhand market. Exclusionary provisions of USM's leases included ten-year terms and a 'full capacity' clause that required lessees to use each machine to the fullest extent possible (Masten and Snyder, 1993). USM would charge shoe manufacturers with violating this clause if they switched to a competitor's machine, but waived the penalties if the cancellation was caused by changes in demand, conversion to manual operations or replacement with another USM machine.

In *United States v. United Shoe Machinery* (110 F. Supp. 295 [D.Mass. 1953]. aff'd. 347 US 521 [1954]), the US Supreme Court upheld a lower court decision that USM had illegally monopolized the shoe machinery market. The trial court declined to order the dissolution of USM, but structured a decree that prohibited USM from designing its lease and sales terms to make it substantially more advantageous to lease machines. In addition, the duration of all new leases had to be reduced to five years or less with an option to return machines after one year. Return charges or deferred payments were banned. The decree was intended to increase competition by encouraging the purchase of machines, thus creating a vibrant secondhand market, and inducing shoe manufacturers to be more receptive to machines offered by USM's competitors.

The decree did succeed in establishing a secondhand market for machines and reducing USM's market share from roughly 85 percent in 1953 to 62 percent in 1963 (Parrish, 1973). On the other hand, USM's revenue gains were more than twice the sum of its four major competitors' gains, and its return on equity remained relatively constant. The heterogeneity of shoe machinery prevents a direct assessment of shoe machinery prices before and after the decree. However, if the decree succeeded in reducing machinery prices, it is highly likely that shoe manufacturers would have incurred lower machinery expenses relative to the value of shoes produced. But based on data from the *Census of Manufacturers,* the ratio of the value of shoe machinery shipments to the value of shoe shipments remained at 0.012 between 1954 and 1967. (It is conceivable that the stability of relative shipment values could have reflected lower machinery prices and a substitution of machinery for labor in shoe production technology during this period, but no evidence exists to support this conjecture.)

In any event, the US Supreme Court was not satisfied that sufficient competition had developed in the shoe machinery market, because following a review of the decree, it recommended in 1969 that the lower court consider 'more definitive means' to achieve competition. As a result, USM was forced to divest itself of roughly one-third of its remaining shoe machinery operations. Unfortunately, the government required structural relief only after the shoe industry' had entered a steep decline because of the rise in imported shoes. It has even been speculated that the USM decree accelerated the demise of US shoe manufacturing, but we are not aware of evidence to support this conclusion.

AT&T

In 1974, the US Department of Justice brought a monopolization case against AT&T, which eventually led to a 1982 consent decree that divested AT&T of its local operating companies, creating in 1984 seven regional Bell companies that provide local phone service. AT&T retained its long distance operations and a telephone equipment company that is now called Lucent. Following the breakup, long distance telephone competition dramatically increased and rates fell, so there is at least some *prima facie* evidence that consumers benefited from this monopolization case.

But on closer examination, the rise in competition and lower long distance prices are attributable to just one aspect of the 1982 decree; specifically, a requirement that the Bell companies modify their switching facilities to provide equal access to all long distance carriers. The Federal Communications Commission (FCC) could have promulgated such a requirement without the intervention of the antitrust authorities. For example, the Canadian regulatory commission imposed equal access on its vertically integrated carriers, including Bell Canada, in 1993. As a result, long distance competition developed much more rapidly in Canada than it had in the United States (Crandall and Hazlett, 2001). The FCC, however, was trying to block MCI from competing in ordinary long distance services when the AT&T case was filed by the Department of Justice in 1974. In contrast to Canadian and more recent European experience, a lengthy antitrust battle and a disruptive vertical dissolution were required in the US market to offset the FCC's anticompetitive policies. Thus, antitrust policy did not triumph in this case over restrictive practices by a monopolist to block competition, but instead it overcame anticompetitive policies by a federal regulatory agency.

Overall Lessons and Recent Monopoly Cases

This brief overview of landmark monopolization cases suggests several reasons why such cases have often failed to increase competition to the benefit of consumers.

One problem is the protracted length of these cases, which often take so long that industry competition has changed before the remedy is implemented, as in *Standard Oil* and *Alcoa*. This problem has also arisen in modern monopolization cases, like those involving IBM and Microsoft. The first monopolization case against IBM was brought in 1952 and settled by consent decree in 1956, but there is little evidence that it had favorable effects on competition in the computer industry, which was rapidly replacing tabulating machines with mainframe computers (Wilder, 1975). IBM quickly vaulted to a dominant position in mainframes, leading the Department of Justice to file another case in 1969. That case was dropped in 1982, in no small part because the market had changed once again (Fisher et al., 1983). The ultimate merits of the *Microsoft* case are not yet clear, but it has already required six years of litigation (excluding the FTC's earlier investigation), and the court's final judgment is still being appealed. By the time it is resolved, the information technology market is likely to have changed substantially.

Another major problem occurs when a monopolization case simply fails to benefit consumers because the remedy turns out to have a negligible practical impact, as may have happened in *American Tobacco, Paramount* and *United Shoe Machinery.* Recently, a number of monopoly cases like those filed against Safeway and A&P were brought in an attempt to stop the replacement of small grocery stores by large national food chains, but these cases have had little effect on market concentration because they could not prevent more efficient chains from replacing less efficient small retailers (Crandall and Elzinga, 2002).

Similarly, airlines that dominate hub airports have been accused of having monopoly power and in some cases of engaging in predatory pricing behavior to protect hub markets. In 1999, the Department of Justice filed a predatory pricing suit against American Airlines – but lost on summary judgment. Morrison and Winston (2000) cast doubt on the claim that airlines are successfully engaging in predatory behavior. They also show that fares may be higher on hub routes than on other routes because a hub carrier has market power or because low-cost Southwest Airlines mainly serves nonhub routes and significantly depresses fares in these markets. In any case, the cost to travelers from a hub 'premium' is clearly offset by hub benefits, including greater flight frequency and agglomeration economies in areas surrounding the airport.

Challenging large firms in court is often politically popular, but neither policymakers nor economists have yet to offer compelling evidence of marked consumer gains from antitrust policy toward monopolization.

COLLUSION

Explicit agreements to fix prices are often treated by the antitrust authorities and the courts as *per se* violations, which means that evidence of an agreement is sufficient to prove guilt. A wide variety of other restrictive practices are potentially collusive – including exclusive contracts, exclusive territories and others. The courts have generally adopted a 'rule of reason' standard for these practices, which means that they are judged on a case-by-case basis with earlier precedents in mind.[4] The Department of Justice investigates about 100 allegations of price fixing a year and often proceeds with indictments.

Retrospective assessments of some of these cases have failed to find much direct benefit from curbing alleged instances of collusion. (Besides price fixing, very few empirical studies exist of cases involving collusive practices.) For example, Newmark (1988) found that an antitrust indictment of bakers in Seattle had no effect on the price of bread, and Morrison and Winston (1996) concluded that a consent decree that prohibited airlines from announcing the ending dates of their fare promotions had no effect on fares. More systematically, Sproul (1993) analyzed a sample of 25 price-fixing cases between 1973 and 1984 for which usable price data were available. He argued that if a cartel succeeds in raising prices, then prosecution should lower them. However, he found that, controlling for other influences, prices *rose* an average of 7 percent four years after an indictment. Sproul also found that prices rose, on average, even if one uses a starting point during the investigation but before the indictment. Even in the most successful cases, prices fell only 10 percent.

One possible explanation for why these cases have not generally resulted in price declines is that the Department of Justice may in some instances be prosecuting firms that are engaging in activities that involve other goals besides raising prices. For example, Sproul (1993) suggests that a cartel may reduce costs through shared advertising and research, which may tend to reduce prices rather than to increase them. Another possibility is that a cartel may be pursuing distributional goals. For instance, MIT and Ivy League colleges established a tradition of coordinating their need-based financial aid decisions. The schools claimed that the so-called Overlap process enabled them to concentrate their scarce financial resources on needy students without affecting their total revenues. The government sued, claiming that the schools were conspiring on financial aid policies to reduce aid and raise revenues. Carlton et al. (1995) found that the process did not have a statistically significant effect on the average 'price' paid per student, but that it prevented the flow of school resources from lower- to higher-income students. Hoxby (2000) corroborates this finding.

To be sure, there are well-known examples where firms have clearly colluded to raise prices, including recent cases involving lysine, citric acid and vitamins. However, researchers have not shown that government prosecution of alleged collusion has systematically led to significant nontransitory declines in consumer prices.

MERGERS

Department of Justice and Federal Trade Commission investigations of proposed mergers absorb more than half of federal antitrust resources. The Hart–Scott–Rodino Antitrust Improvement Act of 1976 requires any firm valued over $100 million to file a premerger notification under various conditions, the most common of which is that it plans to merge with another firm valued at more than $50 million. After filing the notification, firms must wait 30 days before they can proceed with the merger. During this period, the FTC or the DOJ can request additional time and information (known as a 'second request') before deciding whether to approve or oppose the merger.

Mergers may harm or benefit consumers. Mergers that enable firms to acquire market power may only raise consumer prices, while mergers that enable firms to realize operational and managerial efficiencies can reduce costs and thereby lower prices. Economists generally conclude that taken as a group, mergers are not anticompetitive. Andrade et al. (2001) argue that mergers through the 1990s have produced efficiency improvements leading to a modest 1 percent gain in postmerger operating margins. Carlton and Perloff (1994) claim that the increase in shareholder value from a merger in the United States is not typically due to the creation of market power. But even if one accepts that the average merger results in an efficiency gain, antitrust enforcement could be good or bad, depending on how well the antitrust authorities distinguish procompetitive mergers from anticompetitive ones.

How can a researcher sort out whether the mergers that are blocked or that have conditions attached by the DOJ or the FTC are the ones that would have led to anticompetitive outcomes and welfare losses? With a monopoly, one can observe its impact on consumers before and after antitrust action. But a blocked merger is never observed, and thus its effects cannot be compared directly to what would have happened if the merger had been allowed. This difficulty helps to explain why we could not find any case studies that showed that the FTC or DOJ prevented significant welfare losses by blocking or attaching conditions to a proposed merger.[5]

One approach to investigating whether the antitrust authorities can distinguish good from bad mergers is to look at stock price data, which are presumably forward looking, to test the hypothesis that horizontal mergers challenged by the government would have created market power in the defendants' industries. This is done by estimating whether proposed merger-induced changes in expected future product and factor prices translate into positive abnormal stock returns to firms competing in the same industry as well as to the merging firms. Eckbo's (1992) conclusion from this literature is that the mergers that were challenged were not anticompetitive and in all likelihood would have been efficient had they been allowed to go through.

Another approach is to consider whether the reporting requirements of the Hart–Scott–Rodino Act of 1976 have enabled the antitrust agencies to judge a merger's competitive impact better before filing a complaint. Eckbo and Wier (1985) use stock price data to analyze merger cases filed after 1978 and find that the proposed mergers would not have harmed competition. Thus, they conclude that the Act has not helped the agencies improve their case selection record.

Still another approach is to look at mergers that were challenged or opposed by the antitrust regulators, but were consummated anyway. Such mergers have often worked well for consumers. For example, the FTC unsuccessfully challenged Weyerhaeuser's acquisition of Menasha, which led to a decline in corrugated box prices (Schumann et al., 1997). Similarly, the DOJ opposed airline mergers between TWA and Ozark and between Northwest and Republic. However, the Department of Transportation allowed the two mergers. Morrison (1996) conducted a long-run analysis that improved upon previous airline merger assessments by considering fares well before and up to the merger and fares immediately and several years after the merger. He found that the TWA–Ozark merger led to a 15 percent decline in fares and that the Northwest–Republic merger led to a 2 percent increase in fares, which may have been offset by benefits from greater route coverage.

We now turn to a broad assessment of recent merger policy based on price–cost margins across industries. Although there are well-known measurement concerns with using price–cost margins, greater market power should increase them, *ceteris paribus*. We also recognize that using interindustry data to explain price–cost margins can be problematic. But this line of research has matured to the point where it has produced a set of 'stylized facts' about industry competition (Schmalensee, 1989). Our hope is that the suggestive findings from this exercise will be viewed in combination with other researchers' findings about the effects of antitrust merger policy, rather than dismissed on doctrinal grounds.

For our dependent variable, we use price–cost margins from 1984 to 1996 for the 20 manufacturing industries that are defined at the two-digit SIC level (using the pre-1997 classification system). We choose this time period and sample based on data availability. Outcomes of merger cases are available back to 1982. However, we will specify merger enforcement variables with two-year lags (see below), thus we can analyze price–cost margins only as far back as 1984. In addition, case outcomes are publicly available only at the two-digit level of aggregation, while consistent estimates of industry price–cost margins are available only for manufacturing industries.

In our regression, price-cost margins are assumed to be influenced by court-based outcomes, second requests for information and industry characteristics. The court-based outcomes we include are the number of successful and unsuccessful merger challenges, as well as the number of consent decrees reached by the government and the firms proposing to merge. In a given year, the vast majority of these court-based outcomes are consent decrees; during the period covered by our sample, there were nine cases that went to a verdict and 88 cases settled by a consent decree. Our sample also contains 368 second requests for information, which may have discouraged some of the proposed mergers from moving forward. Each case is only counted once even if there were multiple decisions. An industry is not likely to experience the effect of antitrust merger policy immediately; thus, the estimation is based on two-year lags for the court-based outcomes and second requests. Following previous specifications like that of Salinger (1990), we include the following industry characteristics: the import–sales ratio, to control for foreign competition; the capital–sales ratio, to control for technology; and the growth of the number of firms in an industry with a five-year lag (because this lag provided the best statistical fit), to control for entry.[6]

If antitrust interventions against mergers are benefiting consumers, price–cost margins in an industry should fall from what they would have been when the government successfully challenges a merger in court or negotiates a consent decree. Second requests for information may also lower prices by discouraging anticompetitive mergers from moving forward. If antitrust investigations are focusing on mergers that primarily have efficiency effects, price–cost margins should rise from what they would have been when the government successfully challenges a merger in court or negotiates a consent decree because the merger, as proposed, would have reduced firms' costs.[7]

Our results are presented in Table 2.2. The parameter estimates of the industry characteristics are plausible. A higher import–sales ratio and firm growth reduces an industry's price–cost margin, as does an increase in an industry's capital–sales ratio. Salinger (1990) found that the capital–sales ratio had a positive effect on price–cost margins during the 1970s, but that its effect became negative during the early 1980s. This negative coefficient persisted during the 1980s downturn and expansion; the negative coefficient in Table 2.2 is consistent with this finding.

The coefficients of the court-based outcomes are of central interest and suggest that merger enforcement policy is primarily undermining mergers that would enhance efficiency, rather than protecting competition. We

Table 2.2 Price–cost margin parameter estimates (robust standard errors in parentheses)

Variable	Coefficient
Court-based outcomes	
Mergers successfully blocked by FTC or DOJ (2-year lag)	–0.040 (0.032)
Mergers unsuccessfully challenged by FTC or DOJ (2-year lag)	–0.038[a] (0.011)
Consent decrees (2-year lag)	0.017[a] (0.004)
Other outcomes	
Second request for information made by FTC or DOJ (2-year lag)	–0.001 (0.002)
Industry characteristics	
Import–sales ratio	–0.071[a] (0.020)
Log of the growth of the number of firms (5-year lag)	–0.721[a] (0.188)
Capital–sales ratio	–0.105[a] (0.008)
Constant	0.518[a] (0.018)
R^2	0.45
Number of observations	260

Notes:
[a] Statistically significant at the 1 percent level.
The price–cost margin variable is constructed following standard practice as (value added + Δ inventories – payroll)/(value of shipments + Δ inventories). Data for each of the components were obtained from the *Annual Survey of Manufacturers*, published by the Bureau of the Census, for 1984 to 1996.

Sources:
For the import–sales ratio from 1984 to 1996, total imports were obtained from Robert Feenstra, who assembled data from the US Department of Commerce and the *US Industry and Trade Outlook*. Sales data, reported as shipments, were from the *Annual Survey of Manufacturers*.

Growth of the number of firms was obtained from the *Economic Census*, published every five years by the Bureau of the Census and from the annual *County Business Patterns* (CBP), also published by the Census. The *Economic Census* contains firm data, while the CBP contains plant data that were used to estimate the number of firms. The ratio of plants to firms in the 'benchmark' years of 1977, 1982, 1987 and 1992 was used to generate an estimate for the growth of the number of firms on an annual basis.

For the capital–sales ratio, capital is measured as the historical cost of the net stock of fixed private capital and is from *Fixed Reproducible Tangible Wealth*, published by the Bureau of Economic Analysis within the Department of Commerce. For sales, see above.

Data on the number of mergers successfully challenged in court, mergers unsuccessfully challenged in court, consent decrees and second requests are from the Hart–Scott–Rodino *Annual Reports*, which are annual reports to Congress prepared jointly by the FTC and the Antitrust Division of the DOJ. Court outcomes were described in each report, and the SIC codes for the companies involved in the cases were determined by consulting FTC and DOJ case histories.

find that a successful merger challenge does have a negative effect on the price–cost margin, but that the effect is not statistically significant. In contrast, an unsuccessful challenge in which a court eventually allows the proposed merger is associated with a decline in price–cost margins, and the effect is statistically significant. The most optimistic interpretation to place on these findings is that potential challenges from antitrust authorities succeed in blocking or discouraging mergers that would reduce welfare and that the courts do not allow the regulators to block mergers that improve economic welfare. However, we believe that a more plausible interpretation, consistent with the findings reported earlier in the section and the statistically insignificant effect of second requests, is that the mergers blocked by antitrust authorities have no significant effect on price–cost margins in those industries because the regulators are not sorting out good mergers from bad ones with much accuracy. Further, the negative and statistically significant coefficient of unsuccessful court challenges suggests that the antitrust authorities overreach and attempt to block productive mergers, although only a handful of merger cases actually reach a court verdict.

When the government and the potential merger partners reach a consent decree to gain regulatory approval for the merger, price–cost margins in the industry subsequently increase. In our data, the FTC and DOJ negotiated 45 percent of their consent decrees with companies that at that time were in two-digit industries located in the upper quintile of price–cost margins. This finding can be interpreted either as an argument that the antitrust authorities should have negotiated stronger conditions to address potential anticompetitive problems or that the consent decrees allowed mergers to go forward only when the firms were saddled with conditions that compromised production efficiencies. Neither interpretation is complimentary to the antitrust authorities.[8]

We do not want to overstate our confidence in the specific estimated coefficients from Table 2.2. It would clearly be preferable to have more disaggregated data for more industries. As we have noted, the findings can be interpreted in various ways. There are, of course, counterexamples of individual mergers that have raised prices (for example, Barton and Sherman, 1984). But the regression results are not biased in any particular direction and are broadly consistent with the other empirical evidence that we have surveyed. We can only conclude that efforts by antitrust authorities to block particular mergers or affect a merger's outcome by allowing it only if certain conditions are met under a consent decree have not been found to increase consumer welfare in any systematic way, and in some instances the intervention may even have reduced consumer welfare.

DETERRING ANTICOMPETITIVE BEHAVIOR

Given the lack of direct evidence that antitrust actions on monopolization, collusion and mergers have promoted competition and benefited consumers, supporters of an activist antitrust policy are left with the argument that such policy deters firms from anticompetitive behavior. If the authorities had not prosecuted IBM, AT&T, Microsoft and others, who knows what abuses would have occurred? Admittedly, providing evidence on what has been deterred, and therefore did not happen, is a difficult task. In any event, we have not found any evidence that antitrust enforcement has deterred firms from engaging in actions that would have seriously banned consumers.

Historically, it has been suggested that government victories in *Standard Oil* and *American Tobacco* deterred other companies, such as US Steel, from pursuing similar paths to monopoly power. However, Comanor and Scherer (1995) conclude that US Steel's failure to maintain its large share of the country's steel output in the first half of the twentieth century was due to its high costs, not to a concerted effort to avoid antitrust prosecution.

International evidence has been used to assess the deterrence effect of the antitrust laws. Stigler (1966) compared concentration in specific industries in England, which at the time did not have a public policy against concentration of control, with the same industries in the United Stales and concluded that the Sherman Act has had a very modest effect in reducing US concentration. Eckbo (1992) explored whether the antitrust laws deter potentially anticompetitive mergers by estimating whether the probability that a horizontal merger is anticompetitive was higher in Canada, where until 1985 mergers were essentially unconstrained, than in the United States. His analysis compared estimated parameters in cross-section models that explained announcement stock returns to merging firms and their nonmerging industry rivals as a function of industry concentration in the two countries. Based on this comparison, he rejected the hypothesis that the US antitrust laws are deterring anticompetitive mergers.

Although we have not found any evidence that the antitrust laws have had beneficial deterrence effects, we suspect that such effects exist. However, any deterrent effect of the antitrust laws may be relatively small compared with the well-demonstrated ability of competitive markets to deter anticompetitive monopolies, collusion and mergers. We have identified a few of the many instances where erstwhile monopolies have seen their market shares eroded by new competitors: Standard Oil, US Steel, Alcoa and IBM, for example. Moreover, collusion among firms is more difficult than it may appear. Stigler (1964) pointed out that even when few firms compete in a market, it may be difficult for them to reach a consensus on price and market shares, and even if they do, they may not be able to discourage cheating.

Empirical evidence from the rail, airline, ready-to-eat cereal and brewing industries illustrates some of the ways that markets prevent firms from successfully colluding. Beginning in the mid-1980s, electric utilities that received coal shipments from the Powder River Basin in Wyoming were served by only two railroads. Many economists would expect that the two carriers would be able to come to some arrangement that elevates rates above competitive levels. However, Gaskins (2001) found that rail rates in the Powder River Basin approached long-run marginal costs, suggesting that carriers were not colluding on prices. It seems that shippers are able to play one railroad off against another when negotiating long-term contracts to reduce their rates, because if a carrier does not compete fiercely for a shipper's traffic, it may have to wait several years before it has an opportunity to recapture any traffic that it loses (Grimm and Winston, 2000).

In April 1992, the president of American Airlines Robert L. Crandall attempted to introduce some discipline in airline pricing by urging other carriers to adopt American's pricing regimen of four basic fares and reduced full-fare coach and first-class fares. But American's influence was too limited to get other carriers to follow its lead (Morrison and Winston, 1995). By October 1992, Crandall abandoned the strategy, bemoaning: 'We tried to provide some price leadership but it didn't work, so we are back into the death by a thousand cuts' (Lollar, 1992).

In contrast to railroads and airlines, the ready-to-eat cereal and brewing industries are characterized by persistently high price–cost margins. Economists have explored whether market power in these industries is attributable to collusive pricing behavior, but have rejected this explanation. Cereal firms (Nevo, 2001) and brewers (Baker and Bresnahan, 1985) have engaged in nonprice competition, particularly through advertising, to influence the perceived quality of their products and to elevate price–cost margins. Indeed, firms that produce differentiated products face less incentive to engage in and find it more difficult to maintain collusive agreements than firms that produce homogeneous products.

There is a widespread belief that the antitrust laws deter collusion more than they deter attempts to monopolize. Firms and individuals convicted of price fixing are subject to federal criminal penalties and also vulnerable to private suits for treble damages. Block et al. (1981) provide evidence that such class actions are the strongest deterrence against collusion. It is possible that the Department of Justice has succeeded in deterring the most serious instances of price fixing and has therefore been increasingly prosecuting marginal cases, but this surmise has not been documented. Recently, the Antitrust Division of the Department of Justice has attempted to strengthen deterrence by imposing higher fines on corporations for price fixing and expanding the use of corporate leniency for firms that disclose their role in a conspiracy and cooperate with the government. However, Kobayashi (2002) develops a model of optimal deterrence and cautions that these actions may lead to overdeterrence, which would induce excessive investments in monitoring and prevention, raise production costs and result in higher consumer prices.

Finally, the surrounding climate of market competition is also an important reason why most mergers are not anticompetitive. Indeed, Paulter's (2001) survey of the literature on mergers concludes that they 'fail' 35 percent to 75 percent of the time, where failure is determined by survival, profitability, retention of assets and so on. Because of internal and external market forces, mergers have much less predictable outcomes than do most other business investments. It is also noteworthy that although the US economy experienced major waves of large mergers during the 1980s and 1990s, aggregate concentration has not increased over the past two decades (White, 2002).

Most of US industry is structurally competitive. For example, Pashigian (2000) used a government task force's definition of an imperfectly competitive market as one with a four-firm concentration ratio above 70 percent and found that in 1992 only 46 out of 398 four-digit US manufacturing industries met this threshold.[9] In a competitive climate, monopolies will tend to be eroded, collusive agreements will fall apart and mergers will either provide efficiency benefits or fail. Any additional deterrence antitrust policy provides should be evaluated in this context.[10]

CONCLUSION

The apparent ineffectiveness of antitrust policy stems from several causes: (1) the excessive duration of monopolization cases, which portends that the particular issue being addressed will evolve into something different – often of less importance – by the time it is resolved; (2) the difficulties in formulating effective remedies for monopolization and effective consent decrees for proposed mergers; (3) the difficulties in sorting out which mergers or instances of potentially anticompetitive behavior threaten consumer welfare; (4) the substantial and growing challenges of formulating and implementing effective antitrust policies in a new economy characterized by dynamic competition, rapid technological change and important intellectual property (Carlton and Gertner, 2002); (5) political forces that influence which antitrust cases are initiated, settled or dropped (Weingast and Moran, 1983; Coate et al., 1995), including situations where firms try to exploit the antitrust process to gain a competitive advantage over their rivals (Baumol and Ordover, 1985); (6) the power of the market as an effective force for spurring competition and curbing anticompetitive abuses, which leaves antitrust policy with relatively little to do.

We recognize that antitrust doctrines have changed and continue to change over time (Baker, 2002). Our concern is that these changes have not been motivated and guided by empirical assessments that identify which policies have and have not succeeded in increasing consumer welfare.

We also believe, however, that the evidence presented here would be more extensive and persuasive if researchers had greater access to potentially informative sources of data and employed the latest empirical developments in industrial organization. The DOJ and the FTC could help advance our knowledge of the effects of antitrust policy by making more data generated by cases available to researchers. Indeed, we were restricted to using two-digit industry classifications for court-based and other outcomes in mergers, even though the antitrust authorities have this information at a more disaggregated level. Baker and Rubinfeld (1999) survey models that economists have developed to analyze price-fixing, mergers and oligopoly conduct, but fail to identify a single instance where any of these models has been used to assess the welfare effects of antitrust policy. Clearly, economists should make greater efforts to use such methodological tools to aid our understanding of antitrust.

The present state of and gaps in our knowledge suggest a short-term and long-term course of action. Until economists have hard evidence that the current antitrust statutes and the institutions that administer them are generating social benefits, the Federal Trade Commission and the Department of Justice should focus on the most significant and egregious violations, such as blatant price fixing and merger-to-monopoly and treat most other apparent threats to competition with benign neglect. As the antitrust research agenda evolves, we envision that economists may identify cases where antitrust policy has improved consumer welfare. If they do, the long-term task will be to explain why certain policies have been counterproductive and others helpful and to provide guidance for how antitrust resources can be confined to beneficial activities.[11] A research agenda has emerged for those who are truly interested in improving the consumer welfare effects of antitrust policy and enforcement.

NOTES

[*]   This chapter first appeared in the *Journal of Economic Perspectives*, vol. 17, no.4, Fall 2003, 3–26. Reproduced with kind permission of the American Economic Association.
     A long list of people provided us with helpful comments on previous drafts. We are grateful to them and the editors for their help and to David Zipper for research assistance.

1. Our focus is on academic assessments of antitrust policy, not studies conducted by federal agencies. In fact, there are very few government assessments of the economic effects of past antitrust decisions. When the government has examined the outcome of mergers or divestiture orders, its focus has typically not been on competition or consumer welfare, but on the viability of the proposed action. For example, the Federal Trade Commission's Bureau of Competition (1999) examined the viability of divestitures in 35 merger cases between 1990 and 1994 in which divestiture orders were issued as a condition for approving the merger.
2. Our assessment does not include cases involving allegations of price discrimination brought under Section 2 of the Clayton Act, because such cases have been relatively rare during the past 20 years.
3. The court reporter numbers for the key decisions in the Alcoa case include *United States v. Aluminum Company of America*, 44 F. Supp. 97 (S.D.N.Y. 1941); *United States v. Aluminum Company of America*, 148 F.2d 416 (2d Cir. 1945); *United States v. Aluminum Company of America*, 91 F. Supp. 333 (S.D.N.Y. 1950).
4. Under resale price maintenance agreements, for example, a producer of a product sets a price that the retailer may not undercut. The procompetitive argument for such agreements is that they encourage the retailer to invest in knowledge and service about the product. The likelihood of prosecution in such cases was substantially reduced by a 1997 Supreme Court decision (*State Oil Company v. Khan*, 522 US 3 [1997]). Also. Ippolito and Overstreet (1996) provide some evidence that resale price maintenance produced efficiency gains.
5. Pittman (1990) estimates that the Santa Fe–Southern Pacific rail merger, which was opposed by the Department of Justice and blocked by the Interstate Commerce Commission, would have led to annual operating cost savings by the carriers, but deadweight losses of roughly $100 million. Southern Pacific, however, had failed to become 'revenue adequate' and probably could only survive with a merger. Indeed, it subsequently merged with Union Pacific, which led to disastrous service disruptions in the southwest that cost shippers billions of dollars. In any case, many observers of the rail industry envision that the 'final frontier' of the industry is for the two remaining railroads in the East and the two in the West to form two efficient transcontinental railroads (Grimm and Winston, 2000).
6. Of course, we experimented with this specification in various ways. For example, using one-year lags and no lags had little effect on the main findings. Our findings did not change when we specified court-based outcomes and second requests as a percentage of the total mergers proposed in an industry in a given year. They were also not affected when we specified separate coefficients for interventions by the DOJ and the FTC. We tried using industry fixed effects to control for unmeasured industry characteristics, but the parameters for the court-based outcomes and second requests were not affected if the fixed effects were excluded from the specification; thus, they are not included here. It is possible that merger policy could influence the rate of entry; thus, we estimated a model that dropped this variable, but found that this specification did not affect the parameters for the merger policy variables, so we kept it in the specification. We also estimated models that controlled for several other potential influences on the price–cost margin, including macroeconomic variables (unemployment, interest rates, GDP growth), year fixed effects, industry output growth, selected commodity dummies and a time trend, but these variables were statistically insignificant.
7. If antitrust enforcement were fully optimal and complete, then all the enforcement variables should be statistically insignificant because the DOJ and FTC would have thwarted all anticompetitive attempts to raise price–cost margins and not thwarted mergers that would have lowered price–cost margins. The preceding summary of evidence suggests that it is extremely unlikely that merger policy has been optimal.
8. It is possible that the mergers may have involved antitrust markets within a given two-digit industry that had price–cost margins that were quite different from a two-digit industry's average price–cost margin; for example, a merger may have occurred within a relatively concentrated subindustry of a relatively unconcentrated industry. Because we control for other systematic influences on two-digit industry price–cost margins, our methodology

should uncover the impact of merger policy, albeit with a somewhat diluted effect. The extent of this dilution, however, is not clear; after all, we do find that two of the four merger policy variables had statistically significant effects.

9. This theme that the market is largely competitive is compatible with the common finding that the US economy has experienced only a small deadweight loss from noncompetitive pricing. Harberger's (1954) initial finding of a deadweight loss of roughly 0.1 percent of GDP has been revisited by several authors. Cowling and Mueller (1978) found a much larger deadweight loss than other researchers because they included advertising expenditures as part of welfare losses. More recent estimates summarized by Ferguson (1988) indicate a deadweight loss of about 1 percent of GDP. These estimates of deadweight loss are not fully appropriate for our purposes, however. Our focus is on consumer benefits, which would involve transfers from consumers to firms, not just on deadweight loss. Moreover, the estimates of losses from imperfect competition include distortions caused by government interventions such as regulations and trade protection, but do not include possible offsetting dynamic benefits of imperfect competition, such as greater investments in R&D that lead to enhanced product quality and design.

10. In his response to this paper. Baker tries to advance the argument that antitrust policy has significant deterrence effects. But he fails to acknowledge that the influx of foreign competition, deregulation, the entry of new firms and the emergence of new technologies has created an extremely competitive environment for contemporary US industry. Indeed, Baker's evidence regarding deterrence is mainly drawn from episodes that predate the current intensity of industry competition. Moreover, the antitrust authorities may deter firms from actions that either increase or reduce social welfare. Baker fails to provide a balanced quantitative assessment of the effects of deterrence, so we have no feel for the impact or even the sign of this component of antitrust policy.

11. Baker's response initiates an all-purpose defense of antitrust policy, rather than distinguishing good antitrust policy from that which is ineffective, irrelevant or harmful.

REFERENCES

Andrade, Gregor, Mark Mitchell and Eric Stafford (2001), 'New evidence and perspectives on mergers', *Journal of Economic Perspectives*, Spring, 15. pp. 103–20.

Areeda, Philip (1988), *Antitrust Analysis*, Boston. MA: Little, Brown and Company.

Baker, Jonathan B. (2002), 'A preface to post-Chicago antitrust', in Roger van den Bergh, Roberto Pardolesi and Antonio Cucinotta (eds), *Post-Chicago Developments in Antitrust Law*, Cheltenham, UK: Edward Elgar, chapter 1.

Baker, Jonathan F. and Timothy F. Bresnahan (1985), 'The gains from merger or collusion in product-differentiated industries', *Journal of Industrial Economics*, June, 33, pp. 427–44.

Baker, Jonathan B. and Daniel L. Rubinfeld, (1999), 'Empirical methods in antitrust litigation: review and critique', *American Law and Economics Review*, 1 (1–2), 386–435.

Barton, David M. and Roger Sherman (1984), 'The price and profit effects of horizontal merger: a case study', *Journal of Industrial Economics*, December, 33, pp. 165–77.

Baumol, William J. and Janusz A. Ordover (1985), 'Use of antitrust to subvert competition', *Journal of Law and Economics*, May 28, pp. 247–65.

Bittlingmayer, George (1995), 'Output and stock prices when antitrust is suspended: the effects of the NIRA', in Fred S. McChesney and William F. Shugart II (eds),

The Causes and Consequences of Antitrust, Chicago: University of Chicago Press, pp. 287–318.

Block, Michael Kent, Frederick Carl Nold and Joseph Gregory Sidak (1981), 'The deterrent effect of antitrust enforcement', *Journal of Political Economy*, June, 89, pp. 429–45.

Burns, Malcolm R. (1977), 'The competitive effects of trust-busting: a portfolio analysis', *Journal of Political Economy*, August, 85, pp. 717–39.

Carlton, Dennis W. and Robert H. Gertner (2002), 'Intellectual property, antitrust, and strategic behavior', NBER Working Paper 8978, June.

Carlton, Dennis W. and Jeffrey M. Perloff (1994), *Modern Industrial Organization*, 2nd edn., New York: HarperCollins.

Carlton, Dennis W., Gustavo E. Bamberger and Roy J. Epstein (1995), 'Antitrust and higher education: was there a conspiracy to restrict financial aid?', *Rand Journal of Economics*, Spring, 26, pp. 131–47.

Clark, John B. (1901), *The Control of Trusts*, New York: Macmillan.

Coate, Malcolm B., Richard S. Higgins and Fred S. McChesney (1995), 'Bureaucracy and Politics in FTC. Merger Challenges', in Fred S. McChesney and William F. Shugart II (eds) *The Causes and Consequences of Antitrust*, Chicago: University of Chicago Press, pp. 213–30.

Comanor, William S. and F.M. Scherer (1995), 'Rewriting history: the early Sherman Act monopolization cases', *International Journal of Economics and Business*, 2(2), 263–89.

Conant, Michael (1960), *Antitrust in the Motion Picture Industry*, Berkeley, CA: University of California Press.

Cowling, Keith and Dennis C. Mueller (1978), 'The social costs of monopoly power', *Economic Journal*, December, 88, pp. 727–48.

Crandall, Robert W. (1975), 'The postwar performance of the motion-picture industry', *Antitrust Bulletin*, Spring, 2, pp. 49–88.

Crandall, Robert W. (2001), 'The failure of structural remedies in Sherman Act monopolization cases', *Oregon Law Review*, Spring, 80, pp. 109–98.

Crandall, Robert W. and Kenneth G. Elzinga (2002), 'Injunctive relief in Sherman Act monopolization cases', Brookings Institution working paper.

Crandall, Robert W. and Thomas W. Hazlett (2001), 'Telecommunications policy reform in the United States and Canada', in Martin Cave and Robert W. Crandall (eds), *Telecommunications Liberalization on Two Sides of the Atlantic*, Washington, DC: AEI–Brookings Joint Center for Regulatory Studies, pp. 8–38.

Eckbo, B. Espen (1992), 'Mergers and the value of antitrust deterrence', *Journal of Finance*, July 47, pp. 1005–1029.

Eckbo, B. Espen and Peggy Wier (1985), 'Antimerger Policy under the Hart–Scott–Rodino Act: a reexamination of the market power hypothesis', *Journal of Law and Economics*, April, 28, pp. 119–49.

Federal Trade Commission (1999), *A Study of the Commission's Divestiture Process*, Washington. DC: Bureau of Competition, Federal Trade Commission.

Ferguson, Paul R. (1988), *Industrial Economics: Issues and Perspectives*, London: Macmillan.

Fisher, Alan A. and Robert H. Lande (1983), 'Efficiency considerations in merger enforcement', *California Law Review*, December, 71. pp. 1580–1673.

Fisher, Franklin M., John J. McGowan and Joen E. Greenwood (1983), *Folded, Spindled, and Mutilated Economic Analysis and U.S. v. IBM*, Cambridge, MA: MIT Press.

Gaskins, Darius (2001), 'Duopoly pricing of coal transportation', Unpublished paper, August.

Grimm, Curtis and Clifford Winston (2000), 'Competition in the deregulated railroad industry: sources, effects, and policy issues,' in Sam Peltzman and Clifford Winston, (eds), *Deregulation of Network Industries: What's Next?* Washington, DC: Brookings Institution, pp. 41–71.

Harberger, Arnold (1954), 'Monopoly and Resource Allocation', *American Economic Review*, May, 44. pp. 77–87.

Hoxby, Caroline M. (2000), 'Benevolent colluders? The effects of antitrust action on college financial aid and tuition', NBER Working Paper No. 7754, June.

Ippolito, Pauline M. and Thomas R. Overstreet Jr. (1996), 'Resale price maintenance: an economic assessment of the Federal Trade Commission's case against the Corning Glass Works', *Journal of Law and Economics*, April, 39, pp. 285–328.

Kaysen, Carl (1956), *United Slates v. United Shoe Machinery Corporation*, Cambridge, MA: Harvard University Press.

Kobayashi, Bruce (2002), 'Antitrust, agency and amnesty: an economic analysis of the criminal enforcement of the antitrust laws against corporations', George Mason University School of Law, Law and Economics Working Paper Series No. 02–04.

Lollar, Coleman (1992), 'Back to the bad old days', *Frequent Flyer*, December.

Masten, Scott E. and Edward A. Snyder (1993), 'United States versus United Shoe Machinery Corporation: on the merits', *Journal of Law and Economics*, April. 36, pp. 33–70.

McGee, John S. (1958), 'Predatory price cutting: the Standard Oil (N.J.) Case', *Journal of Law and Economics*, October, 1. pp. 137–68.

Morrison, Steven A. (1996), 'Airline mergers: a longer view', *Journal of Transport Economics and Policy*, September, 30, pp. 237–50.

Morrison, Steven A. and Clifford Winston (1995), *The Evolution of the Airline Industry*, Washington, DC: Brookings Institution.

Morrison, Steven A. and Clifford Winston (1996), 'Causes and consequences of airline fare wars', *Brookings Papers on Economic Activity: Microeconomics*, pp. 85–123.

Morrison, Steven A. and Clifford Winston (2000), 'The remaining role for government policy in the deregulated airline industry', in Sam Peltzman and Clifford Winston (eds), *Deregulation of Network Industries: What's Next?*, Washington, DC: Brookings Institution, pp. 1–40.

Nevo, Aviv (2001), 'Measuring market power in the ready-to-eat cereal industry', *Econometrica*, March, 69, pp. 307–42.

Newmark, Craig M. (1988), 'Does horizontal price fixing raise price? A look at the Bakers of Washington case', *Journal of Law and Economics*, October, 31, pp. 469–84.

Parrish, Gordon (1973), 'The Experience with Antitrust Relief in Shoe Machinery', unpublished Ph.D. dissertation. Department of Economics, Washington State University.

Pashigian, B. Peter (2000), 'Teaching microeconomics in Wonderland', Working Paper 161, George J. Stigler Center for the Study of the Economy and the State, University of Chicago, July.

Paulter, Paul A. (2001), 'Evidence on mergers and acquisitions', Bureau of Economics. Federal Trade Commission, Washington, DC, September.

Pittman. Russell W. (1990), 'Railroads and competition: the Santa Fe/Southern Pacific merger proposal', *Journal of Industrial Economics*, September. 39, pp. 25–46.

Salinger, Michael (1990), 'The concentration–margins relationship reconsidered', *Brookings Papers on Economic Activity: Microeconomics*, pp. 287–335.

Schmalensee, Richard (1989), 'Inter-industry studies of structure and performance', in Richard Schmalensee and Robert Willig (eds), *Handbook of Industrial Organization, Volume 2*, Amsterdam: North-Holland, pp. 951–1009.

Schumann, Lawrence, James D. Reitzes and Robert P. Rogers (1997), 'In the matter of Weyerhaeuser Company: the use of a hold-separate order in a merger with horizontal and vertical effects', *Journal of Regulatory Economics*, **11**(3), 271–89.

Sproul, Michael F. (1993), 'Antitrust and prices', *Journal of Political Economy*, August, 101, pp. 741–54.

Stigler, George J. (1964), 'A theory of oligopoly', *Journal of Political Economy*, February, 72, pp. 44–61.

Stigler, George J. (1966), 'The economic effects of the antitrust laws', *Journal of Law and Economics*, October, 9. pp. 225–58.

Tennant, Richard B. (1950), *The American Cigarette Industry. A Study in Economic Analysis and Public Policy*, New Haven, Conn.: Yale University Press.

Weingast, Barry R. and Mark J. Moran (1983), 'Bureaucratic discretion or congressional control? Regulatory policymaking by the Federal Trade Commission', *Journal of Political Economy*, October, 91, pp. 765–800.

White, Lawrence J. (2002), 'Trends in aggregate concentration in the United States', *Journal of Economic Perspectives*, Fall, 16, pp. 137–60.

Wilder, Ronald P. (1975), 'The electronic data processing industry: market structure and policy issues', *Antitrust Bulletin*, Spring. 2, pp. 25–47.

Williamson, Harold F., Ralph L. Andreano, Arnold R. Daum and Gilbert C. Klose (1963), *The American Petroleum Industry. The Age of Energy 1899–1959*, Evanston, ILL: Northwestern University Press.

CHAIRMAN'S COMMENTS

David Arculus

I will give a British perspective on the issues discussed in this paper, though mainly from the point of view of regulation rather than antitrust policy, as I am head of the Better Regulation Task Force and my job is to marry up some of the economic considerations mentioned with some of the political realities.

I became head of the Better Regulation Task Force in 2002, picking up the reins from Chris Haskins. Obviously in establishing the Task Force, the government was acknowledging that some bodies felt that regulation was becoming a big issue. My time in the job so far has involved putting in and refining the tools of Better Regulation, some of which were established by my predecessor – notably what we call the five principles. These are that regulation should be tested against whether it is proportionate, accountable, consistent, transparent and targeted, and we encourage all in government to test their proposals and regulations against these principles.

Government departments are also expected to carry out a Regulatory Impact Assessment – a form of cost–benefit analysis – for any proposal for regulation which has an impact on business, charities or the voluntary bodies. Broadly speaking, if the benefits do not exceed the costs, then the proposals should not go ahead. That has been quite a difficult concept to ingrain. However, with the work of the Task Force, in conjunction with a variety of other measures, we are now getting there, and have around 92 per cent compliance across government. The aim is to have 100 per cent compliance by 2005.

Consultation is also extremely important because generally the answer as to how to achieve the outcome government desires resides with the practitioners. So people should be asked about government proposals before legislation is even considered. In the UK there is a Code of Practice on consultation which is binding on all UK government departments and their agencies. The Code sets out standards for consultations run by government and aims to increase the involvement of individuals and groups in public consultations and to give them enough time to respond, all of which helps to reduce the risk of unintended consequences.

Alternatives to regulation are also extremely important; we recently published a report on this (see below). But there are also other tools government has put in place such as the system of Regulatory Reform Orders which can amend primary legislation without the need for a bill, as long as it removes or reduces burdens. There are, for instance, something like one hundred and twenty-six Fire Safety Acts in the UK, which have obviously been built up over the last hundred years or so. If you are running a small hotel, this is inconvenient because about thirty-five of those Acts tend to impinge on your business in some way. So we recommended in our 'Hotels and Restaurants' report that government should simplify the vast array of fire safety legislation. The government agreed and also accepted our recommendation to use a Regulatory Reform Order, which is now going through. There are a number of other examples of Regulatory Reform Orders, such as on business tenancies.

Those are the five main tools we have. To give them more teeth, the Task Force, with the support of government, has taken on a new role. We can draw to the attention of the National Audit Office (NAO) ten Regulatory Impact Assessments where we feel that departments could have done better. The NAO is investigating and will, it is hoped, produce a report pointing out to departments where they can do better – in other words, helping them to learn from their experiences.[1]

The Task Force itself produces about four or five reports per year into particular areas of regulation and the prime minister has asked the relevant government minister to respond within 60 days.

However, it occurred to me that there are a great many independent regulators, for example bodies such as English Heritage and the Accounting Standards Board, that do not seem to be accountable to anybody in Britain. So we carried out a study to see how many of these bodies there are. We identified 108 independent regulators, and that is excluding the economic regulators such as Ofwat and Ofcom, for example, but there could well be more. So if you are running a hospital, you may have to deal with up to 36 of those independent regulators simultaneously. No wonder the health service is having a few bureaucratic problems at the present time!

In the rest of my period of office as head of the BRTF, I aim to improve how we deal with some of the issues that the authors mention. But we need to try to introduce a culture change into government, as the government is a kind of regulating machine. Ministers go into politics because they want to change things, so when they become ministers they start to pass bills. Civil servants obviously want to please their ministers, so they look at ways of facilitating that. What we have to do is to convince civil servants in particular that they can stand up to ministers and suggest that primary legislation may not always be the only way forward. I am starting to look for examples of good practice in the civil service in terms of coming up with non-legislative alternatives, and writing letters of congratulation to show that alternative approaches do not go unnoticed. It is also important to get business to engage much better with government. There is a huge amount of complaining about regulation in Britain. But also a large number of people do not ever bother to reply to government consultations, do not appeal to ministers and so on. The whole process of engagement with government by business and by public-sector institutions can be improved. And most important of all, we must influence Europe more. It is estimated that 40 per cent of the substantive regulation affecting the UK comes out of Europe at present, and that is certainly not a problem the USA has to contend with. We must engage much better with the European Community. I hope that when we have our presidency in 2005, we will make Better Regulation a key focus.

In respect of alternatives to regulation, the Task Force tries to make it more difficult for ministers arbitrarily to introduce more regulation – we are a bit like a piece of grit in the shoe: when the minister puts his foot down we just make it a little bit uncomfortable for him. We ask him to think again and make sure that he is on the right track. Education and information provision are important as alternatives to regulation. For instance, the government is trying to educate people about health with its five-a-day fruit and veg. campaign. There are areas where classic regulation and education can be mixed, for example the drink-driving campaign, which had a very strong advertising campaign, but also statutory, legal underpinning. Incentives are extremely important. For example, we are struggling to get tradable permits working in the UK. We have a carbon trading scheme and I hope that the USA will likewise introduce one: it is obviously crucial to the whole global warming agenda, and will certainly work much better when the USA participates.

We are also looking at taxes that encourage particular types of behaviour, for example the landfill tax. If you want people to recycle you have to make it more expensive for them to dump waste. Tax incentives have also been important in the UK, particularly in terms of boosting R&D in some areas.

In addition, we have followed experiments in self-regulation with interest. We have bodies such as the Advertising Standards Association, the Press Complaints Commission and the Association of British Travel Agents, which have helped to put into practice tools such as co-regulation and approved codes of practice. One example where alternatives have worked extremely well is in the building industry. Most of the health-related problems in this industry are caused by bad backs, and most of the bad backs are caused, or were caused, by lifting 50 kg sacks of cement. It was a relatively simple matter for the Health and Safety Executive to persuade the six manufacturers of cement in the UK that they should bag their cement in 25 kg sacks: lo and behold, back injury has fallen substantially.

We are experimenting in the UK with all these alternatives to regulation, and what we are saying to government is: we understand the outcome you want to achieve; please do not specify the process. Leave it to the market to find the best way of getting to the desired result. This will encourage a good deal of innovation in the process. The wealthier society gets, the more the public and the press will urge regulation. I do not think we can stop the tide of regulation: we must concentrate on making it better.

Note

1. The NAO published their report, 'Evaluation of Regulatory Impact Assessments Compendium Report 2003–04', in March 2004.

3. Efficiencies in merger control

Jrissy Motis, Damien Neven and Paul Seabright*

1. INTRODUCTION

Two years ago, Paul Seabright presented a lecture in this series in which he observed, on the occasion of the ten-year anniversary of EU merger control, that little was known about the source of efficiencies in mergers. In that lecture, he also put forward a simple framework to think about the motivation behind mergers, as a particular form of corporate restructuring, and the source of synergies between merging partners. In this paper, we report on some of the work that we have undertaken on synergies and the source of efficiencies in mergers in the last few years. We outline the framework that we have developed to think about mergers, summarize some of the empirical evidence that we have gathered and discuss the insights that the framework yields into the role of competition authorities. This work provides some confirmation that the reallocation of intangible assets is a significant motivation for mergers and a source of merger-specific efficiencies. With respect to the role of competition authorities, we will suggest that they should systematically ask about the activities that can only be undertaken through the proposed merger and seek evidence from the merging parties about the plans that they have developed to integrate their activities. We will also suggest that synergies are of particular importance compared to technical efficiencies because the latter are in principle achievable by other means than a merger, and if in practice they are not likely to be achieved otherwise, this will tend to signal that rivalry is weak in the market where the merging firms are active.

Developing a better understanding of efficiencies seems to be essential for improving the precision of EU merger control; indeed, when the current treatment of efficiencies in the EU is considered in light of empirical regularities with respect to the importance and distribution of efficiencies across mergers, it would appear that the EU approach is likely to generate significant type II errors (circumstances where anticompetitive mergers are allowed) as well as type I errors (circumstances where procompetitive or neutral mergers are prohibited or remedies are imposed).

We first consider some empirical regularities.[1] Three methodologies are typically used in order to assess whether mergers lead to efficiencies; these methods consider profits, or the share of the profits that accrue to shareholders, and hence do not directly capture efficiencies. Changes in returns can be estimated *ex ante*, from the change in stock market value of the merging partners when the merger is announced. They can also be estimated *ex post*, when returns accruing to the shareholders of the merging entity are compared with those obtained from companies that are similar but did not merge. Finally, the comparison between the merging partners and other similar companies can be undertaken in terms of accounting profits – rather than returns to shareholders.

These methods have some shortcomings: in particular, they focus on profits rather than efficiency, and profits can be obtained, for instance, through the exercise of market power, without efficiencies. In contrast, enhanced profits arising from the exploitation of efficiencies can sometimes be competed away within a short period of time (for instance, when efficiencies diffuse among competitors). In addition, the choice of an appropriate comparator group to assess performance is often difficult, because the performance of firms that are comparable to the merging partners is often directly affected by that of the merging entity. Keeping these shortcomings in mind, the following hard facts emerge: first, mergers generate small returns on average, and often these returns are not statistically different from zero. Second, the targets obtain on average a very large share of the gains that can accrue. However, these averages conceal a substantial amount of variance across deals. Regarding returns, one observes that many mergers simply fail and generate important negative returns. According to some estimates, as many as 60 per cent of mergers fail. As many as 30 per cent of mergers lead to subsequent divestitures that are acknowledged by firms as resulting from a failure of the merging plans. However, some mergers lead to substantial gains. A similar variance is observed with respect to the distribution of gains and some bidders obtain a significant share of the gains.

Consider now the essential features of the EU procedure. The substantive criterion under which EU merger control has been operating is 'the creation or strengthening of a dominant position as a result of which effective competition would be significantly impeded in the common market' (Art. 2.2 of the EC merger regulation – ECMR). This criterion is further informed by Art. 2.1b, which stipulates that in evaluating mergers the Commission should take into account the 'development of technical and economic progress provided that it is to consumers' advantage and does not form an obstacle to competition'.

The insistence on positive consumers' advantage suggests that the EU operates with a consumer surplus standard and that efficiencies can be used in order to claim that consumers are likely to benefit. At the same time, in the vast majority of cases, the EU does not consider efficiencies and waves mergers through after it has convinced itself that anticompetitive effects are unimportant (in the absence of efficiencies). The EU has only considered efficiencies where, under the assumption that there were none, significant anticompetitive effects were observed.

Consider first the cases where efficiencies are not considered. Given that in the absence of some efficiencies (broadly speaking), mergers cannot be to consumers' advantage, the EU procedure must rely on a presumption that efficiencies are sufficiently significant and widespread to compensate for the (relatively minor) anticompetitive effects that it has identified in those cases. Yet, as mentioned above, there is ample empirical evidence that efficiencies may not be large on average and also that many mergers fail to generate efficiencies. In those circumstances, one can expect the EU to make many type II errors, namely to allow mergers on the presumption that they would generate efficiencies which never materialize. And indeed, there is evidence that the EU has very different expectations from stock market analysts regarding the anticompetitive effects of mergers that it waves through; for instance, Duso et al. (2003) find that a significant proportion of mergers that were cleared by the EU (without remedies) generated a positive reaction in the stock market price of competitors, which suggests at least a reasonable probability that they were expected to lead to higher prices in the industry.[2]

Consider next those cases where efficiencies have been considered because without them the merger would be expected to lead to important anticompetitive effects. There are few cases where according to the published decisions efficiencies were explicitly considered and, to the best of our knowledge, none where efficiencies have be considered to be sufficient to change the Commission's mind. There may also be a number cases in which efficiencies were discussed during the proceedings and many cases where the parties did not put forward any claim regarding efficiencies because they were unclear about the Commission's policy in this area. However, these observations certainly suggest that the Commission will have made some type I errors: it is highly unlikely that in the course of the last ten years, the Commission would not have encountered a merger where efficiencies did indeed make a difference. This presumption is supported by the existing empirical evidence on merger efficiencies, discussed above, which reveals a very high dispersion across mergers. There are some very efficient mergers and, with a sample of more than 1500 units, the Commission should have encountered a few – in which there were also anticompetitive problems.

Overall, it appears that developing a better understanding of efficiencies and reliable procedure to evaluate them would significantly contribute to a more effective screening of mergers.

At the outset, it also seems important to distinguish between efficiencies that could be achieved by other means than a merger and those that can only be achieved through this particular form of corporate reorganization. We will suggest that antitrust authorities should focus on the latter.

There is no well-accepted terminology with respect to efficiencies, and in this study we adopt the terminology used by Farrell and Shapiro (2001), which refers to technical efficiencies to describe those gains that could be obtained otherwise and synergies to describe efficiencies that can only be achieved by merging. Technical efficiencies correspond to changes within the joint production possibilities of the merging parties. In the short term, they can be achieved by a reallocation of output across different units or the achievement of scale economies if capital is mobile. In the longer run, they can be achieved by undertaking investment on a larger scale. By contrast, synergies are associated with a shift in the production possibilities of the merging parties.

Technical efficiencies could thus in principle be achieved by other means than a merger. In the long term, the production possibilities of the merging parties are the same as the production possibilities of an individual firm and efficient production plans can be achieved, for instance, by internal growth. That is not to say, however, that technical efficiencies *would* have been achieved absent the merger and what the antitrust authorities should consider is not whether efficiencies could be achieved otherwise but whether they would.

Still, as emphasized by Farrell and Shapiro (2001), there are good reasons to believe that if technical efficiencies would not be achieved absent the merger, it is likely that the merger will have significant anticompetitive consequences. The reason is simply that the incentive to achieve efficiencies for individual firms and their incentive to grow and achieve scale economies is partly determined by their competitive environment. With a competitive structure inducing limited rivalry, firms will have little incentive to achieve these efficiencies. But these are also the circumstances where a merger is likely to have serious anticompetitive consequences.[3]

This does not mean that technical efficiencies should be given less weight than synergies in evaluating the benefits of the transaction in question. Rather it implies that the very circumstances that justify regarding the technical efficiencies as merger specific will increase the probability that the threats to competition are sufficient to outweigh the benefits from efficiencies whatever their source. This increases the importance of improving our understanding of synergies and their role in the merger process. However, despite their practical importance, the discussion of synergies has been relatively neglected in the economic literature. There is a general recognition that synergies involve either a process of learning across merging parties or the close integration of specific, 'hard to trade' assets owned by the merging parties. But the consequences of this approach for the analysis of mergers and merger control have not been investigated systematically (at least in the industrial organization/antitrust literature), and the importance of synergies in mergers has not yet been properly investigated empirically. Our work attempts to contribute to these research questions.

In order to understand where synergies come from, we ask why firms have chosen that form of corporate reorganization. An answer to that question will identify the private gains that firms could only achieve by merging and help identify synergies, that is, the enlargement in firms' production possibilities that mergers allow for. But the answer will also provide an important key to understanding the role of the competition authorities in evaluating efficiencies. For it will never be reasonable to suppose that the authorities are simply better at evaluating efficiencies than the firms themselves. The view of regulatory authorities as simply wiser than private firms has long been discredited. What the authorities can do instead is to evaluate the procedures that the firms have used in their own evaluation – in order to determine, for example, whether firms have genuinely identified merger-specific efficiencies rather than using the merger as a lazy way to gain market share.

Section 2 develops a simple analytical framework in order to investigate the source of merger-specific gains and synergies. Section 3 discusses the evidence that we have gathered to validate this framework. Section 5 discusses the consequences of this approach for merger control procedures.

2. CORPORATE RESTRUCTURING, INTANGIBLE ASSETS AND SYNERGIES

A firm may have decided to acquire or merge with another because the underlying assets of its partners could not be acquired. Reputation, knowledge and organizational assets are typically difficult to trade in part because contracts regarding the transfer of these assets are highly incomplete. In addition, the interaction between assets, in particular when it involves reputation, knowledge and organizational assets, is typically poorly understood and difficult to codify, so that the ability to make these assets interact efficiently with one another and with physical and human assets is typically not contractually enforceable. Because of the difficulty in describing and codifying their operation, these assets can be described as 'intangibles'. For instance, the productivity of a research team can be contingent on dimensions that are poorly understood and controlled. It may be associated with a mode of communication among researchers which is highly informal and made possible by particular circumstances (the age distribution, the location of the researchers or the culture of the organization). The interaction between physical assets and the knowledge associated with a patent may also be dependent on parameters that are poorly understood. A good example of this is provided by the production of carton packages in aseptic conditions. Aseptic packaging machines have been sold for more than two decades by Tetra Laval, but competitors have been unable to reproduce machines with the same level of reliability, despite the fact that all the necessary technology is in the public domain or licensed. It is widely believed in the industry that the process by which aseptic carton packages are effectively produced is not fully understood even by Tetra Laval itself.

When intangible assets are involved, the bundle of assets operated by the firm will enable it to undertake a range of activities, offer a set of products or services and achieve a level of productivity in producing them that are not easy for others to replicate. The corporation itself only owns the assets that can be traded and enters into formal contracts with others, but its production possibilities are associated with a particular combination of intangible assets that work together in a certain way.

In this framework, when one corporation chooses to buy another it is because it could not replicate what this other corporation does (if it could, it would simply buy its component tradable assets independently – or would accumulate the assets through internal growth). It must be that it is really trying to buy tradable assets in the hope that it will benefit from the combination of tangible and intangible assets operated by that corporation as well. So paradoxically the key to understanding this kind of trade is to see it as a contractual exchange of assets, in which the assets enumerated are not the primary motive for the transaction.

In this perspective, firms will thus engage in mergers and acquisition because they anticipate that additional value will be generated by recombining assets and the source of these gains must be found in the operation of intangible assets. That is, firms must anticipate that the particular bundle of assets operated by each firm can be combined in new ways which generate additional value: firms are trying to generate a specific combination of the assets which will generate value in excess of the value that they generate in their current use. One extreme example of such a situation would be one in which a target firm is a bundle of tradable but intangible assets that generate low returns. Think, for instance, of a portfolio of IP (intellectual property) rights and a manufacturing facility. If IP rights were not to some extent intangible, their interactions with the manufacturing facility could be easily predicted and the inadequate performance could be immediately corrected by management. But the interaction of IP rights with the manufacturing facility is difficult to predict: the improvement in performance may require for instance a different combination of IP rights in the portfolio from that used by the target. The identification and implementation of this remedy may itself require another intangible asset, for instance an organizational asset. An acquirer who has access to this asset will then be in a position to apply his own organizational skills to the target and improve his performance. This would be a situation where the interaction between the intangible assets of acquirers and targets is limited. More generally, however, one would expect that the intangible assets of both firms will be reorganized in complex ways in order to expand the production possibilities of both.

Before turning to the empirical validation of our framework, a number of comments may be in order. First, although the recombination of intangible assets provides a motivation behind mergers, it is by no means the only one. For instance, mergers can be motivated by market power, concerns about investment in specific capital or the pursuit of objectives by managers that may have little to do with profits. These alternative motives should be kept in mind while undertaking an empirical analysis of mergers.

Second, if in general the merger-specific gains that firms anticipate from recombining their assets will be associated with some synergies (an expansion of their production possibilities), it may come at the expense of consumers and competitors. As in the case of technical efficiencies, it will be necessary from a public policy perspective to disentangle the effects that corporate restructuring will have on the merging entity, competitors and consumers. This will be further discussed in the concluding section.

3.   EMPIRICAL EVIDENCE

Three distinct hypotheses can be derived from the theoretical framework discussed above.

Hypothesis 1: Mergers that achieve significant positive returns should be associated with the presence of intangible assets in the merging parties. Hence, we will test whether returns are correlated with the intensity of intangibles.

Hypothesis 2: Given the central role that intangible assets play in mergers and acquisitions, the returns that they generate should be highly variable. Since the operations of intangible assets are hard to predict, the recombination of assets which is taking place in mergers and acquisitions is to some extent a gamble; some recombination may be uncharted territory but attempted on the basis of the firms' limited understanding of how the intangible assets operate. The recombination of assets may have been experienced in other circumstances but the very nature of intangibles is such that the parameters which determine their operation are not all fully understood and controlled. Hence past experience will offer a poor guide to future performance. Overall, mergers and acquisitions involving intangibles will involve high risks: it should not come as a surprise that many of them fail to generate the returns that were contemplated when they were undertaken. In addition, the returns to deployment of intangible assets may take relatively extreme values (see Lev, 2001), with success generating substantial returns but failure generating massive losses.[4] Accordingly, we will test whether mergers involving large intangible assets also display a higher variance of returns.

Hypothesis 3: The allocation of the potential gains from mergers between acquirer and target, or between merging partners, may be affected by the importance of intangible assets. The insight comes from auction theory, which suggests that the winner of an auction is the bidder who has the highest willingness to pay among all bidders for the object being sold and that he/she will pay a price equal the second highest willingness to pay realized among the bidders.[5] Hence, when there is only a single bidder who can manage to generate value from a merger, he/she should pay a price equal to zero, or in other words, should not pay a premium in excess of the market value of the target. He/she will appropriate the value that he/she can generate and, in those circumstances, most of the gains from the merger should thus accrue to the bidder. More generally, if both the assets of the bidder and those of the target are necessary in order to generate value, one would expect that targets and bidders (having equal bargaining power) will share the gains equally. By contrast, when a number of alternative bidders can generate value, the price paid by the winner may be close to the value that he/she expects to generate from the merger (because the second highest bidder will have a willingness to pay which is close to his/her own). In those circumstances, the target will appropriate most of the expected gain from the merger.

As discussed above, when the merger is associated with the deployment of intangible assets, it is unlikely that many acquirers, or many merging partners, will anticipate the same gains from recombining their assets. This will arise because different potential acquirers or different potential merging partners will operate different bundles of assets. Even if assets are similar, the uncertainty involved in operating intangible assets will make it very unlikely that different partners have the same understanding of how the assets are operated and end up with a similar assessment of the potential gains. Hence one would expect that none of the merging partners will face an alternative candidate (bidder) who would anticipate similar gains. In such an environment, it is likely that the gains will be split evenly between merging partners or between the acquirer and the target. By contrast, when no intangible assets are involved, we expect that several merging partners will be able to replicate the gains from the merger. The competition between these alternative partners will then exhaust the rent that they will obtain. In this case, one of the merging firms, typically the target, will obtain most of the gains.

In a companion paper,[6] we investigate these hypotheses in a sample of mergers. The empirical investigation uses two sources of information with respect to the value of intangible assets. We use accounting data on intangible assets in firms' balance sheets, and a market-based measure of intangibles, which also considers the difference between the firms' market value prior to the merger and its book value. With respect to the evaluation of gains from mergers, we rely on stock market data. That is, we assume that the gain in the value of the firms concerned from some suitable date prior to the announcement of the transaction to a suitable date afterwards provides an unbiased estimate of the gain yielded by the transaction to the firms' shareholders, controlling for other factors that may influence that value of the shares of the firms concerned. We control for these other factors by calculating the gain in firm value compared to what would have occurred if the firms' shares had simply mirrored the evolution of the market index for the relevant sector between the two dates (we call such measures index-adjusted). Our data are drawn from the SDC Thomson and Datastream databases. Our sample includes about 330 firms for which we have data on gains and intangibles.[7] Our sample of transactions with index-adjusted gains is about one-third smaller than that with unadjusted gains (that is, about 250 deals).

As discussed in Motis et al. (2003), we do not find a strong support for our first hypothesis; there is no clear pattern suggesting that deals undertaken by firms for whom intangible assets are relatively important generate significantly higher returns than deals involving firms for whom such assets are relatively unimportant.

Our second hypothesis is supported by the data. In particular, we find that the variance of returns conditional on the share of intangibles is strongly increasing in the share of intangibles.

Our third hypothesis is also supported by the data: we observe that when intangibles are relatively unimportant in the acquirer's assets, the bulk of the gains from the transaction accrue to the target firm, while acquirers for whom intangibles are important are able to capture a significant proportion of the gains for themselves. The distribution of gains between partners that we uncover, as a function of intangibles also matches the theoretical predictions; in particular we find[8] that an acquirer in the upper quartile of the intangible distribution would get 48 per cent of the gains accruing from the transaction – while theory would suggest that gains should be evenly split. At the opposite end of the spectrum, we observed that an acquirer in the lower quartile of the intangible distribution would get 15 per cent of the absolute gains – while theory would suggest that they should not obtain any. This evidence certainly confirms that the importance of intangibles plays a significant role in accounting for variance in the share of gains accruing to the acquirer (across deals).

We conclude, therefore, that our data do not provide clear support for the hypothesis that intangible assets are likely to be associated with higher gains to merger transactions. However, they do support the hypothesis that these gains are likely to be more variable. And we have found support for the view that acquiring firms perform better, *relative to targets*, when they have more intangible assets, a view that makes sense in light of the reduced competition from other bidders when the acquirer has significant intangibles. The question arises as to why we do not find clear support for the first hypothesis. One possibility is that the market may actually already discount the fact that firms with high intangibles are likely to be involved in profitable reorganizations: as a result, when a merger is actually announced, the price of firms with high intangibles may not react more than the price of others.[9]

4. THE ROLE OF COMPETITION AUTHORITIES

One response to the complex character of synergies and the considerable uncertainty surrounding their nature and magnitude might be to conclude that competition authorities should not even begin to consider them as factors influencing their attitude towards merger cases, but should rather confine their attention to technical efficiencies. In fact, as we argued above, technical efficiencies are those about which the authorities would do well to be sceptical (though this does not imply that good defences involving technical efficiencies can never be made). However, synergies are those that, if achieved at all, are necessarily specific to the merger. Refusing to take them into account would consequently rule out any mergers whose likely synergies were large enough to outweigh the likely adverse effects of increased market power. Given the uncertainties surrounding predictions about synergies, one can reasonably doubt whether such effects could ever be large enough and probable enough to outweigh *large* risks to competition. However, many cases are not of this kind. There is a wide zone of uncertainty about risks to market power as well (as recent adverse court judgments on EU merger decisions have underlined). Even where the uncertainty is not great, there are many cases where the risk to competition, though not trivial, is not very large, and where the authorities are quite reasonably under some hesitation as to whether the transaction should be blocked. These cases are marginal in terms of the appropriate decision but far from marginal in terms of their importance and their claims on the authorities' time – should evidence about likely synergies not be given some weight in these cases? The evidence may not be 100 per cent compelling but it might still be compelling enough to tip a marginal case in one direction or the other. If so, what kind of evidence might this be?

It is impractical to suppose that competition authorities might ever realistically have access to information better than that which the merging parties could have collected themselves. The two questions it seems reasonable to ask are, therefore: first, how can the authorities induce the merging parties to give them, accurately, the relevant information, and second, how should the authorities evaluate this information?

The key to the answer lies in the fact that efficiency gains from merging intangible assets will never be realized entirely through their passive combination under common ownership. This is because such intangible assets always represent ways of working and managing the *other* assets of the firm; consequently, bringing the intangibles of one firm together with those of another requires a change in behaviour (other than just pricing behaviour) of some of the parties involved, and this will require a change in incentives. This is not always true when intangibles are used to create or consolidate market power. For instance, if two pharmaceutical firms bring together a portfolio of products with no other intention than to raise their prices, they have no need to do anything to change the behaviour of the parts of the firm that research, develop, produce or manage the products themselves – only the sales teams need to be implicated. If there is an intention to bring about real change in the productive parts of the firm's activities, an integration of the intangible assets – the research teams, the production processes or the management methods – has to be put into action, and this will require changing the incentives for some of the individuals who will take part in these activities.

To put the point another way, if the intangible assets of the merging parties are substitutes for each other and have no capacity for being used together in genuinely complementary ways, the attraction of the merger to the parties will consist purely in being able to increase the return to these assets' activities by raising the prices of the goods they are used to produce.[10] If, on the other hand, they are indeed complements, the merging parties cannot know this unless they have some idea how to alter incentives within the merged firm so as to realize their complementarities. Furthermore, for these complementarities to be genuinely merger specific, the parties need to have identified ways of altering incentives within the merged firm that would not be possible between two independent firms ('improving contacts between research teams', for instance, would hardly count as a merger-specific source of efficiency gains). We can conclude from this that for the firm to have identified merger-specific means of implementing the integration of the parties' intangible assets is a necessary condition of their having identified even the existence of any merger-specific efficiencies at all.

We can now turn to the first of the two questions above: how can the authorities induce the merging parties to give them, accurately, the relevant information? If the parties have indeed identified merger-specific means of implementing the integration of their intangible assets, they will have information about this (in the form of board-level memoranda, for example), and it is straightforward to require such evidence to be produced. Ensuring that such evidence is not falsified or manipulated is, of course, an important concern. However, note that what is being asked of firms is to present evidence of definite intentions to undertake actions which, once they have been identified, the firm would have an interest in undertaking anyway *even in the absence of intervention by the authorities*. Firms that have no synergies to claim will not, in the great majority of cases, be firms that promise to implement actions that in fact they will not undertake. Rather they will be firms that can find no relevant, value-creating actions to implement in the first place. This makes the requirement to provide evidence of synergies more naturally incentive-compatible than it would be if such evidence consisted, say, in judgments about the characteristics of the merging parties.

It will remain possible, of course, for merging parties to assert falsely that their intangible assets have certain characteristics which make synergies possible, and then to invent implementing actions that would allow these synergies to be realized if indeed they were possible. However, this will be a costly subterfuge for the merging parties to undertake: falsely asserting characteristics of the merging parties is something that could be undertaken by a report of external consultants without significantly impinging on management time, but asserting plausible implementing actions to realize these will involve a significant commitment of management time (the degree of commitment will of course depend on how rigorously the management expect their assertions to be scrutinized by the authorities). Such an investment of management time would have been undertaken in any event by firms that had genuinely identified synergies, and would not represent an additional cost for them. But for firms falsely asserting the existence of such synergies it would represent a significant additional cost (at a time when the management would in any event be preoccupied with planning the forthcoming merger). So it seems reasonable to suggest that, while fabrication or manipulation of intentions is certainly not impossible, it may be costly enough to make it difficult and infrequent.

It is quite likely, of course, that some firms will reply that, until the merger is actually consummated, it will be difficult or impossible to know what actions need to be taken to implement the relevant synergies. This is indeed a reasonable response in some cases, but it also represents the assertion of a hope that synergies can be realized rather than a well-grounded belief that they can. There may be nothing reprehensible about such a situation, but it does not provide sufficient grounds for asserting efficiencies as a counterweight to risks of market power.

Overall, therefore, our arguments suggest that in considering efficiencies, the authorities may adopt the following procedure.

1. Firms notifying mergers should be asked to state on their notification form, reasonably briefly, what is the business rationale for the merger, and what are main types of efficiency gain they expect the merger to make possible. They should be warned that they may be asked about this in any notification discussions. Firms should not be required (though may be permitted) to submit supporting documentation at the notification stage.
2. The extent of any supporting documentation will obviously depend on the stage of the investigation (notably in that Phase II investigations will typically scrutinize claims about efficiencies much more thoroughly than those in Phase I). Nevertheless we can say something about the *kind* of documentation that is appropriate. This should consist of documents dated prior to the notification of the merger, and identifying two types of information: first, evidence about the *existence* of potential complementarities between the various assets and capacities of the merging parties; such evidence may consist in external consultants' reports. Second, evidence about the *plans* of the merging parties for implementing the integration of their assets and capacities. This evidence must consist in documents signed by executive members of the board and proposing actions, with a reasonable indication of likely timing, which would enable the realization of efficiencies in a way that would not be possible without the merger. Naturally any such documents could be commented, or supplemented, by other documents submitted by the parties in support of their case (for instance, documents explaining why certain proposed actions were in fact merger-specific).

3. In evaluating the evidence submitted, the authorities should note that:

   (a) If the complementarities identified appear to be principally in the nature of what we have called 'technical efficiencies', it is likely that these will be merger-specific only if there are significant elements of imperfect competition. The claimed merger-specific character of such efficiencies should therefore be used as a guide to identify where precisely the most significant obstacles to competition are to be found.

   (b) If the complementarities appear to be principally synergies, the depth and plausibility of the proposed implementing actions will itself be evidence as to the degree of conviction of the parties about the existence of such synergies. Firms will only devote significant management time to planning the implementation of synergies they genuinely believe to exist.

   (c) If the parties provide particularly weak or unconvincing evidence of synergies, this fact of itself may be used as grounds, albeit slight, for concluding that their motive for undertaking the merger is likely to have been the strengthening of their market power. Such grounds may be used to support the case for prohibition or modification of a merger provided the case would already have been reasonably strong on conventional criteria alone. The knowledge that this inference may be made can act as a disincentive for firms to have frivolous recourse to the efficiency defence.

   (d) If the evidence for the existence of synergies appears reasonably strong, it should be used in support of approval of a merger provided the risks to market power are not very great, particularly bearing in mind that the evidence provided by the parties is evidence of their belief in the existence of synergies rather than of their existence *per se*.

   (e) Such evidence should also be used when conditional approval is granted, in order to ensure that, where possible, conditions attached to a merger should not be those that undermine the business rationale for the deal.

5.   CONCLUSION

This paper has argued that developing a better understanding of synergies and a method to evaluate them should be an essential component of merger reform in the EU. We suggest that synergies can be grasped by asking why firms undertake mergers rather than alternative forms of corporate reorganization. In this perspective, we have gathered some evidence suggesting that the reallocation of intangible assets could be an important source of synergies and we have argued that synergies can be assessed by asking firms about precise plans for the integration of their assets.

The merit of the procedure that we outline for competition authorities does not, however, rest on the importance of intangibles as a source of synergies. Its central feature, namely that authorities should enquire why the merger is taking place and evaluate the evidence provided by the firms, is independent of the source of gains. It suggests another approach that authorities may systematically wish to pursue, possibly in parallel with the usual approach (such that an analysis of dominance is possibly followed by an analysis of efficiencies); it is for the authorities to enquire directly into the sources of gains to shareholders as identified by the management, and to form a judgment as to what proportion of these gains are of the kind that can be achieved without significant costs to consumers – the magnitude of the remainder being an indicator of the likely dangers to competition. This approach focuses on the core of the motivation behind corporate reorganization and is more likely to identify synergies that benefit consumers, and hence to reduce type I errors. The ability of the authorities to ask firms explicitly about the business rationale for the deal would make it easier to identify merging parties that did not seem to have thought about the deal other than as a means of buying market power and hence would reduce type II errors. And it is at least possible that some firms might give more careful thought to the rationale for such deals in the first place if they believed they might subsequently have to defend it in front of the authorities.

NOTES

* We would like to thank Cinza Alcidi (HEI, Geneva), who provided excellent research assistance. The financial support of DG ECFIN of the European Commission is gratefully acknowledged. This chapter is also being published in Ilzkovitz, F. and R. Meiklejohn (eds) (2005), *European Merger Control: Do We Need an Efficiency Defence?*, Cheltenham, UK and Northampton, MA, USA: Edward Elgar.
1. See Pautler (2003) for an excellent survey.
2. The market evaluation of the effect on competitors may in some cases have been based on the belief that the merger would cause efficiencies that would diffuse throughout the industry, but it seems unlikely that this is true for all or even most transactions.
3. A particular sharp illustration of this argument is found in Farrell and Shapiro (1990), who show that in the context of the Cournot model, mergers which do not exhibit synergies will always raise price. Hence, in this context, synergies are necessary to generate procompetitive mergers.

4. Jovanovic (2001) notes that such discrete distribution of returns will generate a very high market–book ratio. If an investment involving intangibles generates a normal return *ex ante* but has a probability of success of some 10 per cent, a successful project will have a market–book ratio equal to 100.

5. The process of acquisition is best seen as an affiliated private value auction (in which the value of the target has a common element for all bidders). The result that the acquirer will get a higher share of surplus if few other bidders have high private value also holds in this environment.

6. Motis et al. (2003).

7. Note that the sample using accounting intangibles can be smaller than that using market intangibles despite the fact that market intangibles include accounting intangibles. This arises because accounting intangibles are scaled by total assets, whereas market intangibles are scaled by market value.

8. For some specifications, see Motis et al. (2003).

9. Note that the interpretation of the results that we report for the third hypothesis would be unaffected if we assumed that the market discounts the benefit that might accrue to firms with high intangibles.

10. Other anticompetitive actions might fall under this heading, such as when a firm suppresses some product varieties altogether in order to be able more effectively to raise the prices of others.

REFERENCES

Duso, T., D. Neven and L.-H. Roeller (2003), 'The political economy of European merger control: evidence using stock market data', mimeo.

Farrell, J. and C. Shapiro (1990), 'Horizontal mergers: an equilibrium analysis', *American Economic Review*, **80**, 107–26.

Farrell J. and C. Shapiro (2001), 'Scale economies and synergies in horizontal merger analysis', *Antitrust Law Journal*, **68**, 685–710.

Jovanovic, B. (2001), 'Comments on Intangibles, Management, Measurement and Reporting by B. Lev', Washington, DC: Brookings Institution Press.

Lev, B. (2001), *Intangibles. Management, Measurement and Reporting*, Washington, DC: The Brookings Institution Press.

Motis, J., D. Neven and P. Seabright (2003), 'Merger efficiencies: an empirical evaluation', mimeo.

Pautler, P. (2003), 'Evidence on mergers and acquisitions', *The Antitrust Bulletin*, Spring, 119–221.

CHAIRMAN'S COMMENTS

Sir John Vickers

I want to focus on what the paper's analysis means for competition authorities, and in particular:

- how the OFT (Office of Fair Trading) analyses efficiencies when appraising prospective mergers;
- whether the authors would approve of our procedures; and
- to what extent we could accept the authors' recommendations.

1. Analysing Efficiencies in Mergers

The OFT is, of course, a 'stage 1 assessor' in merger appraisal. In a typical recent year, it considered about 300 deals, of which 40 raised preliminary competition concerns and 15 were referred to the Competition Commission, which carries out detailed 'stage 2' assessments. The law now requires us to apply an explicit 'substantial lessening of competition' (SLC) test and we have a duty to refer mergers to the Competition Commission when there is a significant prospect of an SLC, subject to a 'customer benefits' exception that I will explain later.

Efficiency assessments can come into our work at two points. The first is when we apply the SLC test. Competition is about rivalry, and one can well imagine a situation in which there are efficiency gains to the parties that enhance rivalry. Second, efficiency assessment is relevant when we consider the customer benefits exception. There may be cases (though they are probably rare) where, despite the prospect of a substantial lessening of competition, there is sufficient evidence of a pro-customer effect that we would not refer it. Similar considerations can apply at the Competition Commission stage of an inquiry. So there are two entry points for an efficiency test in the UK's statutory scheme.

Our guidance note, published in May 2003, sets out how we intend to go about our analysis. Chapter 4 deals with the SLC assessment and Chapter 7 explains the customer benefits exception to the duty to refer. But there were also relevant cases under the previous (Fair Trading Act) regime. Let me give two examples. In the Euronext/LIFFE case, which was cleared, there was discussion of procompetitive efficiencies. A quite different case, which was referred, was VNU/Bibliographic Data Services: in this case, we considered carefully whether there were prospective customer benefits which would outweigh the manifest substantial lessening of competition. The Competition Commission's report, which cleared the merger, has a page or so of analysis of possible customer benefits and how they relate to efficiency considerations.

2. Would the Authors Approve of our Procedures?

The authors suggested that the European Commission tends to be too optimistic about efficiency gains from mergers. Large numbers of mergers are cleared and yet we know that many are not particularly successful, even from the shareholders' point of view. I will not discuss in detail the analysis of type I and type II errors in merger control. We know the empirical literature but our job is to analyse cases, rather than to save shareholders from themselves. We become involved in mergers when there might be adverse effects on third parties – in particular consumers.

In SLC cases, our stance on efficiency gains is, in a sense, sceptical. We put the burden on the parties to demonstrate that the claimed efficiencies can be realized, that they are specific to the proposed merger and that they are likely to be passed on to consumers. When we look at customer benefit claims we are quite demanding. But our attitude should not be characterized as pessimism about the prospect of efficiency gains. It reflects our status as Stage I assessor and also our awareness of the problem of information asymmetry: the parties know far more about their businesses than we can do and so we have to be demanding in probing their claims. I think of us more as 'principled pragmatists' than pessimists (or optimists).

Do we distinguish sufficiently between synergistic and other efficiency gains? I am tempted to say that, in a sense, it does not matter so long as our SLC (or customer benefit) tests are met. However, that is really too glib a response. The issue comes down to the merger-specificity of efficiency gains. In our guidance we say that efficiencies must be judged relative to what would have happened without the merger. One of the interesting questions the authors raise is the degree of merger-specificity that should be required.

3. The Authors' Recommendations

The first of the authors' four recommendations is that the authorities should ask for the business case for the merger. We already do that, not just for the reasons given in the paper but because the business case is always illuminating if you are trying to understand how the market works.

Second, the authors suggest that the parties should be asked whether they wish to make an efficiency defence. We do not put it like that – partly because I do not see parties with prospective efficiency gains as being on the defensive – but our guidance is an open invitation to make such propositions to us.

The third recommendation is that we should ask for pre-merger evidence of prospective efficiency gains. That is something we do, where appropriate, since pre-existing plans deserve to be taken seriously.

Fourth, the authors say we should distinguish between synergistic and technical efficiency gains. I am not sure how feasible or desirable that is, but we certainly care about merger-specificity. Remember also that our statutory scheme means that efficiency arguments enter the assessment either through the SLC test or the customer benefits part of the argument.

My last point concerns EU merger appraisal. Some people argue that it is not possible to take efficiency considerations into account if your test is based on dominance. I do not agree with that but I think, as the authors say at the end, that efficiency considerations fit more easily and more naturally into an SLC-based regime – which is yet another argument for the superiority of such a regime.

4. Emissions trading: a market instrument for our times

Charles Nicholson

My role in British Petroleum (BP) in recent years has focused on international sustainable development issues. Sustainable development is a broad church, however, and working in this area takes one down many new and interesting paths.

So it has been for me with carbon dioxide emissions trading systems. One of my commitments through BP is to the UK Emissions Trading Group (UKETG), and another to the International Emissions Trading Association (IETA). The UKETG has been instrumental in working with the government in the pioneering effort to develop the first nationwide carbon emissions trading system. It is now advising the government on the proposed EU scheme. And IETA does an excellent job gathering and collating the growing amount of information and expertise on this topic.

In this paper I will try to give an overview, from a business perspective, of the development of emissions trading systems.

MOMENTOUS TIMES

This is a fascinating, even historic, moment to be discussing carbon dioxide (CO_2) emissions. We are on the cusp of some significant developments. Over the next several months governments throughout Europe will be releasing lists showing how much CO_2 they will allow thousands of individual factories and power plants within their borders to emit, starting in 2005. Already a high-stakes engagement is under way as industries and companies try to position themselves to get as large a share as possible of the allowances with the proper intention of protecting their competitive advantage.

Clearly, there will be winners and losers – there is no way a perfect or fair allocation can be ensured – but this will not become evident for about five months until 31 March 2004, when each of the 15 EU member states is due to propose to the European Commission how they will allocate their emission permits.

After this the ten new member states must submit their permit lists to Brussels by 1 May 2004, when they join the EU. However difficult it will be for them among their other priorities, it seems that these member states will be engaged in this effort from the beginning. Further afield industry in the USA and Japan is watching these developments very closely. Plenty of US and Japanese companies with factories in the EU will be affected by the limits. And, of course, there's an awareness – and a hope – that European industry may gain competitive advantage in terms of experience and business opportunity.

So a topic that has been around in a theoretical way for a long time – certainly going back to the US Clean Air Act of 1990 – and only recently took on a practical form is now on the verge of emerging as a functioning, lucrative, Europe-wide commodity trading system.

TRADING SYSTEMS

At the very least, therefore, we need to understand what is meant by emissions trading. Basically, there are two main types of trading systems:

- *allowance trading*, which gives each participant a defined cap on emissions that can be met by either buying or selling, depending on the level of emissions and the relative cost of abatement.
- *baseline and credit trading*, which involves generating credits by investing elsewhere in individual projects that then generate reductions and win credits for the amount of emissions reduced.

A cap-and-trade scheme involves the allocation of emission allowances that can be bought and sold at prices determined by the market. The total supply of allowances by government determines the total allowable emissions. So reducing allowance volumes each year requires industry as a whole to reduce emission levels progressively.

By contrast, in a credit trading system a company can exceed its allocation both by buying allowances in the market from another business whose emissions are below its permitted level, and by generating credits through low-emissions projects or products. This system tends to encourage investment in new technologies as long as the cost of doing so is lower than the price of allowances in the market.

Given that the impact of climate change is felt globally, and it is global concentrations of greenhouse gases (GHGs) that have to be reduced, the optimum system is a working global scheme. Individual company, or national, schemes do not offer the flexibility for which the Kyoto Protocol aims.

The problem is that up to now much of what I have just stated is still largely untried. Trading in carbon dioxide is rare. The markets that exist are still in their infancy. But as I hope to illustrate, progress is being made on a number of fronts and we have come a long way since 1997.

THE CONTEXT

What follows is divided into three sections: the first sets the wider context; the second describes how my company BP has been approaching the issue; and the third involves looking ahead.

The Wider Context

There is now wide agreement that emissions trading is likely to make a major contribution towards finding the most cost-effective way of reducing carbon dioxide emissions, because the system creates an incentive for companies that can make cheaper emissions reductions to make deeper cuts. Then they can sell their surplus emissions allowances to other businesses that cannot make such inexpensive reductions. So a market develops based on relative energy efficiency and both the seller and the buyer gain.

But emissions trading has not always been seen like this. As recently as 1997, in the run-up to Kyoto, it was widely regarded in Europe – by the European Union, individual governments and by most environmental NGOs – as an essentially American, capitalist device cooked up to avoid tough, government-mandated action.

There were several reasons for this view. There was resistance in most continental European states to approaches based on the market, rather than legislation or technology-driven improvements. In Germany, where the constitution obliges the government to legislate to minimize pollution, there was intense political debate about the whole notion of overachievement that lies at the heart of any emissions trading system, and even whether it is even ethical 'to trade pollution'. From the outset the concept was better understood, and more widely accepted, in the UK at both official and unofficial level. Market mechanisms are viewed with less suspicion in the UK. And business was an early supporter. In a speech at Stanford University in May 1997, for example, BP's chief executive, John Browne, specifically endorsed emissions trading as one way forward.

In any event, the concept finally became one of the three flexible mechanisms endorsed in the Kyoto Protocol at the end of 1997 – basically in response to proposals from the Clinton Administration. Subsequently the Bush Administration rejected Kyoto. But by then opinion in Europe was shifting, as was shown by the stance EU heads of state took at Gothenburg in June 2001, following the US rejection. There were various reasons for the EU's changed attitude. But essentially the political need for the EU to show it could meet its commitments to Kyoto cost-effectively and consistent with economic growth, and bring GHG emissions under control, meant there was an urgent political need for an instrument that could produce results. Emissions trading was seen as that instrument.

The Protocol permits allowances to be traded between countries. It also allows for the trading of project-based credits generated by energy-efficiency or renewable energy schemes in developing countries or economies in transition. So it is a mistake to regard emissions trading as a purely big-business, developed-world process. It is certainly flexible enough in theory to allow poorer, weaker countries and small companies to be included by projects that help to transfer clean technology. It also allows regulatory bodies such as the EU Commission scope to influence outcomes based on the perceived requirement for 'clear rules and a strong framework to ensure compliance' in the words of the EU Commissioner in charge, Margot Wallstrom. So it is very far from a free-for-all. In fact, I would define emissions trading as an enabling bridge – between regulating authorities and the free market.

A key instrument for the EU
However emissions trading (ET) is viewed, by October 2001, when the European Commission made its first ET proposal, it had become a key instrument – probably the key instrument – in the EU's commitment to meet its Kyoto obligations.

The EU must reduce greenhouse gas emissions by 8 per cent between 1990 and 2012 under the Protocol. By the start of 2002 GHG emissions in the European Union were down 2.3 per cent as compared to 1990. But the trend is actually in the wrong direction given that emissions in 2001 were 1 per cent higher than in 2000 and nearly 2 per cent higher than in 1999. Only the UK, Germany and Luxembourg have been making any advances. Austria, for example, which should cut its emissions by 13 per cent by 2012, has so far actually increased them by 10 per cent. Ireland too has a challenge. So now, in Mrs Wallstrom's words, 'what counts is practical action'. The Commission's rationale is interesting and bears repeating:

1. It has come to believe that 'we have to be realistic and start somewhere', as Commissioner Wallstrom puts it. This ideological shift is striking.

2. It believes ET will reduce the costs to companies of meeting the EU's Kyoto targets by as much as 35 per cent (700 million euros per year) – but only if the market is big enough; the trading system is mandatory and a framework exists to ensure compliance.
3. The Commission is concerned that national trading schemes in Europe – just beginning to emerge in 2001 – might offer what it delicately describes as 'divergent design choices'. It is keen to assert control in other words.
4. It wants to 'smooth out' the implementation of the Kyoto EU burden-sharing agreement among member states – taking into account the divergent performances I mentioned earlier – and believes emissions trading may help to achieve this.

There is one other thing Commissioner Wallstrom has said about emissions trading that stands out. She makes the point that ET is flexible – that it allows a lot of room for manoeuvre in terms of how allowances are allocated, the rewards offered for early action, the penalties, who can take part and so on.

The UK system
While this evolution was proceeding in the EU, individual member countries – and in particular the UK and Denmark – were already taking action, in an often used phrase 'learning by doing'.

This is not the place to rehearse the subtleties of the UK system – the world's first economy-wide national scheme. But essentially a voluntary system was set up in April 2002. In its first year it saw around 900 companies exchange rights to emit more than 7 million tonnes of carbon dioxide. The scheme was kick-started by the British government with cash incentives of more than £200 million for 32 organizations. Thirty-one of the 32 met their targets, including BP, which successfully reached its commitment to reduce 353 000 tonnes of CO_2 equivalent emissions to the UK scheme – nearly 10 per cent of the total target for British industry. Another 5000 firms risked losing tax rebates on energy use under the Climate Change Levy if they missed their agreed energy efficiency, or relative targets. More than 860 entered trading, mostly as buyers, and the government announced in April 2003 that national emissions of carbon dioxide had been cut in the previous 12 months by 13.5 million tonnes, or by more than three times the target reduction.

All of BP's UK-operated exploration and production assets participated directly. Many of these assets are joint ventures, which underlines the broad support for ET that exists across the UK oil and gas sector.

For various reasons BP's chemicals operations and refining and retail operations took part through the relative, rather than directly via the absolute, sector of trading. BP Chemicals already has a Climate Change Levy Agreement with the government, which makes participation a more complex process, while project entry rules for the downstream activities hadn't been defined when the UK scheme began. But both are committed in principle to taking part. It is also noteworthy that a BP company, BP Energy, developed a business model to support the UK ET scheme. This service enables customers to access information on the emissions trading market and track their own environmental performance against targets – a good example of opportunity leveraging based on cost-effective innovations that help lower emissions.

There are some other interesting features of the UK system. First, it is voluntary. Second, it is built around incentives to innovate and invest in reducing the cost of complying with targets. Third, it has a competitive element. Any company that reduces its costs relative to the costs of other traders in the system should be able to make a profit from trading. There are three possible entry points. Companies may accept absolute targets for their emissions, or, if they are covered by the UK Climate Change Levy, they can reach agreement with the government that provides a reduction in the levy in return for increased energy efficiency and specified emissions reductions that can be achieved directly or through the trading system. They may also undertake specific projects that result in further emission reductions that they can sell into the scheme.

In May 2003 the UN stated that the UK was well on course to meet its emissions goal under the Kyoto Protocol of a 12.5 per cent cut on 1990 levels by 2010. There has been some criticism of the trading system for not being as active as hoped, and also complaints from NGOs that the government had been too generous initially with the cash it offered. But mostly these are minor complaints. The first year of economy-wide emissions trading in the UK was a success. The system worked and emissions fell. It was a major opportunity to learn by doing, share experiences and be innovative. The great majority of participating companies and organizations made full use of this opportunity.

The EU model
Clearly Brussels has been sufficiently encouraged by the UK experience to press ahead with its own scheme. So in January 2005, one of the most far-reaching environmental policies that industry anywhere has ever seen will be introduced across the 25-member European Union.

It is worth spelling out the features of this policy in detail:

- It is the largest and most ambitious ET scheme in the world and will cover more than 12 000 industrial installations and companies when it starts in January 2005.
- It is intended to allow for reductions to be achieved through projects carried out anywhere in the world provided they lead to measurable benefits that can be verified.
- It will be mandatory. Industries affected account for 46 per cent of the Community's carbon dioxide emissions and include power generation, steel, oil, paper, glass and cement.
- It excludes nuclear projects in line with Kyoto Protocol rules and, for the time being, 'carbon sinks' (forests that soak up CO_2) because of uncertainty about the effects of emission removal by such sinks.
- Existing member governments will have until March 2004 to draw up national allocation plans that will determine how much of the task should fall on industry, and how the task should be divided between individual installations of companies.
- At least 95 per cent of allowances to emit carbon dioxide will be given out free of charge by governments, but they may choose to auction the rest.
- It will be phased in between 2005 and 2007. The UK can exempt companies involved in its own scheme from this pilot EU scheme.

We should not be too surprised at the scope of what the EU is planning. It is part of a worldwide trend. IETA's website lists about 20 countries that are developing or studying market-based approaches to emissions reduction.

In the USA both the public and private sectors have been exploring the potential of greenhouse gas trading systems through initiatives such as the Chicago Climate Exchange (CCX) and the Massachusetts programme to reduce emissions from power plants. At the end of September the CCX – which involves Canada, Mexico and Brazil as well as the USA – announced the results of its first auction of 100 000 tonnes of CO_2 emissions allowances. A sealed-bid mechanism was used to establish a market price. There were 20 successful bids, with an average bid price of \$0.98 per tonne of CO_2 for emissions having a 2003 'vintage'.

In Japan, the Ministry of Economy, Trade and Industry is considering creating a system for trading carbon dioxide emissions rights that is likely to involve more than 100 companies and organizations, though I believe a significant part of Japanese industry is opposed to a cap-and-trade system. In Europe the UK is not alone in setting up domestic systems – Denmark has also done so, and Norway is at an advanced stage of discussion though it will need to consider how the Norwegian and EU schemes will interact.

But this is not just a developed-world trend. A market-oriented emissions trading programme is being introduced in seven regions of China as part of a China–US initiative to curb acid rain. It is based on caps that limit the amount of pollution produced by industrial sources, such as power plants and factories, and in its initial phase is being rated a great success.

One reason for this global interest is the potential size of the markets that may result. In Europe, for instance, estimates of the eventual size of the EU emissions market vary. But one, by Point Carbon, a Norway-based research group, reckons it could grow from about US$1.2 billion in 2005 to US$8.9 billion in 2007.

The BP Experience

None of this is particularly surprising to those at BP. We had already shown, through an internal trading emissions system that we set up by ourselves, that the basic idea could work on a wider canvas. We piloted our system in 1999 with 12 business units, and operated it across the company on a global basis in 2000 and 2001. At the beginning of 2002 we decided to suspend the system to make space for the transition we could see happening to external GHG trading systems. Of course, internal systems are necessarily limited in business signals they can give.

So what did we achieve on our own? Well, first of all, we showed that an ET system was practical. This gave us the confidence to work with the UK government on a national scheme. Second, we got results. The system we devised allowed resources to be applied in the most effective ways. Third, it proved to be cost-effective. And finally, it gave focus to our wider efforts to reduce emissions. All BP operations worldwide were included. Each of about 120 business units was given an annual emissions allocation that could only be exceeded by purchasing allowances from other units that had reduced emissions below their cap. The sum of the allowances represented BP's total emissions, and this cap was reduced each year to help meet the BP Group's wider commitment to reduce greenhouse gas emissions by 10 per cent below a 1990 baseline by 2007. Each business was given the flexibility to decide how it would meet its overall emissions target – which was a commitment, not an aspiration. This had the effect of boosting ingenuity. Emissions trading proved to be a powerful tool because it attracted real rewards for those involved.

The results were impressive. As a group we hit our emissions target seven years early by the end of 2001 at a net saving to the company of about $600 million. We did this, essentially, by eliminating waste and improving competitiveness. But the focus that emissions trading gave to the business issue was integral to this achievement. Looking back, John Browne remarked that BP's experience of trading had been important – not least because it had shown what was possible.

'Trading is crucial to the next stage in the process of resolving the threat of climate change', he said. 'The answer to global warming won't be a simple uniform process applied to every activity in every nation. But everyone can make a contribution and will be motivated to do so if there is a common trading system in which every action can be valued on a consistent basis.'

I now turn to some of the elements which are key to the success of an emissions trading scheme (see the Appendix for more details).

Looking Ahead

So where do we go from here?

For the next few years, and probably until 2006 at least, the UK and EU systems will coexist. The Commission has made it clear that it would like to see the UK system absorbed into the EU scheme. But no dates or processes have yet been agreed. So an immediate issue for UK-based companies is to find a way through this complexity.

Another important point for business is that, regardless of whether or not the Kyoto Protocol is ratified by enough governments to bring it into force – and this is an issue for Russia, the EU is committed both politically and legally to achieve its Kyoto reduction targets.

There are still underlying differences of philosophy within the EU – broadly between the British emphasis on market trading and the German emphasis on 'best available technology' as the best way to impact emissions. Nevertheless there is consensus, both within the existing EU and the 25-member organization from May 2004, that trading should begin on time at the start of 2005.

Then we have a number of what might be termed 'operational' questions about the trading scheme itself. One concerns the likely value of this market. There have been various estimates, and they are only estimates. I have mentioned one already. But another, by the emissions broker CO2e.com, reckons that the average one-ton emissions allowance will be trading at around 15 euros (about $17.75) by 2005 when the EU caps take effect. This would value the 25-nation EU market at roughly 30 billion euros annually – substantial indeed.

Another issue centres on incentives. The majority of the 32 companies that took part in the UK scheme stated (in a survey published earlier this year by Enviros consulting group) that financial incentive (worth £215 m) was the most important factor in their decision to take on absolute emissions reduction targets – because it overcame the risk of the scheme. There is no prospect of similar incentives being envisaged for the EU scheme!

Then there are concerns about knock-on effects. The EU system will cap emissions of power and industrial plants and there have been forecasts by McKinsey, the management consultants, of rises in wholesale electricity prices of up to 40 per cent, and an acceleration out of coal into gas in power plants. Of course, supporters argue that increased electricity prices are beneficial. If the costs of carbon emissions are not passed on to the users of energy, they will have no incentive to reduce their consumption.

There are no definitive answers; but if such consequences are possible they need to be properly considered in advance. Another issue concerns emissions from cars and trucks. At the moment they are excluded from the EU system. But they may be somehow included later, and this will clearly raise a dilemma since any EU country that allocates looser caps now to energy-intensive industries may not be faced with having to impose tougher limits on vehicles.

There is also some considerable concern in the chemicals sector about emissions trading, with companies divided in their approach and willingness to get involved. Industry bodies like the European Chemical Industry Council (CEFIC) worry that the mandatory nature of trading could make the regulatory environment so strict that chemical businesses would be driven out of Europe. At the moment only chemical sites which run from a power generation unit of 20 MW or larger will be affected by the EU system – roughly 50 per cent of all chemical units in Europe. But there are likely to be definitional issues – whether crackers, for example, will be included or not.

There is also some potential for a backlash. Only recently the Australian government dropped a carbon trading scheme designed to reduce GHGs after heeding industry's protest that it would drive investment offshore. As these examples suggest, there is plenty of scope for argument and clarification – and lobbying.

At a governmental level, as I mentioned earlier, at the time of writing, ten of the 15 EU member states are way off track in reaching their EU burden-sharing targets under the Protocol. They are also at varying degrees of readiness in terms of turning the EU trading directive into national law. Several are likely to miss the 31 December 2003 date. Some of the accession states may seek opt-outs. Hungary and Latvia have already requested 'clarification' of the draft EU legislation. All the East Europeans, having endured severe economic contraction in the 1990s that reduced their GHG emissions well below Kyoto-agreed targets, are wary of cutting emissions further ahead of any new climate negotiations. And there are divisive conceptual issues around core EU objectives such as single market competition, lack of harmonization and state aid.

The allocation of allowances, in particular, could prove a significant factor in future business competitiveness. As the chemicals example emphasizes, there is a lot of room for disagreement about which installations should be included in the EU system and about the stringency of targets. Companies would have scope to challenge allocations in the courts. And there is bound to be controversy about the fines levied on companies within the trading system that fail to present credits equivalent to their emissions – currently set at 40 euros ($45) per tonne of carbon dioxide equivalent from 2005 to 2007, and 100 euros thereafter. Many companies in Europe that are also concerned about competitive advantage are likely to press governments for the largest possible allowances. We can also expect to see the Commission being very careful to ensure that governments don't use the scheme as a means of improving their market positions. So it will not all be plain sailing.

CONCLUSIONS

These sorts of concerns are only to be expected when something as radical as an entirely new commodity trading system is introduced. The Kyoto Protocol represents a major change of rules for industry, and emissions trading will be its 'cutting edge' in Europe. Industry has never been faced with such a challenge before. Accurate information about emissions is often lacking, the timeframe for starting the EU system is very tight, and individual companies often have differing views, as do entire industries. But perhaps this is the moment to raise our game and recognize the opportunity in what is being attempted.

The EU system will offer the chance to deliver the climate change architecture foreseen under the Kyoto Protocol. It will be a world first – the first regional emissions trading bloc, the first trading scheme to cover such an extensive number of industries and companies, the first to be mandatory, and the first to establish a true market price for greenhouse gases. We cannot be clear at this point how the details and impact will unfold. Much will depend on the architecture and the willingness to learn and adapt. The response of participants will also be a key. It will bring uncertainty and a new operating environment for many, and there will probably be unforeseen consequences. There are uncertainties, for example, about the initial and subsequent allowances; about levels of participation, the rules on banking; and on what the second commitment phase and beyond will hold.

The cause will not be well served if the trading system is applied in such a way that it becomes discredited and damages the objectives it is seeking to address. But we have come to this point, in the judgement that an emissions trading system does offer the best approach to align a number of potentially conflicting priorities.

If it works, then it will have an enduring impact on the way European industry conducts its operations as well as, it is hoped, on climate change. There are sure to be winners and losers and we must be pragmatic and responsible in ensuring that we recognize the timescales to find and deliver the correct answers, and absorb the goal of managing the transition to a lower-carbon pathway without undermining other proper economic and social policy objectives. The closure of older facilities may happen. But new business opportunities will be created, new investments will be made and new projects will result.

Above all, emissions trading is likely to prove significant for business competitiveness. For those industries and companies that take part, it will not necessarily be easy, but with a sensible and flexible approach the outcome has much to offer.

If the EU scheme fails, it will be a very significant setback to efforts to tackle global warming. But if it succeeds, it might form the basis of a new international currency – a gold standard – which could form the unit of value for judging multiple different options and actions taken in support of the common objective of dealing with the threat of climate change. There is much to play for. The prizes are worth the endeavour.

APPENDIX: KEY ELEMENTS IN THE SUCCESS OF AN EMISSIONS TRADING SCHEME

- ET provides flexibility as well as incentives. ET focuses attention on the climate change issue and rewards sites that exceed targets.
- Target setting is the key. Targets define the environmental goal. Trading is an additional tool to help achieve the goal.
- Fair targets for all are difficult to achieve but when setting base years account should be taken of special cases to reward those who take early action.
- It is crucial that ET participants are engaged in the early planning stages of any scheme.
- An open, transparent and accurate reporting system is vital for the efficient functioning of an ET market and for external credibility.
- Achieving a market price for carbon focuses attention on the cost of carbon in project investment decisions and stimulates innovation.
- Starting slowly, and providing flexibility to change and learn, helps overcome teething problems.
- Rules should reward good behaviour, avoid distortions and encourage energy efficiency or processes that result in environmental benefits.
- The six greenhouse gases covered by the Kyoto Protocol should be included within an emissions trading programme.
- To ensure effectiveness, a wide number of participants will stimulate reductions and engage the economy across sectors.
- Allocation of allowances under a cap-and-trade system should consider that historic emissions levels be distributed in a transparent way, free of charge.
- Allocation methodology for future years should be transparent in order to allow for long-term investment planning.
- Setting allowances over longer periods will improve market liquidity and enable business to take GHG costs into account when making investment decisions that may have environmental consequences.
- Baseline protection should be provided for those participants who have taken action before initiation of a trading scheme.
- Provisions should be made in a cap-and-trade scheme to permit banking excess allowances for future use, as well as enabling positions to be taken in the futures market.
- Markets should be open to those not receiving allowances directly.
- Enforcement and compliance are essential elements of a successful programme. Penalties for non-compliance should be clearly stated.

CHAIRMAN'S COMMENTS

Colin Robinson

As I pointed out in my Beesley lecture last year,[1] energy policy is now converging on environmental policy. It is fascinating to learn from Charles's paper about all the efforts that are going on to establish markets that will help to reduce carbon dioxide emissions – the environmental issue that is now perceived as the most serious. His paper is particularly interesting since he is from a company, British Petroleum, that has been enthusiastic about trading systems for emissions and has helped to pioneer their introduction.

My purpose is not to comment on the details of the systems that Charles describes so well. Furthermore, I take it that most economists would accept that, if global emissions are to be reduced, emissions trading schemes are appropriate instruments for the purpose, with much better efficiency properties than command-and-control measures. However, it is worth commenting on the implicit assumptions behind emissions trading schemes, as follows:

- **A global warming trend has been established**. Despite the popular view that almost any weather event is a consequence of 'global warming', one does not need to be a climate scientist – but merely to have some knowledge of statistics – to realize the problem of separating trends from shorter-term fluctuations in such a complex field. A related concern is that the scientific consensus, as it concerns energy issues, has often been wrong in the past.[2] There is a respectable scientific minority that doubts the evidence that a global climate change *trend* has been identified.
- **Global warming is a consequence of carbon dioxide emissions**. As I understand it, the evidence is inconclusive that supposedly established a causal link between carbon dioxide emissions and such warming as there has been in the past.
- **Collective action is required if global warming is to be avoided**. If we take a leap of faith and assume that there is a warming trend and that the causation runs from CO_2 emissions, it still seems uncertain whether there is a clear case for collective action. The effect on world welfare (itself a nebulous concept) is unclear, because there will be both winners and losers, and economists understand the difficulty of attempting to balance gains to winners against losses to losers.

Even if we accept the three assumptions above, concluding that climate change will clearly lead to a net reduction in world welfare, there are still questions about how to evaluate alternative means of offsetting action – one of which is simply to let people adapt. So I think one should be sceptical of the argument that action is required to deal with a massive and looming global problem.[3]

On a more positive note, if action to reduce emissions is to take place, it is better for it to occur through emissions trading in markets rather than through centralized interventionist measures. I take some comfort, for example, from what seems to have been the British government's partial withdrawal from the interventionist measures with which it toyed when it was formulating its latest efforts at an energy policy in February 2003. It needs to go farther, however. There is still in the Energy White Paper[4] an uneasy coexistence between old-fashioned interventionist steps (such as support for renewables, energy 'conservation' and combined heat and power – CHP – schemes) and trading mechanisms which would either set a price for emissions (a carbon tax) and let volumes adjust, or allow trading to take place, thus setting a price. Let us hope that, as experience of trading systems accumulates, the government realizes that direct intervention is likely to be very costly and that it should be dropped in favour of trading.[5]

Notes

1. 'Gas, Electricity and the Energy Review', in Colin Robinson (ed.), *Successes and Failures in Regulating and Deregulating Utilities*, Cheltenham: Edward Elgar, 2004.
2. Ibid.
3. See Robert L. Bradley Jr, *Climate Alarmism Reconsidered*, Hobart Paper 146, Institute of Economic Affairs, 2003.
4. DTI, *Our energy future – creating a low carbon economy*, February 2003.
5. Eileen Marshall, 'Energy regulation and competition after the White Paper', chapter 6 in this volume.

5.   Ofcom: a converged regulator?

Annegret Groebel

1. OUTLINE OF THE NEW REGULATORY FRAMEWORK (NRF)

One of the major reasons for reviewing the old regime of European telecommunications regulation was the technological development of convergence, creating innovative services offered either via new infrastructure or upgraded existing networks. Convergence causes rapidly changing market situations, both in existing as well as emerging markets. Market dynamics are changing and 'hybrid' markets, on the edge between classical telecommunications markets on the one side and broadcasting markets on the other, are coming into existence with services such as video on demand, where films are delivered via broadband networks on the PCs of individual users. Thus a typical mass (media) service is 'changing colours' becoming an end-to-end (telecoms) service.

To deal with these changing market structures, regulators need more flexibility and also a comprehensive approach enveloping all kinds of services. As shown by the example of films that can be downloaded by individual users, thus becoming a customized service (tailored to the user), or interactive broadcasting services delivered via digital TV networks, once-separated markets converge, the underlying networks over which these services (substitutable in the eyes of consumers) are delivered must be governed or regulated according to the same rules. Otherwise distortions between the various platforms are created and intermodal competition can be distorted as shown by the example of the USA, where the distinction between 'telecommunications' and 'information' services does not work and was recently stopped by a court decision.[1]

Thus regulation can no longer maintain the distinction along the lines of technologically specific services and networks and maintain separate regimes, but has to take into account convergence and the changes created in industry and market structure. The principle of technological neutrality is the natural answer to technological convergence, avoiding the risk of distorting intermodal competition. At the European level, the adjustment was made with the New Regulatory Framework, comprising all electronic networks and services, but leaving content regulation outside its scope (Figure 5.1 and 5.2).

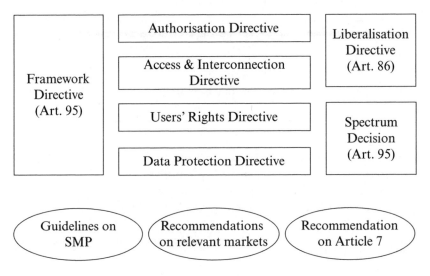

Figure 5.1   The EU regulatory package

2.   SCOPE OF THE NRF

The question resulting from these developments is whether there is merit also in convergence of the separate authorities which up to now have regulated more or less separately in the UK. However, they have had partially overlapping competencies, such as in the markets for telecommunications (Oftel), broadcasting (mainly content: Independent Television Commission, Broadcasting Standards Commission, Radio Authority) and the Radiocommunications Agency dealing with all spectrum issues.

3.   INSTITUTIONAL SCOPE

United Kingdom

In the Communications Bill the decision was made to create one 'converged' regulator called Ofcom (the Office of Communications) by merging the five existing regulators in one authority. Thus, on the one hand, the general idea of having one 'uniform' approach for all electronic communications

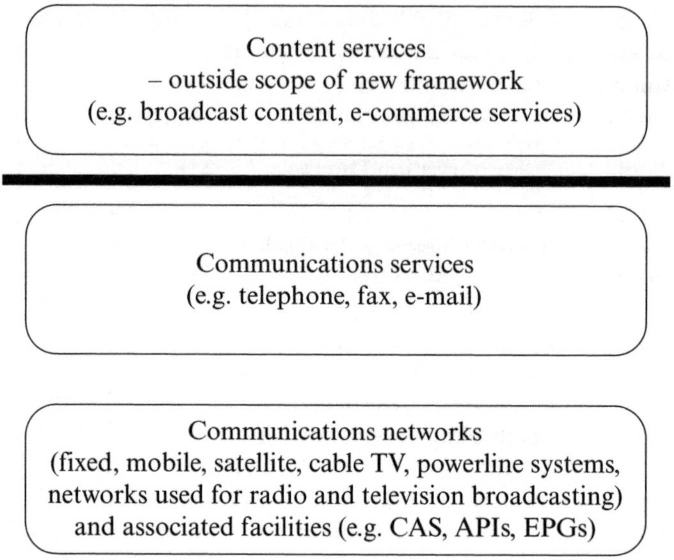

Content services
– outside scope of new framework
(e.g. broadcast content, e-commerce services)

Communications services
(e.g. telephone, fax, e-mail)

Communications networks
(fixed, mobile, satellite, cable TV, powerline systems,
networks used for radio and television broadcasting)
and associated facilities (e.g. CAS, APIs, EPGs)

Note: CAS = conditional access systems; APIs application programming interfaces; EPGs = electronic programme guides.

Figure 5.2   Electronic communications networks and services: scope

markets in a 'single source' followed the logic of converging technologies and markets as outlined above. On the other hand, the reform went further than the European framework as content regulation is also covered by the remit of Ofcom and the three regulators dealing with broadcasting are included, thus going beyond the idea of the NRF, which leaves out content issues. Therefore the questions are to what extent synergies can be found and whether the inclusion of content regulators might lead to diseconomies of scope. Figure 5.3 shows the five regulators of which Ofcom is composed, as compared to the scope of the European framework.

Roughly, one can say that convergence is driven by new technologies of networks and terminal equipment over which innovative services can be offered. In the communications industry, one decisive factor in networks is the use of radio spectrum, which is a scarce resource. Thus different forms of usage such as telecommunications or broadcasting compete for the scarce resource. The liberalizing of new spectrum and the rules for assigning and allocation of spectrum therefore have a tremendous impact on market entry and consequently also on market dynamics and market evolution. Thus spectrum regulation is no longer an issue that can be dealt with under purely technical aspects, but must be seen as part of economic market regulation.

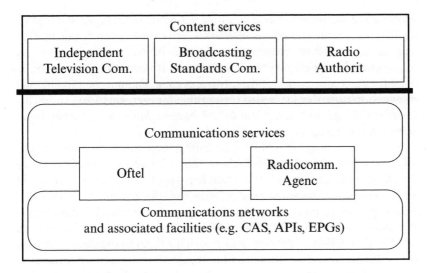

Note: As for Figure 5.2.

Figure 5.3 Electronic communications: institutional scope, UK

Therefore overcoming the separation of telecoms regulation (done by Oftel) and spectrum licensing (done by the Radiocommunications Agency – RCA) is clearly causing synergies for the regulation of markets such as 3G.

For the inclusion of the three content regulators the blessings are less obvious and might even be considered as having negative effects. This results from the different objectives pursued by, on the one side, telecoms/spectrum regulators who are looking at market developments from a competition point of view following economic reasoning, whereas content regulation pursues aims such as plurality of programmes or media literacy, which might – under certain circumstances – run counter to purely economic aspects. Therefore a conflict of interests could emerge, leading to diseconomies of scope rather than synergies. Being composed of both market-oriented as well as content-oriented regulators, Ofcom is related to two departments: the Department of Trade and Industry and the Department for Culture, Media and Sport. Before considering how the organizational structure of Ofcom tries to solve the problem of merging the different organizational cultures of the regulators, the German institutional set-up is examined.

Germany

In Germany, RegTP (the German Federal Regulatory Authority for Telecommunications and Postal Markets) is responsible for both telecommunications and frequency regulation. So, for example, the UMTS auction setting the conditions of market entry for the 3G mobile market was run by RegTP whereas in the UK Oftel did not run the auction. As said above when discussing the UK situation, it is clearly an advantage to combine the competencies for these two areas of communications regulation in one authority. RegTP is also responsible for assigning frequencies for broadcast usage and in general for all issues relating to the underlying communications network infrastructure.

However, as RegTP is not responsible for content regulation, the allocation of programme channels to the assigned spectrum is done by the media regulators as part of content regulation. There are 16 state media authorities of the 16 German states ('Bundesländer'). Content regulation is seen as part of cultural policy, which is a responsibility of the states. There is a clearly defined interface between RegTP, which assigns frequencies, and the state media authorities which allocate them to the chains through the so-called Interstate Broadcasting Treaty, thus minimizing difficulties resulting from a 'split' distribution of tasks as regards the determination of frequencies for broadcast usage. The Ofcom scheme, which internalizes this interface, might have advantages. On the other hand, RegTP does not have any conflict of interest resulting from objectives of content regulation. RegTP is related to only one ministry, the Ministry of Economics and Labour.

The German situation is shown in Figure 5.4.

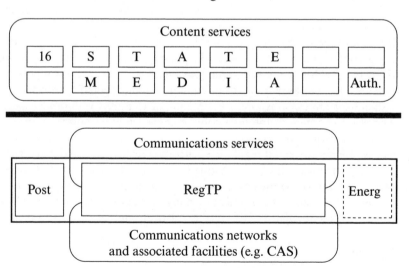

Figure 5.4   Electronic communications: institutional scope, Germany

4. ORGANIZATIONAL STRUCTURE

Ofcom

Whether the synergies of merging telecoms and spectrum regulation outweigh the expected diseconomies of having conduit and content regulation under one roof depends on how the organizational structure of Ofcom manages to overcome organizational cultures of the existing regulators. Four main departments can be distinguished:

*   Strategy and Market Developments;
*   Competition and Markets;
*   Contents and Standards; and
*   Operations.

Figure 5.5 shows the main tasks of the different departments.

Strategy and Market Developments	Competition and Markets	Contents and Standards	Operations

• Strategy development
• Market research
• Technology group
• Chief economist
 	
Dealing with <u>all</u> issues: telecoms, broadcasting, spectrum
	• Strategic Resources
	 – Spectrum Policy
	 – TV/Broadcasting
	 – Broadband,
	   Mobile Planning
	   + Licensing
	 – Numbering
	• Competition
	 Policy + Compliance
	
	Specialists for telecoms, broadcasting, spectrum, but <u>no</u> formal sub-division
		• Broadcasting policing codes
		• Public Service Broadcasting Radio Formats
		• Consumer Policy Media Literacy
		
		Mainly content responsibility cooperation if overlap with competition
			• Complaints
			• Licensing
			 – interference
			 – National
			   Frequency
			   Authorization
			   (NFAP)
			 – satellite
			• Field Operations monitoring
			• Enforcement
			
			Ensure efficient use of spectrum by <u>all</u> spectrum users

Figure 5.5   Ofcom's organizational structure

A 'mixed strategy' is used to try to deal with the problems. Of these four departments, one (Strategy and Market Developments) integrates aspects of all three areas. The biggest potential advantages are clearly in having a 'converged' strategy for all communications markets stemming from an overview and market analysis done for all of them.

The second department, Competition and Markets, combines spectrum usage planning and licensing subdivided into three teams (one each for television, radio and mobile/broadband markets) and the Competition Policy and Compliance Group which includes specialists from all areas, but is not formally subdivided along the lines of expertise. The development of this department, in terms of 'convergence' or 'reorganization' along the lines of the old regulators, is clearly decisive for the success of Ofcom in terms of overcoming the fragmented approach followed hitherto. However, seeing that for spectrum usage the teams are subdivided according to the old lines, there must be doubts about the chances of success.

The third department, Contents and Standards, comprises content regulation. There is little 'convergence' with other departments, except if competition issues are concerned, but it is not clear how this will work out as the department seems to stand as a separate unit. The last department to be mentioned, Operations, monitors interference-free spectrum usage by all users. It is made up mostly of former RCA staff, so there may be a great potential regarding the market surveillance of different users.

RegTP

RegTP has integrated the planning and licensing of frequencies in the Legal Department. The Technical Department is responsible for all tasks regarding market surveillance and may be compared to the Operations Department of Ofcom. The Technical Department, however, is also responsible for standardization, and so has a large number of staff. The organizational structure of RegTP is illustrated in Figure 5.6.

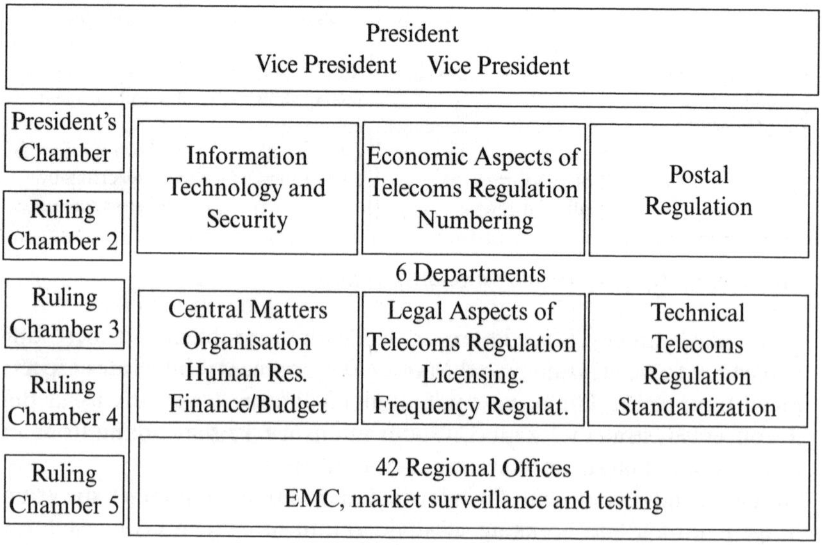

President Vice President Vice President			
President's Chamber Ruling Chamber 2	Information Technology and Security	Economic Aspects of Telecoms Regulation Numbering	Postal Regulation
Ruling Chamber 3 Ruling Chamber 4	Central Matters Organisation Human Res. Finance/Budget	Legal Aspects of Telecoms Regulation Licensing. Frequency Regulat.	Technical Telecoms Regulation Standardization
Ruling Chamber 5	42 Regional Offices EMC, market surveillance and testing		

Figure 5.6   RegTP's organizational structure

A comparison of posts between Ofcom and RegTP shows that RegTP has nearly triple the amount of posts, even though it has no competence for content regulation. The optimistic conclusion that might be drawn from this is that Ofcom may not have diseconomies of scale and not fall victim to 'Parkinson's Law of bureaucracy'.

5. ASSESSMENT OF CONVERGENCE

Criteria

To assess the advantages of a 'converged regulator' it is necessary to develop some criteria where convergence is especially important, that is, where the knowledge of one area helps making decisions in the other area. The following criteria can be used:

- interface between telecoms and broadcasting regulation:
- Art. 9 FD: assignment + allocation of radio frequencies;
- Art. 17/18 FD: standardization in general + interoperability of digital interactive TV services;
- Art. 5 (1) lit. b AD: other facilities: APIs, EPGs;
- Art. 6 AD: CAS and other facilities;
- Art. 31 UD: must-carry obligation, appropriate renumeration;
- Market No. 18 Recommendation on relevant markets – Broadcasting transmission services.

Comparison

As outlined above, the biggest advantage results from the convergence of the responsibilities for telecoms regulation and for frequency assignment and allocation (planning and licensing). This is now the case for Ofcom, so there should be clear benefits.

Convergence also plays an important role in the imposition of 'must-carry' rules, access obligations regarding conditional access systems (CAS) and other facilities such as application programming interfaces (APIs) and electronic programming guides (EPGs). These obligations are at the interface between conduit and content regulation as they are imposed at the network access level, that is, the underlying transmission service, but are strongly influenced by content-related considerations. Thus the knowledge of both areas helps in making sensible decisions.

An advantage of the Ofcom structure is the possibility of drawing on in-house knowledge of content regulation when deciding on access obligations.

In comparison, in Germany it might be much more difficult for RegTP to find the right way through this dilemma as, for example, 'must-carry' obligations would be imposed by the state media authorities whereas it falls in the remit of RegTP to look at the calculation of a reasonable renumeration for the use of the transmission networks for a must-carry service.

Also important for offering a wide choice of different services, especially interactive TV services, is to have open standards for interfaces and ensure interoperability. Here RegTP has an important role to play, whereas the role of Ofcom in this area seems less important.

6. CONCLUSION

As compared to the previous situation, telecommunications market regulation is now being dealt with by the same authority as spectrum issues. Also, the 'single source approach' of having conduit and content regulation under one roof has advantages stemming from the special knowledge of content regulation available in-house when determining obligations such as access to CAS, APIs and EPGs.

However, at the same time, there is a conflict of interest resulting from different objectives of conduit regulation, which is market-driven, and content regulation where public-interest objectives play a major role.

In general, what will be decisive is whether the functional organization planned will work out, or whether staff will 'self-organize' along the old lines of telecoms/spectrum and broadcasting regulators so that the old institutional organization re-emerges to supersede the new.

NOTE

1. US Court of Appeals, Brand X Internet Services v. FCC, Decision of 6 October 2003.

CHAIRMAN'S COMMENTS

Colin Robinson

Communications regulation occupies a special position in Britain's system of utility regulation. After the first utility privatization in Britain – British Telecommunications in 1984 – there was a pioneering leap in utility regulation, based mainly on the work of Michael Beesley and Stephen Littlechild. In a decisive move away from then existing methods of regulating utilities by attempts to control rates of return, the first regulatory office – the Office of Telecommunications (Oftel) – was established. It provided the first test of a system, radically different from previous regimes, which delegated regulation to an independent office charged with applying an RPI-X price cap and attempting to promote competition. That regulatory system, like privatization, has subsequently been exported to many countries around the world, though of course with modifications to suit local circumstances.

But has telecommunications regulation kept pace with changing times? There is room for argument about the extent to which successive regulators have carried out their pro-competition duty, liberalizing markets and reducing regulation over time so that it is restricted to genuine natural monopolies. Compared (say) with British gas and electricity markets, where competition flourishes over separated networks and price controls are now confined to natural monopoly sectors, liberalization does not seem far advanced in telecommunications.

Technological progress, however, has been rapid and inevitably has caused problems for regulators. As Annegret Groebel points out, technological change has resulted in reviews of the 'old regime of European telecommunications regulation'. The 'technological development of convergence' has created 'innovative services offered either via new infrastructure or upgraded existing networks'. Regulators need more flexibility and a comprehensive approach to deal with rapidly changing structures, she argues: 'underlying networks must be governed or regulated according to the same rules' if distortions are not to occur. To deal with technological convergence, the New Regulatory Framework in Europe tries to include all electronic networks and services.

Annegret raises interesting questions in her analysis of the UK's new framework of communications regulation in which five communications regulators have merged in Ofcom: Oftel, the Independent Television Commission, the Broadcasting Standards Commission, the Radio Authority and the Radiocommunications Agency. The logic of convergence has been followed in that all these regulators are now in one body (though the British Broadcasting Corporation still stands apart as an organization that largely regulates itself). However, the British regulatory reorganization in communications, Annegret argues, goes beyond the European New Regulatory Framework in that it includes content regulation (again except for the BBC).

Whether the British reorganization will deal effectively with the 'convergence' issue and improve on its predecessor is as yet uncertain. Evidence from the past is not clearcut and there are few principles to guide us. It is always tempting to amalgamate in one organization supervisory bodies that have overlapping or complementary functions on the assumption that better co-ordination and greater efficiency will result. Such a happy result is certainly possible. But it is also possible that the outcome will be managerial diseconomies in the larger, more complex organization.

Annegret's main concern is not with 'economic' regulation where she thinks there is a good chance synergies will appear (for example, because telecoms regulation and spectrum licensing are no longer carried out by separate regulators). But she raises the question of whether it was wise, in the British reorganization, to give Ofcom responsibility for content regulation. 'Economic' regulation, in her view, is primarily about examining markets from a competition policy viewpoint, whereas content regulators must take a very different 'public interest' view: putting the two functions in one organization might therefore lead to diseconomies of scope.

She has a point, but again it is hard to see what principles might guide us in deciding where content regulation is most appropriately placed – if, indeed, there is any justification for heavier content regulation of the broadcast as compared with the print media. Only a few years experience will reveal how well the new system is working. What is interesting, though, is that in Germany content regulation is the responsibility of the states: there are 16 state media authorities. Regulating content is a particularly difficult task which can easily descend into paternalism and there may be advantages in decentralizing it, as in Germany, rather than making it the responsibility of one body (the BBC apart).

Whatever one's view of the content regulation issue, Annegret's comparison of Ofcom with the German Telecommunications regulator (RegTP) is of considerable interest. She is surely right to say that including telecommunications and frequency regulation in RegTP is advantageous. To British eyes, however, the inclusion of energy regulation in RegTP's functions will seem peculiar. Of course, there are many issues that are common to the regulation of different 'network' utilities but that does not necessarily mean that different markets with very different characteristics should be regulated by one body. The scope of RegTP, which covers both energy and post as well as electronic communications, seems huge and likely to lead to diseconomies, albeit of a different sort from those she foresees in Ofcom. Perhaps significantly, at the time Annegret wrote, RegTP – without content regulation – had three times the staff of Ofcom.

There is plenty of scope for dispute about the issues Annegret raises but the inter-country comparisons she uses are clearly a useful way forward. Different countries have embarked on different regulatory regimes and, once initiated, these regimes develop in ways that are not always predictable. Comparing systems at a point in time and examining how they have evolved is a way we can learn from others and bring about gradual improvements in the ways utilities are regulated.

6. Energy regulation and competition after the White Paper

Eileen Marshall

INTRODUCTION

Following various reports, including the Royal Commission on Environmental Pollution (RCEP)'s *Energy: The Changing Climate* (2000), the Cabinet Office Performance and Innovation Unit's (PIU) review of energy policy early in 2002 and further government consultation on key issues in 2002, a new White Paper was produced in February 2003, *Our Energy Future – Creating a Low Carbon Economy*.

The White Paper set out the four goals of the government's new energy policy as being:

- to put the UK on a path to cut carbon dioxide emissions by some 60 per cent by about 2050, as recommended by the RCEP, with real progress by 2020;
- to maintain the reliability of energy supplies (a term which is used to encompass all aspects of energy security of supply);
- to promote competitive markets in the UK and beyond, helping to raise the rate of sustainable economic growth and to improve productivity; and
- to ensure that every home is adequately and affordably heated.

The White Paper says these four goals are designed to meet what the government considers to be the three main challenges for energy policy in the future:

- addressing the threat of climate change;
- dealing with the implications of reduced UK oil, gas and coal production, which will make the UK a net energy importer instead of a net exporter; and

- over the next twenty years or so, the need to replace or update much of our energy infrastructure, in terms of generation capacity and the gas and electricity transportation networks.

On generation capacity, the White Paper notes in particular that European measures to limit carbon emissions and to improve air quality are likely to force the modernization or closure of most older coal-fired plant, and that in the absence of new build or life extensions all but one of the existing nuclear stations will be closed by 2025.

As regards the electricity and gas networks, the government is especially concerned that electricity transmission and distribution systems can accommodate more renewable and combined heat and power (CHP) generation, both larger scale (including offshore) and smaller scale, distributed energy sources located in homes and businesses such as micro CHP plant and fuel cells. In gas, the government sees the requirement as being to accommodate more imports, both piped and liquefied natural gas (LNG), from a range of sources.

The government did not seek to rank its four energy policy goals, believing that all the objectives can be achieved together by pursuing the policies it has put in place.

However, I want to concentrate on the first two goals, namely control of carbon dioxide emissions and maintenance of security of supply, since presently they are probably the two key issues on the government agenda in terms of their potential effect on the gas and electricity industries, on regulation of those industries and on gas and electricity consumers.

As far as control of carbon dioxide emissions is concerned, both the government's aim and the way it is to be achieved have far-reaching implications, while security of supply has been pushed even further up the public and political agenda since the White Paper was published, because of recent power cuts in the UK and elsewhere in the world.

CONTROLLING CARBON DIOXIDE EMISSIONS

In discussing control of carbon dioxide emissions, I will leave aside a number of important and controversial issues, such as whether climate change is occurring; if it is, whether carbon dioxide emissions are largely to blame; and, if they are, whether it is better to cut emissions than to live with the consequences. Instead I will consider the implications of the *goal* the government has chosen, of setting the UK on a path to 60 per cent reductions from current levels by 2050, with intermediate targets in 2010 and 2020, and the *means* it has chosen to achieve its goal. I then go on to examine how Ofgem might best accommodate the government's goals and targets when carrying out its functions.

The Government's CO$_2$ Goals

The UK's national goal for 2010 is tougher than its Kyoto commitment, a 20 per cent reduction in carbon dioxide emissions below 1990 levels by 2010 rather than the Kyoto commitment to reduce greenhouse gas emissions by 12.5 per cent. Further ahead, the White Paper sets a new aggressive goal for 2020, which it says would put the UK on the path to reducing carbon dioxide emissions in 2050 by 60 per cent, even though international discussions about reductions beyond 2008/12 under the UN Framework on Climate Change (UNFCC) have yet to begin.

The government has chosen to set these aggressive CO$_2$ reduction targets, not because of the direct impact they would have on climate change,[1] but because it hopes that, where the UK leads, others will follow. It also hopes its policy will provide major opportunities for UK businesses to become world leaders in CO$_2$-reducing technologies, such as fuel cells, and offshore wind and tidal power. The idea of pursuing such a policy in the hope of benefiting selected industries seems to me particularly ill founded, given the failure of previous governments to 'pick winners' in this way.[2]

Even without the government's tougher stance, and desirable as it may be to control CO$_2$ emissions, electricity and gas prices look likely to rise significantly. An article in *The Times* recently commented on the EU scheme designed to help achieve greenhouse gas emission reductions between 1990 and 2012 in line with the Kyoto Protocol. The article quoted reports suggesting that the EU scheme (due to be phased in from 2005, with electricity generation being covered in the first phase) could raise wholesale electricity prices by at least 40 per cent in five years and maybe by over 60 per cent, depending on the price of carbon.[3] The expectation is that the move away from coal-fired generation could substantially increase the demand for gas for power generation. UK consumers will presumably see relatively higher price increases given the government's tougher goals.

The White Paper suggests that over the 17 years to 2020, government measures on emissions trading, renewables and energy efficiency might add 5–15 per cent to household electricity prices and less than 5 per cent to household gas prices: to industrial prices they might add 15–30 per cent for gas and 10–25 per cent for electricity. If the reports previously quoted are correct, such increases could come sooner rather than later. Forward UK electricity (and gas) prices for the period after the start of the EU scheme in January 2005 have indeed increased significantly, driven at least in part, one suspects, by the EU emissions trading scheme.

However, I am not trying to estimate the precise effect the government's CO_2 reduction goals will have on prices, save to say that prices will go up and perhaps significantly. The White Paper says that since prices have fallen substantially in real terms over the last 20 years the increases will only be reversing that process and that, since most of the impact is due to the EU emissions trading scheme, which will impact widely on prices, it will also affect the UK's competitors in Europe. I am less sanguine. I believe it will come as a shock to British consumers if they experience significant price increases because of the government's tough stance on environmental protection, especially if the increases are greater than for our neighbours and trading partners.

Moreover, the EU, quite mistakenly in my view, requires governments to allocate, free of charge, most of the permits to emit carbon dioxide, rather than auction them, implying a transfer of funds from consumers and suppliers to generators. As well as having a potentially distorting effect on competition in generation, depending on how the permits are allocated, free allocation will not be popular with consumers. All in all, then, I would not be surprised if some time in the future consumer pressure made the government reassess its CO_2 goals.

The Means of Achieving the Goals

If we look at the means by which the government is seeking to achieve its CO_2 goals, there is the starkest contrast between the government's support for the current framework of independent utility regulation, based on competitive wholesale and retail markets, and its heavily politicized and interventionist approach to the delivery of environmental protection.

The White Paper acknowledges the merits of a carbon trading scheme, and says that in the longer term carbon trading should be the central plank of emission reduction policies designed to achieve its carbon targets. But, for now, the government has chosen to continue with – and indeed substantially enhance – its centrally planned approach to meeting its CO_2 goals in 2010 and 2020, around half of which it sees as being attained by reducing energy demand and the rest through a significant increase in renewables and CHP.

Energy demand reductions are divided more or less evenly between savings from households – 5 million tonnes carbon (Mtc) a year by 2010 (of which the government believes its current measures will deliver 1.5 Mtc), and another 4–6 Mtc a year by 2020, and business and public sectors – where the expected savings are 6 Mtc by 2010 and another 4–6 Mtc a year by 2020. The government envisages strengthening the use of a variety of policy instruments to control energy demand by the targeted amount, including, for example, higher building and product standards. But, in particular, it expects its energy efficiency commitment (EEC) to have a major role in reducing energy demand in homes and is considering whether to extend it beyond the household sector.

Since April 2002 the government's EEC has required all major gas and electricity suppliers to meet a given energy savings target: these targets must be achieved between 2002 and 2005 by installing energy efficiency measures in homes, financed by raising a levy from other gas and electricity consumers. Now, as I mentioned, there is the prospect of a much-expanded scheme from 2005, possibly extending in scope beyond households. The White Paper suggests the possibility of extending the scheme to run from 2005 to 2008 at twice its current level.

The government has taken a similar approach to the expanded use of renewables as it has to energy efficiency in setting physical targets. It has a target that renewables should supply 10 per cent of UK electricity in 2010, subject to the costs being acceptable to the consumer, with a doubling of the target to 20 per cent by 2020.

As with energy savings, the White Paper acknowledges that much-strengthened policies will be required if the renewables targets are to be met. It says that in 2000 renewables (excluding large hydro and mixed waste incineration) supplied 1.3 per cent of electricity and to hit the 10 per cent target by 2010 will require installing 10 000 MW of renewables capacity, an annual build of over 1250 MW, in contrast to a total installed capacity so far of 1200 MW. The variety of policies being used to support renewables includes the renewables obligation, which requires electricity suppliers to source 3 per cent of their electricity requirements from renewables in 2002–2003, rising to 10.4 per cent in 2010–11, then remaining constant until 2027 when the obligation ends – a policy that subsidizes renewable electricity and finances it by increases in customers' bills. The White Paper estimates that by 2010 the England and Wales Renewables Obligation,[4] together with Climate Change Levy exemption for renewables will amount to a £1 billion a year subsidy to the UK renewables industry, with other funding coming through other means such as increased capital grants. For comparison, the total annual value of wholesale electricity in Great Britain is at present about £6 billion.

The White Paper reiterates the government's commitment to the current Renewables Obligation, saying it will maintain the level of support it provides as planned until 2027, and that in 2005–2006 it will review progress and decide policy for the decade to 2020 with the doubled renewables target as the aim.

In addition to the energy demand reduction and renewables targets, the government has other targets to help meet its CO_2 reduction goals, including the achievement of 10 GW of 'good quality' CHP by 2010. The White Paper gives CHP presently installed as 4.8 GW and expects that meeting its 10 GW target would save a further 1.25 Mtc per year.

The government has rightly taken upon itself, rather than leaving it to the discretion of the regulator, the establishment of the Energy Efficiency Commitment and the Renewables Obligation, and the level at which the subsidies (financed by gas and electricity consumers) will be set, since setting up such services that benefit particular groups at the expense of others is usually a matter determined by Parliament and funded from general taxation. But that does not mean there are no problems with the EEC and the Renewables Obligation and with the government's environmental stance more generally. I have two particular concerns.

First, making apparently precise calculations about how much carbon can be saved from using less energy, more renewables and more CHP, then calculating similarly precise goals for each of these intermediate targets, then devising policies in the confident expectation that both the targets and the carbon reductions will occur as expected, flies in the face of the lesson that governments and regulators all over the world have had to learn and accept. That lesson is that even the most gifted central planners do not (and cannot) possess the information necessary to bring about the efficient results that competitive markets produce since the necessary information is only revealed through the market process. It follows that, in the absence of such information, central planners are likely to make misguided decisions and costly mistakes which harm economic prosperity. Moreover, the government's chosen way of setting many different individual targets and using many policy instruments makes environmental decision making heavily politicized, since it provides numerous pressure points which particular interest groups can use to persuade the government to direct policy in a way that benefits them, often at the expense of general economic well-being.

Ofgem estimated that the Renewables Obligation implies a value of around £210–380[5] per tonne of carbon. Soon, when the EU emissions trading scheme begins, there will be an indication of the price of carbon and therefore how cost-effective the Renewables Obligation is. More generally, it is extremely unlikely that the government has opted for policies that can reduce carbon emissions at least cost to consumers.

My second concern is about the unintended consequences for the hard-won competitive gas and electricity markets of the government's pursuing its CO_2 goals in this way. The government's CO_2 policies could adversely affect gas and electricity markets in at least two ways: first, through forcing retail gas and electricity suppliers to become increasingly important tax collectors and providers of subsidized energy efficiency services alongside their main job; and second, by creating a managed market in which the government decides on the amount of energy that should be used and then the share of total energy to be met from different fuels.

At present both the Renewables Obligation and the EEC are relatively small, with a cost equivalent to about an additional 2 per cent on domestic bills. However, with extended programmes, the roles of gas and electricity suppliers will change quite dramatically: retail supply, not only to households but also to businesses if the scope of the EEC is widened, will become different and more complex. That would play into the hands of incumbent suppliers, which might well welcome an increase in their 'public service' role, since it would involve extra tasks and more bureaucracy to check that those tasks had been performed, which would most likely deter prospective new entrants. In the absence of these energy efficiency and renewable obligations, given that competition in gas and electricity supply has developed to the point where all price controls have been removed, these two markets could become much more like other competitive markets in the economy, in terms of the way they are regulated – that is, subject only to economy-wide competition and consumer legislation. The government's current plans could dampen competition and keep these markets subject to more rather than less sector-specific regulation. They would also, of course, discourage market-led provision of energy efficiency services (including by the gas and electricity supply industries) because others will not be able to cross-subsidize their offerings.

In a similar vein, although the White Paper says the government is not equipped to decide on the fuel mix and it therefore does not propose to set targets for the shares of fuels in total energy or electricity supply, its 'targets' route to CO_2 reduction seems to lead perilously close to such a managed market. Having specified the amount of energy saving that should take place (and hence the total demand that will be allowed), then specifying the quantity of renewables suppliers must buy, including the contract term, then targeting specified amounts of CHP, it seems hard for the government to avoid making an explicit decision about other fuels, especially the future place of new nuclear power stations in the energy market – a decision about which the White Paper has put on hold.[6] The place of coal-fired plant will be heavily constrained by EU and domestic environmental regulations, which leaves gas in the difficult position of a residual producer, constrained not only by the government's targets for demand and other fuels but also facing the uncertainty as to whether or not these targets will actually be met.

These negative consequences could be avoided if the government moved swiftly to a competitive approach to the reduction of carbon emissions by the adoption of a carbon trading scheme. If it moved directly to the allocation of tradable emission rights, as far as possible by a price auction, up to its chosen level of carbon emissions and removed all other measures presently in place, there would be four desirable consequences:

1. Participants in the new competitive retail and wholesale markets could assist in delivering the government's environmental objectives in the most efficient way by incorporating the additional carbon cost into their own decision making. Environmentalists should be pressing for such an approach because it can deliver more environmental protection for the money consumers are willing to spend on it. If the government's calculations are right, then schemes presently in place (such as the Renewables Obligation and EEC) would hold their ground under the new arrangements. If they do not, the sooner we stop wasting money on them the better it will be for consumers and the environment. I believe the approach I suggest would actually be better in the long run for the development of renewables. Given a general approach to controlling carbon emissions, renewable developers could find their own place in the market. They would thus no longer be reliant on specific political support nor on the vagaries of particular instruments, such as the renewables obligation.

2. The cost of achieving the government's CO_2 goals would become much more transparent to consumers, enabling them to make a better informed input into future environmental policy making. The government should also see such transparency as an advantage since it has qualified, for example, its renewables target by saying that the cost to consumers must be acceptable. Yet at present the costs are far from transparent, especially since they come partly through gas and electricity industry-specific measures and partly from direct subsidies paid for from taxation.

3. Using one transparent instrument could greatly reduce the scope for special interest groups to influence policy outcomes.

4. The pursuit of the government's CO_2 objectives would complement and not interfere with the functions that competitive gas and electricity markets would otherwise perform.

THE REGULATOR'S ROLE

Should the regulator help the government attain its CO_2 targets and, if so, how? The answer to the first question is clearly yes. Besides its principal objective of protecting the interests of consumers, where appropriate by promoting competition, the Utilities Act 2000 placed other duties on Ofgem, including promoting the efficient use of gas and electricity and having regard to the effect of licensed activities on the environment. The Utilities Act also provided that the Secretary of State should give the Authority *guidance* as to the contribution the Authority should make to the attainment of the government's social and environmental policies.

The new draft guidance published in June 2003, updated in the light of the White Paper, confirms that where the government wishes to implement specific social or environmental measures which would have significant financial implications for consumers or for the regulated companies, they will continue to be implemented by ministers rather than by the Authority, by means of specific primary or secondary legislation. Otherwise the new guidance says that the government expects the Authority to help secure the targets and aims, including those for renewables, CHP and energy efficiency set out in the White Paper, and to bear in mind that the achievement of its objectives is likely to require new electricity generation in widely dispersed parts of the country, including offshore.

The White Paper says that some had urged the government to legislate for a power of direction over Ofgem which it rejected, considering it would undermine the independence of the regulator and politicize the regulatory process so as to cause unacceptable levels of uncertainty in the markets. Thus, as the preamble to the guidance itself points out, it is not the role of the guidance to instruct the Authority to take any specific step.

How then should the Authority go about assisting the government in reaching its CO_2 targets? Some people have suggested that the type of regulation practised successfully to date by successive regulators – which focuses on improving the efficiency of the industries by actively promoting competition and by the application and extension of incentive-based regulation of the monopoly gas and electricity networks – may be less suited to the new challenges and goals identified by the government. Quite apart from the prospect of new legislation, there is probably sufficient discretion in the regulatory regime to allow a less economically rigorous regime to be adopted in future. However, I firmly believe that, considering the challenges, goals and targets as set out in the White Paper, economic regulation of the industries is more important than ever.

As I noted earlier, it appears inevitable that cutting CO_2 emissions by subsidizing energy efficiency, renewables and CHP and by expanding transmission capacity to cope with more distant power stations, as well as reconfiguring the distribution networks to cope with smaller-scale distributed generation, cannot help but raise consumer prices, probably substantially. Even if consumers, large and small, generally support the government's environmental aims, they are hardly likely to welcome such increases, which would break the downward trend that has accompanied market liberalization. Economic regulation can help to contain, as far as is possible, the likely price increases facing consumers. It should, for instance, help to ensure that renewables generation, which seems destined to play a major role in future, is as efficient and as efficiently located as possible.

And the regulatory focus does not have to shift away from attempting to improve the efficiency of the industries, since the White Paper does not seek to make substantive changes to the regulatory framework and indeed reaffirms the government's support for independent regulation and reliance on competition to secure the best deal for consumers.

I was pleased to see also, in the Introduction to the Secretary of State's proposed new social and environmental guidance, a statement that the government intends that the regulatory system, *through economic regulation*, should make an appropriate contribution towards achieving the government's wider social and environmental goals, and where possible be supportive of them.

Given what I have already said, it will come as no surprise that I consider one of the most valuable steps the regulator can take is to assist the government in rationalizing its present CO_2 policies with a view to employing carbon trading as its main, preferably only instrument. Ofgem has been consistently supportive of the adoption of a broad-based instrument to deliver carbon dioxide emissions reductions and regulatory resources devoted to this task could help to work out a practical way of achieving such a transition.

As to the government's specific aims and targets, one of the most important requirements in promoting the efficient use of gas and electricity is to ensure that consumers face the full costs of energy provision. This will help them make well-informed decisions about cutting demand in response to price increases and/or investing in energy efficiency items such as boilers, appliances or home insulation. Effective competition in retail and wholesale markets, supported now by more competitive trading arrangements, will help, tending as it does to align prices with costs and drive out cross subsidies.

Policing effective competition is therefore an important component of promoting energy efficiency. But there are also central constraints that, at present, prevent smaller consumers in particular from facing cost-reflective prices, such as the decision when retail electricity competition was extended to below 100 kW customers, for the settlement system to be based on the use of standard profiles to estimate consumption of these users, half hour by half hour. The alternative at the time was to insist on the installation of expensive half-hourly metering which is used in the above 100 kW market. However, the use of profiles inhibits the introduction of real-time pricing by suppliers, reduces these customers' responsiveness to price increases and distorts their decisions about energy efficiency investment. If market-led, as well as subsidized, energy efficiency is to be encouraged, it would be helpful to see if better, alternative arrangements might now be possible.[7]

In terms of the government's aims of expanding the use of renewables and CHP, there are good and bad ways of helping to achieve them.

One of the most controversial issues since the new electricity trading arrangements (NETA) were introduced in March 2001 is whether renewables and CHP should be given favourable treatment in relation to the imbalance charges they face. NETA removed the restrictions that the England and Wales Electricity Pool had placed on the way generators and suppliers traded, whereby all electricity produced had to be sold into and bought out of the Pool, enabling them to trade in more normal ways through bilateral contracts and power exchanges.

But still the transmission system has to be balanced as between supply and demand on a continuous basis to ensure quality and continuity of supply and the responsibility falls on National Grid Transco (NGT), as system operator, to maintain the balance.

Under the Pool, the generators' offers of power were non-firm, so that any additional costs, say from the need to buy in alternative power because of a sudden generator plant failure, were passed on to suppliers in the prices they paid for their Pool purchases. Similarly, suppliers did not have to make firm commitments about how much power they needed to cover their customers' requirements, so that the costs of meeting a particular supplier's demand variations were borne by suppliers generally and ultimately by consumers. Under NETA, these arrangements too were changed: the costs incurred by NGT in balancing the system are visited on the generators and suppliers that cause them to be incurred, due to being out of balance with their notified contracted positions.

The introduction of firmness into the generators' and suppliers' contractual commitments was a very important aspect of NETA design since the balancing arrangements now support rather than undermine the establishment of electricity trading as a normal market. As compared with the Pool, it has sharpened the incentives for generators to ensure their plants are reliable and for suppliers to understand their customers' demand.

As many renewables (such as wind energy and solar power) are intermittent and would therefore frequently be expected to face paying imbalance charges, there has been a concerted campaign, before and after the introduction of NETA, to exempt them from those charges, even though such generation can cause significant additional system costs. As David Currie said in his October 2000 Beesley Lecture on NETA – and it bears repeating – 'if the future is to be renewables, it is very important that we encourage more reliable, more predictable renewables plant'. It is therefore crucial that calls for special treatment under NETA should be resisted. Many of the Balancing and Settlement Code (BSC) changes accepted by Ofgem, which improve the arrangements generally, have helped such generators in particular, for example accepted modifications have sought to ensure imbalance prices are properly reflective of the energy-balancing costs. Efforts have also been made to avoid unintended barriers which might prevent smaller generators, including CHP, from participating fully in the new trading arrangements. But that is very different from giving them favourable treatment through the market rules. Any such treatment should come through the special provisions put in place by the government to subsidize renewables and CHP.

A further, possibly even more controversial, issue came before Ofgem earlier in the year in the form of proposed modifications to the BSC which suggested altering the way in which electricity lost during transmission was charged to users, from an averaged charge to one that took account of the user's location, thus making the charge more reflective of costs. Such a change had been heralded since before privatization, but nevertheless provoked controversy since generators located far from the centres of demand – including, in the future, peripheral and offshore renewables – would incur increased charges. Having regard to the objectives of the BSC and its statutory duties, Ofgem accepted one of the modifications for differentiated charging of transmission losses. Now, however, there is the prospect of new primary legislation being introduced to implement, for the first time, trading and transmission arrangements covering all Great Britain, and part of the arrangements will be the introduction of a government-designated Balancing and Settlement Code for Great Britain, replacing the present one that covers only England and Wales. After consultation, the government is apparently proposing not to include in the new code the modification which introduced locational charging of transmission losses into the England and Wales code.

Whilst the government is clearly free to introduce whatever primary or secondary legislation it wishes, should this occur then it seems a retrograde step. If there is to be a lot of new generation, including renewables, built in the future to replace existing plant, then it is important that transmission charges, including charges for transmission losses, properly reflect costs. More cost-reflective charging will save resources used in transmission by providing an incentive to build plant closer to centres of demand. Presumably, too, special arrangements would have to be made to prevent further modifications to the way transmission losses are dealt with being proposed and agreed after the new GB code is brought into existence, since it seems by no means certain otherwise that the arrangements put in place by the government will remain unchanged.

There are important decisions yet to be made about how the additional costs arising from installing extra transmission capacity (onshore and offshore) is to be recovered. If, as with transmission losses, the government chooses to influence the use of system transmission charges to cross-subsidize distantly located generation so as to help achieve its renewables targets, it could compromise the efficient location not only of renewables but of all new generation (and load) and northern consumers will be cross-subsidizing southern ones. It would be a situation not dissimilar to that which occurred under nationalization when industry prices were pushed up or down in pursuit of the government's social and macroeconomic objectives: the resulting inefficiencies are well recorded.

Again, there are good ways of helping new generators, including renewables and CHP, in relation to the way they connect to and use the electricity networks. Both distribution and transmission companies have specific obligations, which Ofgem must enforce, which prohibit the licensee from discriminating as between any persons or classes of persons in the provision of use of the system or in the carrying out of connections. Ofgem has been undertaking an important review, in this regard, to ensure that the way distribution companies charge and treat generators embedded in their systems is not discriminatory. Similar reviews are under way into the connection and use of system arrangements of NGT and the Scottish transmission companies. But ensuring that CHP and renewable generators are not discriminated against in terms of connection and use of system charges is very different from giving them preferential terms, and different again from creating a situation where use of system charges as a whole are distorted.

Finally, I want to consider briefly one of the most important issues facing Ofgem, the industry and customers – how best to accomplish the expansion of the transmission systems and the reconfiguration of the distribution systems to accommodate the government's renewable and CHP targets.

The amount of money required promises to be very large indeed. The *Financial Times* reported that an electricity system working group established by the Department of Trade and Industry (DTI) estimated that transmission costs could be more than £1 billion to connect the 10 GW of new renewable capacity required to meet the 2010 10 per cent target, because it is envisaged that much of the renewables capacity will be built in the north of England, Scotland and offshore. As a comparison, NGC has invested about £3.5 billion in total in its network since privatization.

The challenge then is to find a way of estimating how much investment is needed, to ensure extra capacity is available where and when required, without expanding the system in a way that covers all eventualities – which could be extremely costly and inefficient. Both the industry and Ofgem

will be mindful of the statutory duty on network licensees to develop and
maintain an efficient, coordinated and economical system.

In particular, the policy adopted must cope, not only with the uncertainty
as to where and when the new generation will connect to the grid, but also
with inevitable doubts as to whether the full target will actually be met.
The government has already cautioned that the 2010 renewables target is
subject to the cost to customers being acceptable and has said that it will in
2005–2006 review progress and elaborate a strategy for the decade to 2020.
There are also potential planning delays, and in addition, as the White
Paper again points out, the development of offshore wind generation is
in its infancy with only 250 MW having been installed so far in the world,
whereas the government is expecting some 4.5 to 5.5 MW could be built
here by 2010. Moreover, as I mentioned earlier, there must be *some* chance
that the government's tough CO_2 stance will not survive if other significant
countries do not follow its lead.

A similar situation to this, although on a smaller scale, faced the gas
industry in the 1990s when one of the issues for consideration by Transco,
Ofgas and ultimately the Monopolies and Mergers Commission (MMC)
when Ofgas's proposals for the 1997–2002 price control were rejected by
British Gas, was by how much the gas transmission system should be
upgraded to accommodate the soon-to-be-opened interconnector with
Belgium. The interconnector gas shippers were keen for major expansion
while the domestic shippers and customers were concerned that over-
expansion would leave them with increased bills at the same time that
outward flows across the interconnector promised to put upward pressure
on gas prices. What was agreed by the MMC was a middle course. The
result was that in the summer and autumn of 1998 there was considerable
excess demand for capacity at Transco's beach entry point at St Fergus in
Scotland, exacerbated by Transco's being behind in its schedule to increase
capacity, but also because demand had been underestimated.

It was clear that, with the expectation of substantially changing patterns
of supply and demand in the gas system in the future (especially as imports
began to replace indigenous supplies), a new way was required, at least
to supplement if not to replace Transco's central planning approach to
estimating the total amount of new capacity required and where and when
it would be needed.

It was this situation that led Ofgem, Transco and the industry to develop
and eventually introduce in 2002 a new way of selling entry capacity on to
the natural gas transmission system alongside a new incentive scheme on
Transco to encourage it to respond quickly to changing patterns of demand
between price control reviews. The new incentive scheme runs from 2002

to 2007, the same period as the traditional price control put in place at the same time, and which it complements.

Since October 1999, gas shippers have had to purchase entry capacity in order to land gas at the beach entry terminals. But whereas up to now the capacity has been auctioned only six months ahead, the new regime enables shippers to purchase firm, tradable, long-term capacity rights. The first long-term auctions were held in January 2003, when capacity rights were offered out to 2017, with another tranche in September. They are expected to occur at least annually in the future. As part of the price control, the transmission company must commit to providing a baseline level of entry rights. If market signals suggest that additional capacity is required, the company would have the freedom to carry out investment and earn additional revenues from selling the extra access rights. Conversely, it would be exposed to the costs of buying back access rights at market prices if it failed to provide the baseline level of capacity allowed for in the price control.

A regulatory arrangement along those lines in electricity could help deliver the transmission reinforcement necessary to accommodate larger volumes of renewable generation, while at the same time providing for the uncertainty associated with the renewables programme. Something similar could also be appropriate for the distribution networks.

The development of renewables is only one of the challenges, albeit an important one, for the current transmission investment regime. For example, the possibility of new interconnectors (for example, with Norway, Holland and Ireland) will also make it more difficult for NGC to assess future capacity requirements. The only alternative to a market-based mechanism is to continue to rely, in this increasingly complex world, on central planning to determine how much investment is needed and when. But without clear market signals of demand, how can the companies and Ofgem ensure that the capital investment requirements are not being over- or understated and that individual projects are well chosen? It is quite possible, without a new approach, that a lot of money could be spent and still the growth of renewables generation might be held up by insufficient capacity at the right places and at the right times.

SECURITY OF SUPPLY

Security of supply is an imprecise term: no energy form and no source of supply can offer absolute security and it would be prohibitively expensive to try to cater for all eventualities. But the term is used to cover both sudden and widespread price shocks which can disrupt the economic and social life of the country and, of course, physical interruptions.

Security of Gas Supplies and Gas Infrastructure

The first longer-term challenge identified by the government in its White Paper as having a potential impact on security of supply is the expected move from being a net energy exporter to a net importer: by 2020 the White Paper estimates the UK could be importing about three-quarters of its total energy requirements. A particular issue affecting gas and also electricity consumers, given that about 40 per cent of generation capacity is presently gas-fired and that the percentage could well increase, is concern about whether wholesale supplies of gas would remain secure when, in a few years' time, the UK may be a net importer.

There is sometimes a perception, influential with past governments, that fuel self-sufficiency guarantees fuel security, without due recognition of the security-enhancing properties of imported supplies. The UK's past mistaken heavy reliance during nationalization on indigenous coal, which played into the hands of the British coal industry and created insecurity in power supplies, is the most obvious example.

But the White Paper does not take this line. Instead the government has adopted a generally non-interventionist stance and seems ready, subject to monitoring the position closely, to accept whatever degree of self-sufficiency results from the competitive markets which it champions as its third energy policy goal. It says that relying neither on imports nor an increased dependence on gas in themselves pose security of supply problems, and quite rightly points out that competitive markets incentivize suppliers to achieve reliability.

Already, in anticipation of a decline in indigenous production, there has been a very significant market response to bring gas to the UK from 2005 onwards. There are plans for three LNG import terminals, two new interconnectors with Norway and Holland and a planned upgrade to the existing interconnector with Belgium.[8]

As I mentioned earlier, the government is also concerned to ensure that the gas transmission system responds effectively to increases in imports of both piped gas and LNG from a range of sources, and the new arrangements for the sale of entry capacity to the natural gas transmission system, coupled with the new incentive scheme on NGT to respond quickly to market demand, were put in place in 2002 to achieve this. The demand signals coming from the sale of long-term entry rights gives NGT additional information about where investment is needed and when, while the firmness of the transmission rights provides an additional incentive on NGT to make the capacity it has sold available on the day and also provides users of gas with realistic levels of compensation if NGT does not deliver, since NGT must buy back the rights at prevailing market prices.

Security of Wholesale Electricity Supplies and Infrastructure

I now turn to security of supply in electricity, which has gained greater
prominence and caused more immediate concern than when the White Paper
appeared earlier in 2003. Initially the talk was of electricity generation and
whether, given the steep falls in prices which accompanied the introduction
of the new trading arrangements, there would be enough generation to
meet peak demand that winter and in the longer term. Now, because the
London power cut of 2003 was apparently due to transmission system
failure, worries about the robustness of the electricity network have been
added to the previous concern about generation availability.

In terms of the transmission system, some press comment suggested
that the London power cut was due to underinvestment in the system
post privatization. Both Ofgem and NGT were quick to refute this claim,
pointing out that transmission investment has been higher over the past
10–12 years – averaging £300 million per year – than immediately before
or after privatization when investment was running at less than £100
million per year. In total, Ofgem estimates that about £16 billion has been
invested in electricity networks since privatization. They also point out that
security of electricity supply has improved post privatization. Up to now,
the national transmission system has been nearly 100 per cent reliable and
on the distribution networks, where most problems arise, especially when
extreme weather conditions affect overhead lines, according to Ofgem power
cuts have fallen by 11 per cent since 1991/92 and also fallen in duration by
nearly one-third.

It is clearly right that Ofgem should investigate the causes of these power
cuts, especially given the widespread disruption caused in London from
quite a short interruption to supplies. And, since the Utilities Act 2000
came into force, there is the possibility of the regulator imposing financial
penalties up to 10 per cent of turnover should a company be found to be
in breach of its statutory and licence duties.

But, in addition, the introduction of firm transmission rights for the users
of transmission systems, the merits of which I discussed earlier, in ensuring
sufficient targeted investment in the transmission system, could also improve
security of supply. They would further sharpen the commercial incentive
on NGT to deliver the capacity rights it sells, and would also provide direct
compensation to users if there were transmission-related interruptions to
supplies, which the imposition of financial penalties for breach of duties
does not achieve.

What about generation? Are there sufficient incentives in place to ensure
enough capacity is available when required? It is inevitable that generators
will lament the steep fall in prices that accompanied the introduction of

NETA when it replaced the Pool system which had helped keep electricity prices excessively high during the 1990s.

Now the new competitive framework for trading wholesale electricity works hand in hand with the competitive supply and generation markets, and allows the market to provide appropriate levels of generation capacity in response to price signals. In the short term, the NETA balancing arrangements encourage suppliers to ensure they have contracted enough power from generators to meet their customers' requirements, especially over periods of likely peak demand when imbalance prices might be high. Large customers, too, under NETA are much more able to participate fully in the market, and generators have strong incentives to have reliable plant in order to meet their contractual obligations. Further ahead, forward prices help guide existing plant owners to decide whether to run their plants or to mothball units or whole stations, while further ahead still forward prices assist decisions about plant closure and investment in new capacity. Under the Pool, none of these incentives was present to help ensure capacity was available when required.

Experience in 2003 has shown the market responding as one would anticipate. After the shake-out in prices following the introduction of NETA, and against rising demand, a 25 per cent increase in forward prices over 2002–3 led several generators to make previously mothballed plant ready to start generating that winter. And the plant margin, the excess of peak capacity over estimated peak demand, is reportedly close to the 20 per cent with which NGT presently says it feels comfortable.

Nevertheless, there is a persistent call by some generators, though not all, for the reintroduction of fixed capacity payments which generators previously received under the Pool for keeping power stations available. Capacity payments under the Pool were intended to provide both a short-term and a long-term signal of capacity requirements. However, they failed to provide effective short-term signals since they did not accurately reflect short-term change in the capacity margin. Over the longer term, capacity payments varied arbitrarily between years, and a high or a low level of payment in a particular year was not a good signal of likely capacity payments in subsequent years. Although significant new entry occurred during the time the Pool was operating, it seems to have been more associated with the overall high price level during the period: neither the level nor the pattern of entry appeared to have had much to do with the level of capacity payments.

Now of course there are capacity payments under NETA, but they are determined by the market itself, not fixed by the government. In the dynamic market that now exists they are much more likely than any administered arrangement to send timely and appropriate signals to investors and existing generators about when additional plant is likely to be needed.

The White Paper says that the government had reviewed the case for some kind of capacity payment or obligation and concluded that the case had not been made for such an instrument in the UK market. It also noted that experience with such instruments in other countries has been mixed, some being subject to material alterations within short time periods, which is the kind of regulatory risk the instrument is supposed to offset.

But one of the reasons for calls for some administered arrangement that raises prices above market levels is the worry that some time in the future the government might be tempted to hold prices down below market levels. Even the fear that this might happen can have a profound adverse effect on security of supply. Neither suppliers nor producers will have the incentive to enter the market if they believe they may be prevented from supplying their product at competitive prices in the future.

Mindful that, for markets to work, firms need to be confident that the government will not interfere, the White Paper gives a categorical assurance that the government will not interfere in competitive energy markets, except in extreme circumstances such as to avert, as a last resort, a potentially serious risk to safety. Generators who are inviting government intervention in the market now presumably appreciate the downside of such a position: government intervention, depending on the political pressures of the day, can keep prices down as well as up.

Yet it is not only through a direct influence on prices that the government affects the decisions of existing and would-be generators. Its decisions on targeting specific amounts of energy savings, renewables and CHP plant have a similar effect. The White Paper says that, given current levels of capacity, including mothballed plant, and the government's expectations of growing renewables generation and energy efficiency improvements over the coming years, it calculates that we are unlikely to need significant new investment in non-renewable power stations over the next five years or possibly longer.

The implication of this statement is that, if the government's targets are not met, there *will* be a need for non-renewable power stations within the next five years. This statement makes it clear that meeting the government's CO_2 reduction targets is crucial not just for its CO_2 goals but also for future security of supply. Yet the government has said that the market should be relied on to produce security. And indeed, if free to do so, it would. The cost of carbon would be incorporated in the calculations of market participants and separate judgements would be made about the reliability of different fuels, fuel sources and technologies. But, in creating specific demand and generation targets to meet its CO_2 reduction goals, the government is effectively simultaneously making decisions that have a crucial bearing on security of supply, thereby restricting the role of the market in this respect. It is a sobering thought that whether or not the targets the government has set to reach its CO_2 reduction goals are met can also have a profound effect on security of supply. More generally, whether or not the government's energy efficiency, renewables and CHP targets to 2010 and 2020 are fully met will have a *major* and *increasing* influence on the price of *unsupported* wholesale electricity and thus on market decisions about plant closures and new investment.

The Operation of the Gas and Electricity Transmission Systems

But investment alone is not sufficient to ensure security of supply. Even if there is sufficient production capacity to meet demand, and if there is enough transportation capacity in the right locations, still if the transmission systems are not kept in balance in real time, then security of supply will be threatened. This is a particular issue for electricity, where supply and demand must be kept in balance all the time, but it is also important for the gas system to be properly balanced day by day, and the presence of gas-fired generation means there are important on-the-day interactions between the two systems. Over short time scales, then, NGT – as system operator for both the gas and electricity transmission systems – plays a major role in ensuring security of supply by balancing the systems. Commercial incentives, put in place by Ofgem, help ensure it carries out these roles efficiently. It can buy and sell gas and electricity to keep its systems in balance and to match overall demand and supply. Where supply is tight relative to demand, on-the-day imbalance prices may rise to very high levels to ensure security of supply is maintained.

To make sure their customers enjoy security, suppliers are obliged to continue to purchase electricity and gas, whatever the close-to-real-time price, if they have not already contracted ahead with producers to cover all their customers' requirements. Most suppliers do contract ahead for the majority of their customers' demand, so close-to-real-time balancing trades represent only a small proportion of the total gas and electricity trade (around 2–3 per cent to date). But the system operators need to rely on market participants and to have adequate and timely information if the unexpected happens. There is an obligation in the licences of all gas shippers not to prejudice the efficient balancing of the system, but no such condition exists in electricity: that is a deficiency I believe the government could usefully rectify if new legislation is forthcoming, in order better to ensure security of supply.

However, there is also a deficiency in the gas arrangements. Much of the system-balancing information Transco needs is offshore with gas producers, a part of the industry regulated by the DTI. There has been a long-standing concern by other market participants that offshore production information, which can affect market prices, is not so readily available as similar information in electricity. But more specifically in relation to the system operation, Transco has been concerned for some time that it has not been informed quickly enough about offshore events that can affect its system-balancing role. A report by Ofgem into gas interruptions which occurred in the summer of 2003 suggested that lack of offshore information contributed to the interruptions. And in its Winter Operations Report for 2003–2004, covering both the gas and electricity systems, NGT said it was very supportive of the Ofgem/DTI initiatives already under way, following the summer interruption events of 17/18 June 2003, to improve data provision from upstream parties. It is clearly important that NGT's on-the-day information requirements are addressed as soon as possible.

But perhaps the key challenge is to deal effectively with the interactions of gas and electricity system operation, given that a large proportion of power generation is gas-fired. Problems with gas supply or on the gas system can therefore easily affect electricity supplies, while the within-day operation of the gas-fired power stations can also cause problems for gas system balancing.

Several years ago Ofgem sought to ensure that the then gas and electricity operators took fully into account events on the other system and has also tried to ensure that the necessary near-to-real-time information exchange could take place between the two system operators to help ensure secure supplies. Now NGT operates both the gas and electricity systems, although working under separate licences for each. And the Joint Energy Security of Supply group (JESS), involving both Ofgem and the DTI, monitors energy security, particularly market responses to key market indicators, such as forward prices. At Ofgem's instigation, the gas and electricity system operators also produce a report annually on the expected operation of each system, including interactions between the systems, with a commentary on the arrangements in place to ensure security of supply for the forthcoming winter. This has become known as the Winter Operations Report.

Winter Power Cuts?

Nobody could give a categorical answer to the question of power cuts in the winter of 2003–4, but NGT in its Winter Operations Report concluded that there were sufficient gas supplies and power stations to meet demand during a normal winter. It went on to say that in a 'worst case', including a long, cold winter, combined with gas shortages, power station failures and no electricity coming over the interconnector from France, voltage reductions might be required. But, as noted earlier, no energy form or source of supply can offer absolute security and it would be prohibitively expensive to try to cater for all possible eventualities. Therefore, even if there are power cuts, it does not necessarily mean there is something fundamentally wrong with the arrangements.

CONCLUSION

To conclude, I would reiterate the two important general messages I hope I have been able to convey.

First, economic regulation is as important and relevant now as it has ever been. Policing and promoting competition in retail and wholesale markets is not only important in ensuring customers are protected in respect of the price they pay for gas and electricity; it is also essential to give suppliers and producers the right incentives to provide the supply reliability that customers also demand. And, if they are allowed to, our liberalized gas and electricity markets could help also to deliver the government's CO_2 goals economically, putting the UK ahead in that area, as they have done in driving greater industry efficiency.

The second general message I consider particularly serious. In terms of how the government is seeking to achieve its CO_2 and security of supply goals, there is a major difference of approach. As regards security of supply, the government is looking to competitive wholesale and retail gas and electricity markets to deliver reliable supplies of gas and electricity to consumers and has pledged that it will not under all normal circumstances interfere with the operation of those markets, being fully aware that government intervention, or even the threat of such intervention, could jeopardize the security that the government, as well as customers, seeks.

To date, however, to achieve its CO_2 goals the government has chosen not a market-based but an interventionist approach which is likely to make attainment of the goals more costly and less transparent than necessary. Its approach also has the effect of interfering with the proper functioning of the competitive gas and electricity markets, including in electricity the role of markets in determining the appropriate choice of fuels to deliver security.

I do not believe the two approaches can live together compatibly. A change in stance to the adoption of a carbon trading scheme could harness the competitive markets in the provision of environmental improvements and leave markets performing their other roles, including security provision. If such a change in stance does not take place, then it seems likely, especially since missing the CO_2 targets could have important implications for security of supply, that government intervention will creep further into the functions that the competitive markets now perform. Gas and electricity regulation will expand, rather than contract, and the government may well become more directly involved in network regulation.

Thus I do not believe it is too far-fetched to see independent economic regulation seriously compromised in the years ahead if the government does not change its stance on the way it seeks to achieve its CO_2 reduction goals. But we are still close to the beginning of seeking seriously to control CO_2 emissions and there is still time to make that change.

NOTES

1. The UK currently accounts for only about 2 per cent of the global total.
2. See, for example, John Burton, *Picking Losers? The political economy of industrial policy*, Hobart Paper 99. Institute of Economic Affairs, 1983.
3. 'Electricity bills set to surge in war on CO_2', *The Times*, 8 October 2003.
4. The Scottish Executive launched the Renewables Obligation Scotland on 1 April 2002. The White Paper also reported that the Northern Ireland Executive had recently brought forward provisions to introduce a Northern Ireland Renewables Obligation.
5. For example, see 'Energy Policy Objectives and Instruments', *The Utilities Journal*, September 2002.
6. The White Paper says that, while nuclear power is currently an important source of carbon-free electricity, the present economics of nuclear power make it an unattractive option for new generating capacity; there are also significant issues about nuclear waste to be resolved. It goes on to say that the government does not rule out the possibility that at some point in the future new nuclear plant might be necessary to meet its carbon targets, but such a decision would be preceded by public consultation and another White Paper.
7. See Ralph Turvey, 'Ensuring Adequate Generation Capacity', *Utilities Policy*, 1(2003), 95–102.
8. Sir John Mogg, Speech to the Gas Forum Annual Seminar, 2 October 2003.

CHAIRMAN'S COMMENTS

Stephen Littlechild

Having worked with Eileen for many years, both at the University of Birmingham and at Offer, I know the high and professional quality of her work and the rigorous thinking that underlies it. This paper is no exception. It comprises a masterful survey of three interrelated topics of great importance and topicality, namely, controlling carbon dioxide emissions, the regulator's role and security of supply. I agree with her general thesis, but she has opened up some controversial and important ideas, and with some reluctance I must confine myself to a few of them.

The Regulator's Role

Eileen suggests that the regulator should resist special treatment for renewables in the NETA regime. She makes the point that ensuring that CHP and renewables are not discriminated against is very different from giving them preferential terms and distorting the system in their favour.

As regards network charges, she suggests that the regulator should help ensure that renewables generation is as efficient and as efficiently located as possible, and that the government's intention not to include zonal transmission charges in the new arrangements for Great Britain seems a retrograde step. As those who have followed this saga over the last 15 years will expect, I agree with her view. Uniform charges favour renewable and other generation in one part of the country at the expense of renewable and other generation in other parts, and reduce the signals for efficient location. Hiding the costs of renewable energy generally is not conducive to the interests of consumers or of public policy making.

Renewable generators have been very concerned about some aspects of NETA, particularly the spread of imbalance prices in the early days. This is understandable. Eileen notes that the regulator should continue to modify imbalance prices to ensure that they are properly reflective of energy-balancing costs. The economic logic of dual cashout pricing, and the identification and measurement of the relevant costs, could usefully benefit from further analysis and examination.

Eileen rightly notes that transmission and distribution expansion to accommodate the government's plans for renewables and CHP could be very expensive (reportedly over £1 billion to meet the 10 per cent target by 2010). How best to ensure efficient investment here, and in particular how to avoid spending large sums of money yet still not getting the needed capacity? Effectively, the suggestion is that auctioning capacity rights will remove or reduce the need for the regulator to commit at a price control review in advance of the need being substantiated, will enable the company to go ahead with investment before the next price control review if and when the demand does materialize, and will encourage the company to respond quickly.

These are understandable and laudable objectives. But how these auctions schemes and associated regulation will develop is as yet somewhat unknown. The auction prices seem likely to depend on the timing of the auctions, the quantities of capacity involved, and on various other terms of sale. How should the resulting prices be interpreted, how should they be translated into regulatory guidance to the company, how should the price control and the incentive mechanism be calibrated? The answers to these questions are not entirely clear as yet, and the possibilities of manipulation by the companies cannot be ruled out. It would be helpful to know more of the thinking behind this approach, and of the experience to date in the gas transmission sector. Of course, no regulation is perfect, so the hurdle to beat is the present version of electricity regulation rather than some kind of theoretically ideal outcome.

Controlling Carbon Dioxide Emissions

The paper considers the implications of the government's goal – establishing a path to 60 per cent reduction in carbon emissions – and the means chosen to achieve this goal. It notes that significant gas and electricity price increases are likely as a result. It identifies the present interventionist means of achieving this goal: half to come from reducing energy demand and half from increasing renewable energy and CHP. To this end the government has established energy efficiency commitments and energy-savings targets.

For renewables, the targets are daunting. Meeting the 10 per cent target by 2010 will involve building more renewable capacity per year from now until 2010 than the total capacity of renewables built over the last 15 years. This rate of construction is to be subsidized by the renewables obligation. The target for CHP, perhaps more modest, still requires more CHP to be built from now to 2010 than in the last 15 years, that is, at more than double the previous rate of investment.

Eileen's concerns are twofold. First, such government planning is unlikely to be as efficient as markets, and is vulnerable to political influence from pressure groups at the expense of customers generally. Second, such government involvement could adversely impact on competitive energy markets by forcing suppliers to become tax collectors and subsidized energy efficiency providers, and by creating a managed market with respect to total supply and the shares to come from different fuels.

Her main argument is that all 'these negative consequences could be avoided if the government moved swiftly to a competitive approach to the reduction of carbon emissions by the adoption of a carbon trading scheme' (p. 124). Such a scheme would involve tradable emissions rights, and would enable the removal of all other measures. Indeed, the benefits would depend on the latter occurring. These benefits would be fourfold:

1. The market will deliver carbon reductions in the most efficient way, and reveal whether present measures are viable (and if not, the government could stop wasting money on them).
2. The cost of the policy would be more transparent.
3. There would be reduced scope for special interest groups to influence policy.
4. Such measures would complement rather than interfere with competitive energy markets.

In general I agree on these advantages of such a trading scheme. If it is necessary to reduce the level of carbon dioxide emissions, it is sensible to discover and encourage the most efficient ways of doing so, and the trading scheme would assist with that. However, there is still the issue of what level of carbon emissions to commit to, and how that might evolve over time. That will impact not only on the kinds of trades that take place, but also on the underlying investment.

To illustrate, consider the difference between such a carbon trading market and the normal electricity and gas markets. In the latter, market participants can be reasonably confident that there will continue to be a demand for these fuels well into the future. Their task is to estimate the extent of demand in relation to available supply, and the viability of their own actual and potential investments.

In contrast, with carbon trading it is a matter of guessing what future government policy will be. What will be the levels of future commitments and obligations? Can market participants even be sure that there will be commitments and obligations at all? The government might talk of long-term commitments, but can any government be believed on such long-term matters and can any government bind its successor? There must be an election, and therefore a new government in place, within a couple of years. By 2020 there will have been at least four new governments, perhaps more, and surely they will be of various different political and philosophical complexions. If there is one thing of which we *can* be confident, it is that government policy in future will *not* be the same as government policy today.

This suggests that carbon trading, like renewables trading, may be more efficient for short-term decisions than for long-term ones. That is, it will tend to find the best ways of saving carbon or producing renewables given present capacities, but whether market participants will have the confidence to base significant investment decisions on carbon trading markets is another matter. The same, incidentally, goes for renewables investment in the light of the market for renewables certificates. The market price for renewables today is known, but for how long can the obligations that underlie it be assumed to remain in place?

This takes us to the 'important and controversial issues' that Eileen noted at the beginning of her remarks: 'whether climate change is occurring; if it is, whether carbon dioxide emissions are largely to blame; and, if they are, whether it is better to cut emissions than to live with the consequences' (p. 119). These are perhaps becoming more controversial issues rather than less. A recent monograph[1] has surveyed the climate science literature and emphasized the uncertainties involved. But there seems reason for moderate optimism. Climate change may be occurring at a slower rate than was previously believed to obtain; there is increasing doubt as to whether carbon dioxide emissions are the sole or main contributor to climate change; there may be means of reducing climate change other than by reducing carbon emissions; and there may be significant benefits as well as costs associated with global warming.[2]

Now consider that these costs and benefits lie many years into the future, so that their discounted value today is relatively small compared to the very high costs of trying to reduce carbon emissions today. Consider that, although the Kyoto commitments appear to be accepted and taken relatively seriously in parts of Europe, they are much more controversial in North America, and flatly rejected by some of the major and fast-growing nations in Asia and Africa. And consider finally that with the passage of time scientists will inevitably discover much more about the nature and likelihood of global warming, and new and better ways of dealing with the situation are very likely to emerge as technologies and understanding develop.

In all these circumstances, is it really rational to impose high costs on customers today to deal with a possible eventuality a century or two in the future, of which we presently know very little? And is it likely that government policy on this issue will remain broadly constant over the whole of this next century or two?

Carbon trading would indeed have the merits that Eileen identifies, and in particular it would make the costs of such a policy more apparent. However, it would only encourage new investment to the extent that market participants considered the government's policy commitments to be credible. It would not remove the scope for special interest groups in seeking support for their preferred investments or policies.

Suppose it is accepted that significant carbon reduction is the government's decided policy. Does it follow that renewables and energy efficiency are the best way to achieve this? Part of Eileen's case for carbon trading is that it would test this claim. What do recent economic appraisals tell us? Emerging research suggests that renewables are a very expensive means of reducing carbon, and that nuclear energy, despite its various problems, could be cost-competitive under certain conditions and is likely to be significantly cheaper than renewables.[3] Of course, there are different ways of producing nuclear electricity and dealing with nuclear waste. Reprocessing technologies used in the UK in the past may well not be the most efficient methods in future (compared to storing). But this is a detail. The point is that nuclear energy could well be more economic and efficient than renewables at reducing carbon emissions, if carbon emissions really needed to be reduced.

This then raises the obvious question. Would a carbon trading scheme give sufficient confidence to finance the construction of a nuclear station, or indeed of a series of such stations, on a scale sufficient (with other methods) to meet the government's carbon policy?

I do not know the answer to this question, but it suggests that, despite its many undeniable advantages, carbon trading does not eliminate a very active role for government. This role would include setting (and probably resetting) the levels of reductions to be achieved. But it would also seem to extend to facilitating the kinds of major and longer-term investments – notably in renewables or nuclear – that might be deemed appropriate and necessary to secure those reductions. That being the case, and given the very high direct and indirect potential costs of such investments and such a government role, it surely seems appropriate to give further serious thought to the need for, and implications of, its carbon emissions policy.

Conclusions

Eileen has argued the potentially serious consequences if the government does not change its stance on the way it seeks to achieve its carbon dioxide reduction goals. She notes that there is still time to make that change. Her argument might be extended. At the present point in time, is it prudent to commit to such carbon dioxide reduction goals in the first place?

Notes

1. Robert L. Bradley Jr, *Climate Alarmism Reconsidered*, Hobart Paper 146, Institute of Economic Affairs, 2003.
2. See the comments by Colin Robinson on page 104 of this volume
3. E.g. John Bower, 'UK Offshore Wind Generation Capacity: a return to picking winners?', Oxford Institute for Energy Studies, *Energy Comment*, July 2003. Dan Lewis, *Recharging the Nation*, report for National Economic Research Council, November 2003. *The Future of Nuclear Power. An Interdisciplinary MIT Study*, Cambridge, Mass: MIT, July 2003. Also Bradley, *Climate Alarmism Reconsidered*, pp. 38–9.

7. Regulating London Underground

Chris Bolt

INTRODUCTION[1]

My job title – which is, in the Greater London Authority (GLA) Act 1999 that establishes the role, the 'Public–Private Partnership Agreement Arbiter', or 'PPP Arbiter' for short – is perhaps not the most self-explanatory. The reaction from most people is 'What is the PPP?' More informed audiences, such as this, do not need to have those initials expanded, and generally understand that my role relates to the London Underground PPP. But almost everyone still asks 'What does an Arbiter actually do?'

At least the job title does make the point that my role is one of an Arbiter – not regulator, or for that matter arbitrator – and that the Arbiter is concerned with specific contracts, not companies or a particular utility sector. So the title of this paper is misleading. If 'regulation' is defined as consumer protection achieved through continuity of service and safe and efficient delivery, while allowing a reasonable return for efficient service providers, then no one person 'regulates' London Underground. Certainly as Arbiter I do not.

The PPP arrangements for London Underground are new and still relatively unfamiliar. The model adopted by London Underground Ltd (LUL) for the PPP is fundamentally different from that familiar in other infrastructure sectors, including the national rail network; and the role of Arbiter has no close parallels – either in the UK or (so far as I am aware) internationally. So I will start by describing the PPP Agreements and the Arbiter's role within them. I will then contrast these arrangements with those applying to regulated networks and to Private Finance Initiative (PFI) projects, under three broad headings:

- the allocation of responsibilities between the different players;
- the handling of important 'technical' issues such as establishing efficient costs and allowing for appropriate financing costs; and
- the provisions for amending 'contracts', and the respective roles of customers and regulators.

As well as highlighting similarities and differences, I will draw some tentative conclusions about the pros and cons of the different models. I also identify areas where further consideration may need to be given to consistency of approach and the possible case for future convergence.

AN OUTLINE OF THE PPP AGREEMENTS[2]

LUL has entered into three PPP Agreements for the maintenance and enhancement of its infrastructure over the next 30 years. Under these PPP Agreements, three private sector companies (Infracos) have been contracted to maintain, renew and upgrade discrete parts of LUL's infrastructure – track, stations and rolling stock. LUL will remain responsible for delivering services to customers. Two of these contracts have been awarded to the Metronet consortium, which took control of the Sub Surface Lines (SSL) and Bakerloo, Central and Victoria (BCV) Lines on 4 April 2003. The other contract, for the Jubilee, Piccadilly and Northern (JNP) Lines, was awarded to Tube Lines and commenced on 31 December 2002.

The PPP enables an intensive programme of work on a scale never previously undertaken on the Underground. The PPP Agreements deliberately do not specify the work to be undertaken, and set deliverables in terms of the service provided to passengers. To meet the output specifications in the contract, the Infracos' plans include:

- 336 new trains by 2014 and an additional 42 trains by 2019;
- all rolling stock currently more than ten years old replaced by 2019;
- all lines to have modern signal and control systems by 2016, providing automatic train operation and automatic train protection;
- a total of 80 per cent of the Underground's 400-plus kilometres of track replaced over the life of the contract;
- capacity increased within ten years by 22 per cent on the Jubilee Line; 14 per cent on the Victoria Line; and by 18 per cent on the Northern Line, with increases on other lines over the period of the Agreements;
- ten of London's busiest stations modernized or refurbished within ten years: Oxford Circus, King's Cross, Liverpool Street, Piccadilly Circus, Waterloo, Leicester Square, Tottenham Court Road, Charing Cross, Paddington and Victoria;
- a programme of modernization and refurbishment at other stations, including a network of 'step-free' stations, with ongoing refurbishments every seven-and-a-half years; and
- all infrastructure fully maintained and renewed to achieve a network-wide state of good repair by the end of the third review period.

The PPP Agreements create a long-term relationship between LUL and each Infraco, many aspects of which are fixed at the start. However, the designers of the PPP concluded that it would not be practical for Infracos to submit fixed prices for the whole 30 years, nor would it be good value for money. Similarly, LUL could not confidently predict its service requirements for the distant future. So the Agreements allow LUL to restate its requirements for the service to be delivered at Periodic Reviews every seven-and-a-half years[3] and for the Infrastructure Service Charge (ISC) payable to the Infracos to be reviewed to reflect changes in costs for an efficient 'Notional Infraco'.

The required deliverables result in a front-loaded expenditure profile, which is not fully reflected in the ISC (Figure 7.1). So the Infracos are cash-flow negative in the first period, and have put financing arrangements in place to allow for this. Whilst raising broadly comparable amounts within each Infraco (some £4.5 billion in aggregate), these arrangements differ between the two Metronet-owned Infracos and the one owned by Tube Lines in the following respects:

- Metronet has accessed fixed rate and index-linked capital markets for a material part of its debt, with the remainder coming from the European Investment Bank and other project finance banks; while
- Tube Lines has borrowed from the EIB, raised conventional project finance debt and raised a credit-enhanced tranche which has the benefit of a AAA credit rating (but is currently considering a refinancing of these initial arrangements).

Given that the funding arrangements are closer to the project finance model underlying PFI projects than to those familiar in the privatized utility sector, the Agreements contain extensive provisions to protect the position of lenders and allow them to recover their investment (through a process of 'Mandatory Sale') if LUL's requirements change to such an extent that there is a fundamental change to the nature of the deal.

Under the PPP Agreements, requirements are, so far as possible, specified in terms of the service experienced by passengers.[4] There are three main measures:

- capability – measured through reduced journey times as a result of major line enhancements involving expenditure on track, signalling and rolling stock;
- availability – reflecting 'in-service' performance of the infrastructure measured through the reduction of delays; and

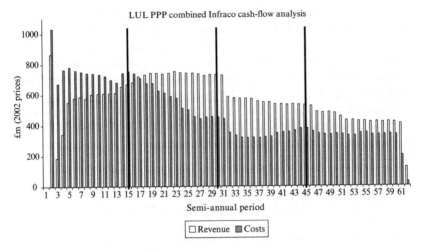

LUL PPP combined Infraco cash-flow analysis

Semi-annual period

□ Revenue ■ Costs

Source: Office of the PPP Arbiter.

Figure 7.1   Infraco costs and revenues (at 2002 prices)

- ambience – reflecting the condition and cleanliness of trains and stations measured through mystery shopper surveys.

For the purposes of calculating financial abatements and bonuses, actual performance is assessed on the basis of two main measures: Lost Customer Hours and Service Points. In order that incentives on Infracos reflect customer interests, Lost Customer Hours are valued at £6/hour – LUL's estimate of its passengers' average value of time – with rates of £9 above an 'unacceptable performance' threshold, and lower rates of £3 for improvements beyond benchmark.

PRECEDENTS FOR THE PPP

The form of the PPP has its origins in the model of project financing developed over the last decade in the Private Finance Initiative. But the LU PPP is unique – not just in terms of its scale, but in terms of the pattern of financing and also the change provisions built into the contract from the outset.

   Although the intention, in entering into long-term contracts, is to improve incentives on the Infracos to look at whole-life costs and performance, as with a DBFO (Design, Build, Finance and Operate) contract, the PPP does not have distinct 'build' and 'operate' phases. This has a number of consequences, not least the need for extensive performance arrangements to reflect the complex nature of the service being delivered. But this complexity, and the ongoing nature of the Underground network, makes it more difficult to specify requirements than for a single asset such as a school or hospital.[5]

This, and the corresponding difficulty of capturing long-term future efficiency potential through a competitive tender process, led to the introduction of a Periodic Review mechanism, similar to that in the price-regulated network industries (although at 7½- rather than 5-year intervals). In addition, provision was made for Extraordinary Reviews, similar to the 'shipwreck' clause in water company licences, to allow charges to be modified within a review period if Infracos experience cost shocks outside their control.

Most disputes under the PPP Agreements are dealt with through a contractual Disputes Resolution Agreement involving internal escalation, adjudication and ultimately the Courts. But it was recognized that this was not appropriate for disputes at Periodic and Extraordinary Reviews because of the nature of the issues involved and the need for decisions to be taken independently of the Parties. So the PPP arrangements also provide for the appointment of a PPP Arbiter, who can be asked to determine the key financial terms[6] of the PPP Agreements at Periodic Reviews, and at an interim Extraordinary Review should one be necessary, and to give guidance on any aspect of the Agreements at any time. This is a standing appointment, created by statute, and it was envisaged that the Arbiter would have a small permanent staff to support him.[7] So although the role is not that of a regulator, it is also very different from that of an arbitrator.

I was appointed to the role of Arbiter on 31 December 2002 (the date the first PPP Agreement became operational), for a four-year term.

THE ARBITER: FUNCTIONS AND DUTIES[8]

The role of PPP Arbiter was established by the GLA Act 1999. The Arbiter is appointed as an individual, with the power to employ staff and incur expenses. Costs are met by the Secretary of State for Transport, although the Arbiter is independent of Ministers (and of the PPP Parties); for example, the Secretary of State can only dismiss the Arbiter on grounds of incapacity or misbehaviour, or where he considers that there has been unreasonable delay in the discharge of the Arbiter's functions.

Under the provisions of the GLA Act, the Arbiter has two principal functions:

- to give directions on matters specified in the PPP Agreements, when referred to him by one of the parties to a PPP Agreement (section 229); and
- to give guidance on any matter relating to a PPP Agreement, when asked to do so by either (or both) of the parties to a PPP Agreement (section 230).

In addition the Arbiter is given further powers 'for the purposes of the proper discharge of the functions conferred on him' by the GLA Act (section 232). For example the Arbiter may do 'all such things as he considers appropriate for or in connection with the giving of a direction or guidance and ... do such other things as he considers necessary or expedient ... for purposes preparatory or ancillary to the giving of directions or guidance generally ... notwithstanding that there is no matter in relation to which a direction or guidance is required'. The powers conferred on me are exercisable therefore on the giving of directions and guidance or in circumstances preparatory or ancillary to the giving of a direction or guidance.

My function in respect of directions is limited by the terms of the PPP Agreements: if there is no specific provision in a PPP Agreement for the Arbiter's involvement, any disputes are dealt with through contractual routes. Even on matters within my remit for directions, I am only brought in if the PPP Parties fail to agree and seek a direction from me. I therefore have no unilateral power as Arbiter to change, or propose to change, provisions in the PPP Agreements. Even where I have made a direction on a disputed matter within my remit, the PPP Parties may, under the provisions of section 229 (7) of the Act, jointly agree to set aside that direction.

My second function under the GLA Act is to issue guidance on any matter relating to a PPP Agreement, although again only at the request of one (or both) of the PPP Parties. An important issue in developing my future work programme will therefore be to understand from the PPP Parties whether guidance is likely to be sought only on matters where I can also give a direction, or whether they may seek guidance on a wider range of issues relating to the PPP Agreements.

In giving directions or guidance, the Arbiter is under a statutory duty to 'act in the way he considers best calculated to achieve' four public interest objectives (section 231). These are:

- to ensure that London Underground has the opportunity to revise its requirements under the PPP Agreements if the proper price exceeds the resources available;

- to promote efficiency and economy in the provision, construction, renewal, or improvement and maintenance of the railway infrastructure;
- to ensure that if a rate of return is incorporated in a PPP Agreement, a company which is efficient and economic in its performance of the requirements in that PPP Agreement would earn that return; and
- to enable the Infracos to plan the future performance of the PPP Agreements with reasonable certainty.

In giving directions or guidance, I am also under a duty to take account of any factors notified to me by both PPP Parties, or are specified in the relevant PPP Agreement, as ones to which I must have regard. The concept of 'taking account of', or 'having regard to', also features in the legislation governing the sectoral economic regulators. For example, the Rail Regulator is under a duty to 'have regard to any general guidance given to him by the Secretary of State about railway services or other matters relating to railways'.[9]

'Taking account of' or 'having regard to' a matter does not mean 'must follow', and does not therefore oblige me to adopt a particular position; in the same way, a requirement to 'take account of' a matter is not the same as being instructed to take a particular approach. But the duty does imply that I must consider the particular matter fully as part of my decision-making process, giving due weight to it and to the expressed intention of the PPP Parties.

The GLA Act does not explicitly prioritize between the four specified objectives in giving guidance or directions. In principle, I will need to consider the interaction between them in exercising my functions. My initial view, however, is that in practice there is unlikely to be significant conflict between them, particularly if decisions are taken only after full and effective consultation.

Similarly, the GLA Act does not prioritize between the duty 'to take account of' factors notified to me by the PPP Parties and achievement of the four objectives other than stating that I 'shall' act in the way best calculated to achieve those objectives. A situation may arise where the apparent intention of the PPP Parties may be in conflict with achievement of the four objectives identified in the GLA Act. Where I consider that this may be the case, I would expect to set out the reasons for this view, explain how my proposed decision has balanced achievement of my duties and seek representations from interested parties before taking the final decision.

The GLA Act also gives me powers to seek from the PPP Parties, their associates and any PPP related third party such information as I consider relevant to the proper discharge of my functions. Any failure to provide information can lead to enforcement action in the High Court.

Any information provided to me which relates to a particular individual or business can only be disclosed with the consent of the relevant individual or business or in specific circumstances set out in the GLA Act. These circumstances include facilitating the exercise of functions under the GLA Act by the Secretary of State, Mayor and Transport for London (or indeed the Arbiter) or to facilitate Ministers, the Mayor and other regulators to carry out statutory functions under other Acts such as the Railways Act. The provisions of the GLA Act have been amended (through the Railways and Transport Safety Act 2003) to introduce reciprocal arrangements which allow, for example, Ministers and the economic regulators to disclose information obtained under their statutory powers to me.

THE ARBITER: CONTRACTUAL PROVISIONS

The main contractual provisions in respect of the Arbiter are contained in Schedule 1.9 to the Service Contracts.[10] They fall into four main categories:

- the specification of matters which can be referred to the Arbiter for direction;
- the process for carrying out Periodic Reviews and Extraordinary Reviews;
- matters which are agreed between the PPP Parties and which they do not require the Arbiter to consider; and
- joint guidance from the PPP Parties to the Arbiter.

Under the provisions of the GLA Act, I can only be asked to give directions on matters specified in the PPP Agreements. For the most part, matters are only referred for direction in the context of a Periodic or Extraordinary Review. However, in addition, all three PPP Agreements allow the PPP Parties periodically to seek direction as to the amount of cost increases or revenue shortfalls that can be 'logged up' towards an Extraordinary Review.

Schedule 1.9 also indicates the matters that the PPP Parties agree can be referred to me for guidance.[11] The matters are the same as those that can be referred for direction, with one exception: in the Metronet PPP Agreements there is specific provision that my guidance can be sought annually, as from April 2005, in the form of a reasoned report on whether the Infraco has 'performed its activities in an overall efficient and economic manner and in accordance with Good Industry Practice'.

Paragraph 6.6 of Schedule 1.9 indicates that the PPP Parties may agree to express the terms of a reference to the Arbiter 'so as to advise him that they do not request or require him to consider any aspect of the matter being referred on which they state they have reached agreement'. So it is clearly open to the PPP Parties to frame any reference to me for directions to exclude matters which have been agreed between them. However, I am also able to give binding directions on any other matter ancillary or incidental to a matter on which I am requested to give direction. This allows me to deal with related issues that were not raised in a reference, where I consider that this is necessary in order to comply with my statutory duty, although it creates no general requirement to consider issues outside the scope of the reference.

It is possible therefore that I may consider matters covered by paragraph 6.6 as being matters ancillary to the giving of directions or guidance where, for example, this is needed to 'make sense' of the original reference. The scope of matters which are ancillary and incidental to a particular reference will clearly depend upon the precise terms of the reference given to me by the PPP Parties.

The guidance contained in Schedule 1.9 refers explicitly to section 231 (6). The terms of the guidance accordingly constitute factors which the PPP Parties notify to me as ones to which I must have regard in giving guidance or directions. As explained above, I am under a statutory duty to take such factors into account in giving guidance or directions.

The PPP Parties' guidance covers the following main issues:

- the nature of the process for a Periodic or Extraordinary Review;
- certain financial issues relating to a Periodic Review;
- the specification of the Notional Infraco, with guidance on factors relevant to the assessment of efficient and economic performance and Good Industry Practice;
- the specification of a Net Adverse Effect;
- the treatment of refinancing benefits; and
- the behaviour expected of the PPP Parties operating within a spirit of partnership.

Given the statutory duty on me to take account of the matters contained in the PPP Parties' guidance, I have indicated that I will pay particular attention to it, and to follow it where this does not create a conflict with my other duties. I have indicated that I would expect to explain in any direction or guidance my reasons for departing from the PPP Parties' guidance where I consider that this is required as part of my overall statutory duty.

THE ROLE: A SUMMARY AND COMPARISON

Table 7.1 summarizes the Arbiter's role, and contrasts it with a 'traditional' regulatory role. Key differences are:

- the restricted remit – not covering for example the specification and enforcement of delivery;
- the reactive nature of the role – only giving guidance or directions when requested by the parties; and
- the possibility of being given 'narrow' terms of reference, even at the time of a Periodic Review.

Table 7.1   A comparison with regulation: the Arbiter's role

Arbiter	Regulator
• Involved only when requested by parties	• Active role, with broad public interest duties
• No general power to modify contract	• Modifies licence and enforces licence conditions
• No role in monitoring or enforcing performance	• Monitors overall performance in meeting objectives
• Contractual framework sets issues considered at Review	• Determines framework for Periodic Reviews
• Gives directions on elements of, or total, ISC	• Sets revised price limits at Reviews
• Only appeal is through Judicial Review	• Competition Commission as appeal body
• Rail Regulator has competition powers in respect of Underground rail services	• Concurrent jurisdiction with OFT under Competition Act

Source: Office of the PPP Arbiter.

AN ASSESSMENT OF THE PPP ARRANGEMENTS

The approach adopted for the modernization of the Underground is clearly very different from that in other UK infrastructure networks, and in particular the national rail network. In contrast to the standard utility model of a privatized company operating under a licence monitored and enforced by an economic regulator, the design of PPP Agreements derive more from a PFI model.

At first sight, the existence of a single public sector body, London Underground Ltd, specifying and purchasing services from private sector Infracos, makes a contractual approach look an obvious choice. But the nature of the deliverables – ongoing maintenance and enhancement of an existing network rather than construction and operation of an asset on a green-field site – and the need to allow for the specification of deliverables to change over the contract period make this a far from typical PFI project. Also, a licence structure could still accommodate the existence of a single direct 'customer' – not least given that there are millions of individual users of the Underground dependent on the services provided.

In terms of the closest parallel, the national rail network, we might ask whether the situation on the Underground is really that different from the Strategic Rail Authority (SRA) specifying the services it wants to run on Network Rail's network[12]. And if the economic reality is in fact similar, why are the contractual and regulatory arrangements so different?

In order to assess the similarities and differences between the London Underground PPP arrangements and the standard utility model, I will consider three broad aspects of the arrangements:

- the underlying customer/client structure, with particular reference to the national rail network;
- the basis on which common 'technical' issues such as establishing efficient costs and allowing for appropriate financing costs are handled under the two models; and
- the provisions for amending 'contracts', and in particular the contrast between contractual and licence models.

STRUCTURE

There have been many comments on the restructuring of British Rail, when the single vertically integrated nationalized industry was broken into over 100 separate companies, linked together by contracts with government (through the franchising agreements with OPRAF/SRA) and with each other, through licences, and multilateral industry arrangements. My purpose here is not to assess that restructuring,[13] but to compare it with that put in place for London Underground under the PPP arrangements as a basis for understanding the strengths and weaknesses of the different models.

Comparison with the National Rail Industry Structure

The PPP model is in essence very simple: LUL, a public sector company (whose ownership transferred from the Secretary of State to Transport for

London on 15 July 2003), has overall responsibility both for specifying services and operating the network – that is, signalling, trains and stations. Three private sector Infracos maintain and upgrade the infrastructure – track, trains and stations – on different parts of the network. Those Infracos take full responsibility for procuring the services needed to deliver their contractual obligations, and are doing so through a combination of in-house resources, single-tender supply chain contracts and competitive tendering. In line with this division of responsibility, other line-specific contracts (such as the PFI contract for the supply and maintenance of trains on the Northern Line) have been novated from LUL to the relevant Infraco. Only system-wide contracts, such as that for the provision of power supplies, have been retained by LUL.

The contrast with the national rail sector is marked. Table 7.2 shows the primary responsibility for different aspects of the business in the national rail sector and in the Underground.[14] In the LUL PPP arrangements, responsibilities lie either with the Infraco or with LUL. In the national rail sector, responsibilities are more diverse.[15]

Table 7.2   A comparison with the national (passenger) rail sector

Prime responsibility for:		
Strategy and service specification	SRA	LUL
Network ownership	Network Rail	LUL
Network operations (signalling etc.)	Network Rail	LUL
Train operations	TOCs	LUL
Station operations	TOCs, Network Rail (major stations)	LUL
Network maintenance and renewal	Network Rail	Infracos
Network enhancement	Network Rail, SPVs	Infracos
Rolling stock	TOcs, ROSCOs	Infracos

Note: SRA – Strategic Rail Authority; TOCs – train operating companies; SPVs – special purpose vehicles; ROSCOs – Rolling Stock Companies.

Source: Office of the PPP Arbiter.

But while it is easy to identify these differences, what are the relevant criteria for assessing the pros and cons of the different models?

Planning v. Market Mechanisms

One possible criterion is whether there needs to be a single strategic focus for planning and specifying requirements for the infrastructure, or whether this can be left to bilateral contracts or to market mechanisms.

In the gas sector, for example, Transco has (under pressure from Ofgem) developed long-term auctions of system entry capacity for its transmission system, allowing for additional capacity to be constructed where auction bids are sufficient to fund this, at least up to the next price review. In a similar way, the original vision for the national rail network was for Railtrack to develop its network where this could be justified commercially by higher access charges paid by individual train operators.[16] Critics have argued that relying on bilateral commercial mechanisms will result in inadequate network provision,[17] and that investment either needs to be underpinned by centrally determined standards, or set by a strategic planning body.

In essence, therefore, the issue is whether consumer needs – in terms of the appropriate balance between price and standard of service – are best met through a planning mechanism or through a decentralized market.

Characteristics which will help to determine the balance between planning and market-based approaches include:

- the extent to which demand depends on the existence of a network, rather than simply point to point flows, and the consequent need for coordination of service provision and investment across the network;
- the costs of supply interruptions to individual users, and whether these can be properly captured through market mechanisms (i.e. the scale of 'free-rider' problems);
- whether there is effective competition for the product being supplied;
- whether the direct customers of the infrastructure company compete, and consequently reflect their true valuation of network capacity in contracting for capacity on a long-term basis; and
- the need for locational (as opposed to system-wide) price signals to incentivize investment properly.

In the case of London Underground, it is clear that passenger demands depend in part on other aspects of transport and planning policy, which is in part the rationale for creating a body such as Transport for London with overall responsibility for all modes of transport. Given the limited development of market mechanisms in other modes, and the clear evidence that policy decisions in respect for example of bus use and congestion charging will have an impact on Underground patronage, the need for a single strategic body to specify requirements is clearer than for some other networks.

The Public/Private Split

Although, almost by definition, a strategic planning function needs to be located within a strong public interest framework, this could be provided by statutory controls or licences (e.g. the requirement on Transco to provide capacity to meet expected demand on a 1 in 20-year cold winter day) rather than through public provision. In principle, therefore, train and station operations on the Underground could be provided through outsourced contracts, in the same way that the SRA procures train operation services through contracts with train operators, or through licences. Although common standards and a common 'appearance' are obviously important for the Underground, this could be achieved through outsourcing as with London buses. Indeed, most franchising operations are designed to achieve that commonality (unlike those for train operations, where the original aim of promoting competition *in* the market as well as competition *for* the market made differentiation an objective of policy).

In some ways, the most important issue for effective operation of the network is not whether train operations and infrastructure management are undertaken in the public or private sectors but how network operation objectives can best be aligned with user requirements. This alignment can be achieved through incentives on private operators (as with the system operation incentives schemes for National Grid and Transco) and does not necessarily require public provision. But where the only mechanism for delivering appropriate coordination is through a series of bilateral contracts rather than through a licence, effective private operation of the network may be difficult to deliver.[18] So it is not surprising that network operation has been retained by LUL.

Minimizing Transaction Costs

This discussion does, however, beg the question that has underpinned much of the discussion about the PPP, namely whether the problems of managing contractors on a network where safety considerations dominate are so great that all activities need to be controlled by one body – LUL in the case of the Underground.

One framework for assessing these issues is that provided by Coase in his discussion of the nature of the firm:[19] are the benefits of external contracting in terms of lower prices greater or less than the transaction costs involved to deliver the same standards (including safety, and risk of service interruption).

Where goods or services are relatively standardized and are supplied by a number of firms, the case for outsourcing is overwhelming. Very few firms make their own paperclips! But already questions are being asked about whether the recent (and apparently inexorable) trend towards outsourcing of services such as IT is in fact delivering lower costs (for the same service standard) than in-house provision.

One question that is relevant for many network industries is whether supply markets are sufficiently competitive to ensure that effective procurement delivers efficient prices. If they are not, companies risk becoming dependent on particular suppliers. Although the challenge of discovering competitive prices is emphasized by Coase as one of the costs of contracting, a more significant cost for a safety-critical network is likely to be that of ensuring delivery to appropriate standards (particularly where requirements are specified in terms of outputs, as makes sense if suppliers are to be incentivized to innovate) and of coordinating between different suppliers where safe operation of the overall system depends on such coordination.

This issue has been at the heart of debate in the national rail network about the consequences of splitting the 'track/wheel interface', and more generally about using contractors to carry out work on the network, particularly for routine maintenance. As the Health and Safety Commission noted in its report on the use of contractors in the rail sector, 'contractorisation is a feature of all industrial sectors worldwide [and] there are well-established principles for good contractor management that, if followed, will provide the basis for safe operation; [however] recent rail history indicates that there have been significant problems related to contractor management'.[20]

There are two main differences between the PPP arrangements and those which have applied in the national rail sector hitherto:

- the Infracos are responsible for both track and rolling stock maintenance and renewal, thereby ensuring that there is one body responsible for decisions across the track/wheel interface; and
- Infracos generally use in-house staff (who in the main are the same people as previously employed by LUL) for routine maintenance, with contractors only used for renewal and enhancement projects.[21]

In addition, the three-year period of 'shadow running' of the PPP contractual arrangements before transfer of the Infracos to their new private owners allowed many of the interface issues to be resolved before transfer.

The Length of Contracts

A further difference between the two sectors is in respect of the contractual structure itself. The length of contracts in the national rail sector varies, but all are of significantly less than the 30 years of the PPP Agreements. In

large part, the 30-year period for the PPP was driven by the need to have a
sufficiently long period to accommodate the work needed to modernize the
network, and to provide for the remuneration of the private sector financial
input. By contrast, investments in station facilities and rolling stock by
train operating companies could generally be funded over no more than
15 years, making this the maximum length of the initial franchises on the
national rail network.

There is, however, a further difference that is worth considering, namely
the trade-off in terms of incentives between a longer contract with periodic
reviews, as with the PPP, and shorter contracts with no explicit review
provisions. In the case of the initial train operator franchises, many were
let on 10- or 15-year periods with no review provisions. The key economic
question is whether the existence of reviews which effectively rebase costs
to efficient levels (as well as allowing for requirements to be restated) will
undermine the incentives to manage assets on an efficient whole-life basis.
The answer to this question depends in large part on the techniques used
to judge efficient costs, to which I turn shortly.

In practice, none of the original 15-year rail franchises has survived. They
have all either been shortened (and in one case terminated), or converted
into management contracts. While it is too early to judge the robustness
of the PPP Agreements, it is therefore very clear that long-term contracts
with no explicit review provisions have, in the national rail sector, proved
to be unsustainable.

Fixed Contract v. Rolling Licence Period

A further important difference in contractual structure is between a contract
which has a fixed end point, as with the PPP, and perpetual contracts with
rolling notice periods.

There are obvious problems with 'rolling' contracts if that notice period
is too short: in the case of the water industry, for example, the notice period
has recently been extended from 10 years to 25 years, on the grounds that
it would 'provide greater regulatory stability, assist companies' long-term
planning, deliver a lower cost of capital and better reflect the lives of the
assets of the industry' (Ofwat, 2002).

However, there are also problems with fixed-period contracts as the
termination date approaches if appropriate incentives to invest and to
continue to improve efficiency are to be maintained. Again, experience
with the passenger train operator franchises is illuminating: there have been
numerous short-term extensions, and, where a franchise has been awarded
at renewal to a new operator, that operator has generally taken over the
remaining period of the existing franchise.[22] But whether these issues will

start to affect incentives from, say, the middle of a 30-year contract, or only start to create problems in the last few years is more difficult to judge. Important issues in practice will be the effectiveness of the termination arrangements, and the willingness and ability of LUL to assume (and transfer to new operators) liabilities reasonably taken on by the existing Infracos in the later part of the contract period.

The other important factor in deciding between a perpetual licence and a fixed-period contract is the value to consumers of retaining the ability to retender a contract other than on the grounds of failure to perform: will this add sufficiently to competitive pressures to improve efficiency when contracts are re-awarded to outweigh the transaction costs? Evidence on this issue is, at best, mixed. In the national rail sector, the existing involvement of the SRA in investment decisions, including its ability to underwrite rolling stock leases to avoid terminal value risk being reflected in leasing charges, means that management of a train operating company can be transferred reasonably easily – even to an 'in-house' management team as with the South Eastern franchise.

The more the transition requires effective due diligence of the existing operation to support bids, including for example valuation of work in progress, and the greater the extent of new staffing and supply chain arrangements that have to be put in place by a new operator, the less effective will competition for the market be at a retendering. Artificially levelling the playing field, as happened with the re-award of the National Lottery franchise by requiring the existing operator to replace all its equipment as part of the new bid, may simply increase transition costs to a level that outweighs the potential benefits of improved competition.

There are, none the less, issues with a evergreen contract, particularly if the periodic review process is seen as in effect creating separate five-year contracts. The impact this can have on incentives has been widely recognized.[23] Allowing for efficiency savings to be retained for a five-year rolling period is one way of reducing these effects.

While it seems clear that long-term contracts with no review provisions are generally inappropriate for circumstances such as the PPP, the balance between an evergreen licence and a fixed-period contract is more difficult to assess. Much will depend on the expected scale of the benefits from improved long-term incentives and from locking in higher efficiencies at retendering in the PPP, and whether the more restrictive framework created by a project finance model for the PPP Agreements makes it more difficult to achieve levels of financing costs comparable to those in the privatized utility sector. This in turn depends on the provisions for amending the contracts, considered below.

Conclusions on Structure

So what conclusions can be drawn on the structure adopted by the PPP arrangements for London Underground, at least in comparison with those for the national rail network? Although there are clearly many issues with the PPP that cannot be assessed at this early stage in the life of the Agreements, I suggest there are two main features which tend to favour the PPP arrangements:

- the smaller number of direct contractual relationships, and in particular the responsibility of Infracos for both track and signalling and rolling stock maintenance and renewal; and
- the clear 'customer' focus on LUL, within Transport for London, which is not mirrored in the national rail network.

ANALYTICAL FRAMEWORK

The area where there is, in principle, greatest commonality between the work I need to undertake as PPP Arbiter and that of the economic regulators of network industries is in the analysis of factors such as efficiency and financing costs. Even here, though, the approach adopted in the PPP Agreements differs from the traditional utility approach. Some of these differences are set out in Table 7.3. But are these differences more apparent than real?

Assessing Efficiency: the Concept of the 'Notional Infraco'

In the PPP Agreements, adjustments to costs are made by reference to those that would be incurred by a 'Notional Infraco'. The Notional Infraco is defined as being 'an assumed entity ... that carries out its activities in an overall efficient and economic manner and in accordance with Good Industry Practice, that has specified characteristics including the same contractual commitments as Infraco and also has Infraco's responsibilities for future performance of the Contract ...' 'Good Industry Practice' is in turn defined as meaning 'the exercise of the degree of skill, diligence, prudence and foresight and practice which could reasonably and ordinarily be expected from a skilled and experienced person ...'.

The guidance from the Parties to the Arbiter expands on these definitions. For example, it says that what should be expected of an Infraco working to Good Industry Practice is:

(a) establishing and maintaining whole life asset planning and maintenance regimes;
(b) considering the issues relevant to each stage in any project and putting in place a strategy to deal with them;
(c) ensuring the right competence is available, including appropriate external advice when needed;
(d) planning for operational, contractual and financial contingencies;
(e) recognising that systems and assets must be useable in practice and taking appropriate steps to ensure this, looking at comparable industries where relevant and taking account of practical constraints;
(f) recognising the time and resources needed for systems integration and taking appropriate steps to make it possible;
(g) understanding the degraded operation of complex systems so as to ensure controlled degradation;
(h) planning, and monitoring projects effectively, and monitoring and taking account of critical constraints;
(i) designing to take account of buildability and operational constraints; and
(j) effective change management.

Table 7.3   A comparison with regulation: analytical framework

UK regulation	PPP
'Economic and efficient'	
• Adustments to base year	• Costs incurred by notional 'good (i.e. not 'best') practice' Infraco
• Capex and opex efficiency targets – approach to frontier	
• Use of comparators/benchmarks	• Use of contract prices
	• Scope for benchmarking?
WACC	
• Single WACC used in assessing allowed revenue	• Separate consideration of new/ old debt/equity
• Optimal, not actual, gearing?	• Market testing for new debt
• Embedded debt cost not generally allowed	• Arbiter may be asked to determine return on new equity
RAB	
• Based on initial flotation value	• No RAB, but consider financing of 'logged-up' costs at Periodic Review
• Logging up between reviews	

Source: Office of the PPP Arbiter.

The guidance also emphasizes the distinction between good and 'best' practice, and indicates for example that the Arbiter should not base his determination on 'an assumption that all the Infracos could reasonably be expected to achieve the financial performance previously demonstrated by the best Infraco, unless there is a clear reason for this assumption'.

At first sight, this specification of a Notional Infraco is rather different from the approach used by utility regulators of assessing an efficiency frontier and the appropriate speed of movement towards it for individual companies. However, the difference is perhaps more apparent than real: in both cases the intention is to determine the cost of a 'reasonably' efficient company, leaving opportunities for individual companies to outperform the cost allowance. Thus in advising me on the relevance of the practice of utility regulators, Cambridge Economic Policy Associates (CEPA) concluded that 'the concept of the Arbiter seeking to determine the costs that would be incurred by a 'Notional' Infraco that carries out its functions in a economic and efficient manner is the same as for utility regulators'.[24]

There remain, however, possible differences in the information available to the Arbiter, and the relative weight given to different benchmarks in reaching his decisions. An early priority for my Office is therefore to put in place a framework of appropriate measures, supported by the relevant information flows, both to monitor outturn against the original financial model (updated for any agreed changes in deliverables) and to compare performance with appropriate benchmarks.

Assessing Efficiency: Reliance on Competitive Tendering

A particular feature of the PPP arrangements is that, as well as tendering the initial contracts, the contracts establish a presumption that subsequent competitive tenders for subcontracts should be the basis for judging the costs of the Notional Infraco – always assuming that appropriate procedures have been followed in order to obtain the best market price.

This too may appear to be a rather different approach from that adopted by economic regulators, who generally focus on costs at the level of the regulated company and do not regard themselves as being bound by costs under existing subcontracts or the outcome of forward-looking tender exercises. Nevertheless, in assessing the scope for future efficiency savings, regulators have often reviewed procurement practices.[25]

This issue has added significance because of the rather different approaches to the supply chain adopted by the two Infraco consortia. In the case of Metronet, the main contracts were put in place with its sponsors concurrently with financial close. In the case of Tube Lines, major supply contracts have been awarded by competitive tender following financial close.[26] Although the guidance from the parties specifically recognizes that different approaches to procurement can be consistent with Good Industry Practice, Infracos will still need to demonstrate how their approach going forward takes account of changes in infrastructure services supply markets to ensure that subcontracts continue to be economic and efficient.[27]

Allowing for Financing Costs

The PPP Agreements take a similar market-based approach to financing costs. The Agreements distinguish between 'base' and 'additional' finance (i.e. in broad terms between that committed at financial close, and the further finance to be raised either to meet existing obligations in future review periods or new requirements established by LUL). In brief, the contracts assume that, provided the Infraco has operated in an efficient and economic manner:

- Infracos will receive the equity returns specified in the contract in respect of base equity (which is indeed one of the objectives specified in the GLA Act);
- base debt costs will in effect be passed through;
- additional debt costs will be passed through on the basis of advice to the Arbiter from a 'financial adviser of international repute', which is to be based on 'preparation and circulation of an appropriate Information Memorandum to interested parties and the indicative commitments they are willing to offer in response and the terms of offers of finance that Infraco may reasonably expect to be able to obtain in those markets'; and
- the cost of additional equity may be referred to the Arbiter for determination.

In addition, the Agreements contain specific provisions in respect of sharing the benefits of any refinancing, broadly reflecting PFI precedents.

If Infracos did not need to raise additional finance over the life of the Agreement, and operated in an economic and efficient manner, then any change to the ISC at Periodic Review would effectively pass through the cost of embedded debt and preserve the initial equity return. But in practice additional finance will almost certainly be required.

While the fixed term of the PPP Agreements creates particular challenges for funding at later reviews, reducing opportunities for long-term funding unless arrangements can be made for LUL to take responsibility for funding after the end of the contract, the issues are otherwise similar to those considered by economic regulators in assessing the weighted average cost of capital for network utilities. In particular, in determining the appropriate return on any additional equity, the Arbiter would need to consider the overall risk profile of the Infraco, and whether this had changed since the contract was originally awarded, changes in market returns, and the impact of gearing and taxation. I have argued elsewhere[28] that there remain differences in approach between the economic regulators on issues such as the cost of capital which are not fully explained, and that this risks distorting decisions by investors operating in international (and cross-sectoral) investment markets.

Conclusions on Treatment of Technical Issues

Although the PPP Agreements appear to approach some of these issues differently from traditional utility regulation, the underlying concepts are in fact comparable. So I will need to ensure that any differences in approach are identified, explained and justified. The work programme and procedures which I am developing are designed to do this.

AMENDING 'CONTRACTS'

In this final section, I consider three issues:

- the merits of a contract compared with a licence;
- the role of Arbiter in comparison with that of an arbitrator; and
- the role of guidance to the Arbiter.

Contract or Licence?

Reference is often made to the existence of a 'regulatory contract' for companies with a licence, which is reviewed and reset by the regulator generally every five years. This description suggests a basic similarity between a commercial contract and a licence. Both impose obligations on the supplier, in terms of services to be provided, and establish the price to be paid, although the circumstances of the initial award of a licence or contract are generally very different. But is the analogy a reasonable one? And given the similarities and differences, are there reasons to prefer a licence or a contract as the basis for the provision of infrastructure services in terms of subsequent enforcement and modification?

Two differences that may be important are the identity of the counter-party and the procedure for modification.

A practical argument for obligations to be set out in licences enforced by an independent regulator in some industries is that it would be impracticable to contract with individual consumers. This impracticality is not, however, because of administrative complexity; supply competition in energy markets has required these issues to be addressed and resolved. Rather the problem is that individual consumers cannot determine their own standards of service: interruptions to supply because of network problems will generally affect groups of consumers, and greater resilience can only be achieved by individuals investing in back-up supplies. So to avoid problems of free-riding, standards for networks (as opposed for example to customer service) need to be established centrally.[29]

This does not, of course, of itself make the case for the regulator to be the counter-party to the regulatory contract. In some sectors, most obviously rail and energy, many aspects of service delivery are set out in bilateral commercial contracts which are consistent with the high-level price controls and service standards in licences. Enforcement of contractual obligations is then through normal dispute resolution mechanisms and need not involve the regulator. Review and change provisions at the behest of the regulator can be written into those contracts. However, the distinction between what goes into a licence and what is more properly part of the contractual matrix is not always clear, which can lead to disagreement between the company, customers and the regulator.[30]

Clearly not all standards are set by the economic regulator. Many are set by other independent regulators such as the Environment Agency, Drinking Water Inspectorate or Health and Safety Executive. But in all current models for the regulated networks, price controls remain an issue decided by the regulator.

It is easy to see why it is important for an independent regulator to have such a role, given the need to provide assurance to the financial markets that the considerable funds invested in network industries will be appropriately remunerated. But even here, it is not necessary for the regulator to take a proactive role in a price review. If there is a single 'customer', as with LUL in respect of the Underground, then there are clear advantages in giving that customer a leading role in determining both the affordable level of charges and the mix of services it wishes to purchase. In those circumstances, both parties can have the right of appeal to an independent regulator or arbiter but also have the ability to frame the reference in a way that makes clear the points at issue, and the points which are agreed. It follows that the Arbiter cannot intervene if the parties are content with the position reached in negotiation.

There is no precise analogy to the position of LUL in other sectors. Even in respect of the national rail network, 'customers' include the Passenger

Transport Executives and open access operators as well as the SRA. But harnessing the views of customers more directly – for example in the shape of the Gas Forum for Transco's shipper customers or in terms of the airlines using airports subject to price regulation by the Civil Aviation Authority – could help to remove some of the information asymmetries in the current regulator/regulatee relationship, and thereby reinforce the role of the independent regulator.

A second apparent difference between contractual and licence models concerns the processes for modification of the 'contract'. This might be characterized as a distinction between an approach based on legal procedures and one based on public law. On this view, a licence framework gives the regulator the ability to propose changes to the 'contract' at any time, subject to public interest tests established in the relevant statute – which effectively seek to maintain the basis of the 'economic deal' in terms of the legitimate expectations of the company[31] and its customers – and subject to appeal to the Competition Commission or to the courts through judicial review. By contrast, a contract establishes a defined commercial relationship that can be modified by the agreement of both parties, but where the role of the courts in the event of dispute is merely to determine the meaning of the contract, not to consider the intentions and expectations of the parties in entering into it.

However, this view of the law of contract is increasingly being challenged by practice, where courts have shown a willingness to consider more than the contract documentation. The development of concepts relating to unfair contract terms is one example. More generally, contracts can be seen as summarizing commercial understandings rather than simply providing the basis for legal action if one or other party fails to meet its stated obligations.[32] Recourse to the courts can then be seen as evidence of a breakdown in the business relationship, given that most contractual disputes are resolved through alternative routes which are better able to take account of the evolving market conventions that underpin commercial relationships.

In part, this broader interpretation recognizes the impossibility of creating complete contracts, particularly where the deliverables are complex and extend over a long period. There is undoubtedly value in trying to define the service to be provided at the outset, not least to ensure that the customer has properly thought about its requirements and to avoid the significant cost increases following specification changes during the contract. But the future is inherently uncertain, and while those drafting the contract may attempt to identify all possible outcomes, and define the allocation of risk between the parties in each, there will inevitably be gaps.[33]

Development of alternative dispute resolution mechanisms is in part a recognition that a fair resolution to a dispute needs to consider more than the words in the contract. In the case of the LUL PPP, recognition of the inevitable incompleteness of the contract and the need for independent resolution of disputes, particularly where either party exercises its rights in respect of the flexibilities in the contract, has gone beyond this and led to the creation of the statutory role of Arbiter.

So in terms of the basis for modifying the initial agreement to take account of changing external circumstances, the comparison between a licence and a contract is not as great as might at first sight appear – although the process is obviously different. Those who use the term 'regulatory contract' may well have recognized this. And the current debate about widening the appeal provisions to industry codes and allowing consumers some right of appeal all move in the direction of narrowing the gap.

It is also worth noting the views of the National Audit Office and Public Accounts Committee (PAC) in relation to the need for effective change control processes in PFI contracts. For example, the PAC has noted that change control procedures had been triggered in more than half of the PFI contracts it considered in 2002, but there was a need to avoid change control procedures being 'abused as a covert means for increasing the profit margins for contractors'.[34]

Arbiter v. Arbitrator

Look in a dictionary, and you may well find that the definition of an arbiter includes being an arbitrator – and vice versa! Given that the PPP Agreements contain well-developed dispute resolution procedures, including resort to adjudication and ultimately the courts, and that they draw a clear distinction between issues where the Arbiter decides disputes rather than an adjudicator, what are they key differences?

A further search of the Internet comes up with the following: 'the arbitrator's job is to decide disputed fact and decide disputed law then apply the decided fact to decided law',[35] although there is clearly also a presumption that arbitrators will consider the norms and conventions within which a contract has been developed.[36]

The LUL PPP Agreements are notable in having two specific forms of dispute resolution – those issues coming to the Arbiter and those dealt with through normal contractual routes. In addition the Agreements create the role of a 'Partnership Director'.[37] So what are the distinguishing features of the Arbiter?

One key feature of the PPP Arbiter role is that it is created by statute with statutory duties rather than simply duties to the parties to the contract. The Act clearly envisages that it is a continuing role, with an ability to give guidance as well as directions, whereas an arbitrator or adjudicator will be appointed only when the parties have reached a specified point in dispute resolution procedures. A corollary of this continuing role is that the Arbiter will seek to establish the framework for dealing with issues, and put in place the necessary information flows to support his analysis.[38]

Given developments in arbitration provisions, there is perhaps less difference between the powers of the Arbiter and of an arbitrator in respect of investigations within the context of a particular reference. For example, the Arbitration Act 1986 provides that the tribunal can decide 'whether and to what extent the tribunal should itself take the initiative in ascertaining the facts and the law'.[39] However, the GLA Act gives the Arbiter similar statutory information-gathering powers to those of the economic regulators, which extend for example to the Infraco subcontractors. An arbitrator does not have such statutory powers in any investigation he decides to carry out.

The nature of the issues referable to the Arbiter perhaps provides the best basis for distinguishing the roles. These issues, which cover both the costs of maintaining and renewing the network and the costs of the finance raised by the Infracos, clearly go to the heart of the economic deal. Some of the concepts will be difficult to define and assess in practice, and the relevant 'conventions' will need to draw on experience in both the regulated network industry sector and the PFI.

One obvious example is in the very definition of the Notional Infraco. The PPP Agreements do not attempt to define what is 'efficient and economic', and go no further than identifying some of the relevant features of Good Industry Practice. Although the guidance provides some further pointers, the Agreements recognize that it is impossible to provide a cookbook recipe that will produce *the* right answer if followed properly, not least given that the assessment is dynamic and needs to be relative to changes in the market.[40]

For issues such as these, which go to the heart of the PPP deal, arbitration would be inadequate. It is no surprise that the GLA Act created an independent Arbiter as a public body, with statutory duties, whose functions focus on responding to references from the parties but with further powers which enable those references to be dealt with expeditiously and in accordance with best practice in public administration – as befits agreements involving costs in excess of £1 billion a year and affecting a key transport system in London.

The Role of Guidance

Drawing this distinction between the role of the Arbiter and that of an arbitrator may appear to put the Arbiter's role close to that of a traditional economic regulator. Nevertheless, for all the reasons outlined earlier in this paper, it would be wrong to equate the Arbiter with a regulator. One particular difference worth further consideration is the existence of guidance to the Arbiter from the PPP Parties.

As explained above, the Arbiter cannot give guidance or directions unless asked to do so by one or both of the Parties to an Agreement. The Parties can set out the terms of reference,[41] and can also indicate matters which they do not wish the Arbiter to consider (but which may none the less need to be considered as matters ancillary or incidental to the matter referred). The approach they expect the Arbiter to take is also set out in guidance, which the Arbiter is under a statutory duty to take into account.

Guidance to a regulator is a feature of other sectors. But it is generally in the form of guidance from a Secretary of State on matters of general government policy,[42] rather than from the parties to a contract; and it is generally issued only after public consultation. The different nature and status of contractual guidance to the Arbiter has been seen by some as constraining the ability of the Arbiter to consider issues relevant to longer-term economy and efficiency.[43]

It is clearly right – and consistent with the principles of incentive regulation and minimization of regulatory risk developed in other sectors – that the terms of the initial deal are protected until a Periodic Review[44]. It is also right that Infracos should have the ability to subcontract major projects beyond the Periodic Review period (7½ years in the case of the PPP) where this can be expected to deliver efficient and economic outcomes and is consistent with Good Industry Practice – and of course delivers the requirements of the main contract. Given these provisions, the guidance from the parties to the Arbiter on these issues does not create unreasonable expectations of the approach that should be taken.

Guidance which sets out the intentions and expectations of the parties is, in any case, an important part of understanding the economic basis of the deal. While the statute gives the Arbiter the ability to give directions which go outside the specific terms of a reference, this can only be done where achievement of the statutory duty means that it would not be possible or appropriate to do otherwise. Seeing the guidance as rebuttable, but requiring such rebuttal to be fully argued and justified, and with decisions only taken after full and effective consultation with affected parties, is consistent both with minimizing regulatory risk and achieving best practice in public administration.

Conclusions on Mechanisms for Amending Contracts

In considering whether regulation and contracts are substitutes or complements, Jon Stern has concluded that 'the existence of a regulatory agency allows for better and simpler contracts, which are easier to monitor, enforce and revise. This is what would be expected from the theory of incomplete contracts'.[45] This is indeed what the PPP provides; and it does so in a way that avoids some of the uncertainties seen in other sectors where licences and contracts exist in parallel.

Some other aspects of the arrangements, such as giving the customer a greater role (and responsibility) in negotiating changes to the 'contract', with recourse to an independent arbiter only when necessary, also set the PPP apart. The reactive nature of the Arbiter's role certainly makes it more difficult to plan ahead with any certainty. But taken overall, the arrangements in the PPP would seem not just appropriate for the Underground PPP itself, but may offer a possible model for developments in other regulatory regimes and in PFI projects[46] where the absence of an independent 'appeal' body on the lines of the PPP Arbiter may undermine long-term value for money.

SOME TENTATIVE OVERALL CONCLUSIONS

I have only been able to sketch in this paper some of the similarities and differences between the LUL PPP Agreements and 'traditional' utility models and PFI contracts, and to outline some of the issues to be considered in assessing their strengths and weaknesses. There is much material here for further consideration and analysis – and in any case it is too early to draw on much practical experience of the PPP.

When I took on the role of Arbiter, some people suggested that it was an impossible one – and certainly in their view more difficult than that of a 'traditional' regulator. My view is rather different: difficult, yes; challenging, yes; but not impossible. Apart from the technical challenges, and the need to take forward a broad work programme with only six permanent staff, one of the key challenges will be to develop trust and credibility, while maintaining independence. One measure of success will be if the parties can resolve differences without recourse to me – not because (as is sometimes suggested with the Competition Commission) that appeal is costly and unpredictable, but because the framework is clear and transparent, and uses information and analysis which they themselves can carry out and share.

So, taking an overall view, I am optimistic about the prospects for the PPP and for the role of Arbiter. In particular, I believe that:

- the structure of the PPP arrangements seems more robust than that for the national rail network;
- differences in the treatment of 'technical' issues need to be considered further across the network and PFI sectors if investors are to face a

level playing field in choosing between investment in PPP/PFI and
regulated networks, but this can be achieved;

• the arrangements for modifying contracts offer some useful alternatives
  to licence approaches which could help to clarify the appropriate
  boundary between the role of an independent re-setter of prices and
  those determining the services to be provided; and
• the model of Periodic Reviews with an independent Arbiter could
  usefully be considered in other PFI/PPP deals.

The London Underground PPP therefore sits between the two current
models, and has tried to learn from the experiences with both. So might
this be the start of a new chapter in the history of infrastructure funding
and 'regulation'?

NOTES

1. This paper reflects my proposed approach to the role of PPP Arbiter as set out in OPPPA
   (2003). It was prepared before consultation responses were received and considered.
2. For further details of the PPP deliverables, see TfL (2003). Details of the shareholders
   in the three Infracos are contained in the Appendix.
3. In addition, LUL is able to exercise certain 'specified rights' to modify required services
   in the early years, for example to add a seventh car to Jubilee Line trains.
4. The main exception is in respect of station refurbishment and modernization.
5. This is not to imply that determining the appropriate specification for such projects is
   straightforward.
6. This covers both the costs of maintenance and enhancement that would be incurred by
   a Notional Infraco, and the financing costs of debt and equity funding.
7. The expectations of the Department for Transport, Local Government and the Regions
   in 2001 are set out in DTLR (2001).
8. For further details of the functions and duties of the Arbiter, including extracts from the
   Greater London Authority Act 1999, see OPPPA (2003).
9. Section 224 (6)Transport Act 2000.
10. The text of schedule 1.9 is published on the Arbiter's website (www.ppparbiter.org.
    uk).
11. This agreement that specific matters may be referred for guidance does not, however,
    preclude a Party from seeking guidance on other matters.
12. Albeit that in that case of the national rail network, train operations are also
    outsourced.
13. Previous Beesley lectures have considered these issues in some detail, for example Beesley
    (1997) and Helm (2002).
14. In both sectors, some of the primary responsibilities are delivered through contracts.
    Thus, for example, track renewal is delivered through contracts rather than in-house
    staff in both sectors.
15. Even in respect of service specification, the strategic role of the SRA is diluted by the
    responsibilities of, for example, the Passenger Transport Executives in their areas of
    responsibility.
16. Department of Transport (1993).
17. See for example Stern and Turvey (2002).
18. For example, recent changes to the priority given to long-distance passenger services on
    the national rail network, to avoid situations where small delays cumulate into significant

disruption for individual services, were achieved following SRA intervention rather than through bilateral negotiation.
19. See for example Coase (1937).
20. HSC (2002).
21. The recent decision by Network Rail to bring track maintenance in house therefore brings its structure into line with that of the Infracos in this respect.
22. For example, the South Central franchise was taken over by the new operator, GoVia, two years before the end of the previous franchise.
23. For example in NAO (2002).
24. CEPA (2003).
25. See for example the review by Accenture of Network Rail's procurement practices in ORR (2003).
26. For example, a track renewal contract has been awarded to Grant Rail, with Jarvis (one of the Infraco shareholders) being an unsuccessful bidder.
27. For a discussion of some of the issues to be considered in awarding contracts, and the circumstances in which this can deliver results which are superior to traditional regulation, see for example Littlechild (2002).
28. Bolt (2003).
29. Central establishment of standards could, however, be through a market mechanism (as with electricity generation), rather than through imposition of standards. The key point is that individual consumers cannot choose their *own* preferred level of network security.
30. For example, in the case of Transco's long-term auctions of system entry capacity, the requirement for an auction and the reserve price provisions are in the licence; the detailed auction mechanisms are in the Network Code.
31. Including, through the financing duty, the company's shareholders and lenders.
32. See Collins (1999) for an exposition, for example (p. 165): 'If the courts wish to do justice between the parties rather than referee the quality of the lawyers in devising comprehensive risk allocation, they should not attach such weight to the paperwork, but concentrate their energies on an investigation of the context, the market conventions, and the assumptions of the parties in framing their core deal.'
33. This is particularly likely in respect of what have traditionally been termed 'public services', as evidenced by the many National Audit Office reports on contracts which have run into difficulty.
34. PAC (2002).
35. Bingham (2003).
36. Collins (1999), p. 164.
37. An individual appointed by LUL (in its capacity as a special shareholder in each Infraco) as a non-executive member of the Boards of all three Infracos. The Shareholder Agreement, which creates the role, notes for example that 'The parties wish the Company to have the benefit of an eligible person who is able, as an independent and non-executive director, to act in a public interest capacity for the good of the Company ... The parties wish the Partnership Director to apply his independence and expertise in areas where there are or may be perceived to be conflicts of interest between the Company and the Special Shareholder and/or the Sponsors ...'
38. My own proposed approach is set out in OPPPA (2003).
39. Section 34 (2) (g).
40. The issues are similar to those considered by John Kay in his parable of the BT dress code, and the doomed attempt to define what is 'suitable business dress', Kay (1996).
41. Which in the case of directions must be consistent with the issues identified in the Agreement as ones which can be referred to the Arbiter.
42. Such as guidance on social and environmental issues to the Gas and Electricity Markets Authority.
43. See for example Glaister (2003).
44. Given that the Arbiter had no part in the specification and negotiation of the PPP Agreements, or in the selection of the winning bids, it is clearly for LUL alone to justify

the terms of the Agreements. The National Audit Office has already carried out one study of the contract award process, and is currently undertaking a second review.
45. Stern (2003).
46. The Public Accounts Committee has noted the risk that contractors may 'seek to increase their profit margins through variations and claims for additional work', PAC (2002).

REFERENCES

Beesley, Michael (1997), 'Rail: the role of subsidy in privatisation', in Michael Beesley (ed.), *Regulating Utilities: Broadening the Debate*, IEA Readings 46.
Bingham, Tony (2003), 'Arbitration', http://www.tonybingham.co.uk/arbitration. htm
Bolt, Chris (2003), 'The future of RPI-X and the implications for utility investment in the UK', in *The UK Model of Utility Regulation: A 20th Anniversary Collection to Mark the 'Littlechild Report' – Retrospect and Prospect*, Centre for the Study of Regulated Industries.
Cambridge Economic Policy Associates (2003): http://www.ppparbiter.org.uk/pdf_ folder/cepa_r1_0703.pdf
Coase, R.H. (1937), 'The nature of the firm', reprinted in *The Firm, the Market and the Law*, University of Chicago Press, 1988.
Collins, Hugh (1999), *Regulating Contracts*, Oxford: Oxford University Press.
Department of Transport (1993), *Gaining Access to the Railway Network*.
Department for Transport, Local Government and the Regions (2001), 'The role of the PPP Arbiter', Supplementary Memorandum to the Select Committee on Transport, Local Government and the Regions: http://www.publications. parliament.uk/pa/cm200102/cmselect/cmtlgr/387/387ap32.htm
Glaister, Stephen (2003), 'The London Underground Arbiter: effective public utility regulation?', in *Regulatory Review 2002/2003*, Centre for the Study of Regulated Industries.
Health and Safety Commission (2002), 'The use of contractors in the maintenance of the railway infrastructure', http://www.hse.gov.uk/hsc/contrail.pdf
Helm, Dieter (2002), 'A critique of rail regulation', in Colin Robinson (ed.), *Utility Regulation and Competition Policy*, Cheltenham: Edward Elgar.
Kay, John (1996), *Financial Times* column 12 January 1996: http://www.johnkay. com/regulation/70
Littlechild, Stephen (2002), 'Competitive bidding for a long-term electricity distribution contract', *Review of Network Economics*: http://www.rnejournal. com/articles/littlechild_bidding_mar02.pdf
National Audit Office (2002), *Pipes and wires*, HC 723 Session 2001–2002: http:// www.nao.gov.uk/publications/nao_reports/01–02/0102723.pdf
Office of the PPP Arbiter (2003), 'The PPP Arbiter: Role, approach and procedures', An initial consultation paper: http://www.ppparbiter.org.uk/pdf_folder/ppp_ cd1_0903.pdf
Ofwat (2002), *Modification of licence condition O*, MD182: http://www.ofwat.gov. uk/aptrix/ofwat/publish.nsf/Content/md182
ORR (2003), *Review of Network Rail's supply chain capability by Accenture*: http:// www.rail-reg.gov.uk/filestore/consultants/accenture_nr-supplycap.pdf

Public Accounts Committee (2002), *Managing the Relationship to Secure a Successful Partnership in PFI Projects*, 42nd report of Session 2001–2002: http://www.publications.parliament.uk/pa/cm200102/cmselect/cmpubacc/460/460.pdf

Stern, Jon (2003), 'Regulation and contracts for utility services: substitutes and complements', London Business School Regulation Initiative Working Paper, Working Paper Series Number 54: http://facultyresearch.london.edu/docs/Sternpaper54.pdf

Stern, Jon and Ralph Turvey (2002), 'Auctions of capacity in network industries', London Business School Regulation Initiative, Working Paper Series Number 53: http://facultyresearch.london.edu/docs/paper53.pdf

Transport for London (2003), *Focus on London's Tube*: http://www.tfl.gov.uk/tfl/downloads/pdf/tfl-focus-on-tubes.pdf

APPENDIX: THE INFRACOS

Tube Lines (Holdings) Limited is a company with three equal shareholders:

Shareholder	Parent company
JNP Ventures Limited	A wholly owned subsidiary of Amey Ventures Limited ('Amey') and ultimately in the group of Grupo Ferrovial S.A., a company listed on the Madrid Stock Exchange
UIC Transport (JNP) Limited	A wholly owned subsidiary of UIC Transport (JNP) LLC and ultimately in the group of Bechtel Enterprise Holdings, Inc. ('Bechtel'), a privately owned company
Jarvis JNP Limited	A wholly owned subsidiary of Jarvis plc ('Jarvis'), a company listed on the London Stock Exchange

Metronet BCV (Holdings) Limited and Metronet SSL (Holdings) Limited are companies with five equal shareholders:

Shareholder	Parent company
Atkins Metro Limited	A wholly owned subsidiary of WS Atkins plc ('Atkins'), a company listed on the London Stock Exchange
Balfour Beatty Infrastructure Investments Limited	A wholly owned subsidiary of Balfour Beatty plc ('Balfour Beatty'), a company listed on the London Stock Exchange
Bombardier Transportation (Holdings) UK Limited	An indirect wholly owned subsidiary of Bombardier Inc. ('Bombardier'), a company listed on the Toronto Stock Exchange
SEEBOARD Metro Holdings Limited	A wholly owned subsidiary of SEEBOARD Asset Management Limited, itself a wholly owned subsidiary of EdF Energy plc ('EdF') and ultimately in the group of Electricité de France (which is wholly owned by the French state)
Thames Water plc ('Thames Water')	A subsidiary of RWE AG ('RWE'), a company listed on the Frankfurt Stock Exchange

CHAIRMAN'S COMMENTS

Tom Winsor

As a Scots lawyer, I was interested in Chris Bolt's paper. I know about arbiters and arbitrators. In Scots law, an arbiter is an arbitrator. However, London is not in Scotland!

You told us that it is very early days in the life of the PPP: the role of the arbiter, the functions and duties of the office, and the relationship with contracts all have to be worked out. I was interested in the seven-and-a-half-year reviews. You might never get to do a review, unless you get reappointed, which I expect you will be, but the guidance role is clearly very important, when LUL can respecify its requirements and restate its outputs (and there is an interesting parallel with the heavy rail network, which I shall come to). It is, as Chris said, difficult, if not impossible, to specify requirements for 30 years ahead.

You mentioned your objectives and how they might conflict; I expect the legal solution to that will be the same as in the Telcom case, where you have to start off with a predeposition to achieve all your objectives, but if they pull you in different directions you can go down one or other route. As arbiter, you are a creature of statute, independent of ministers. That is very important. I was at the first convention of European rail regulators in Vienna. It was very clear that because European law enables the rail regulators in other European countries to be part of the Ministry, most governments, which have no intention of allowing regulators to have power, have established them as parts of the Ministry. As far as the French regulator is concerned I think he just has lunch and that is all he does, because there is no way the Ministry is going to let him interfere with SNCF!

You mentioned that one of the things you can be asked for is to give a definitive certificate to show whether the company in question has been economic and efficient. That would be a dreadful thing to have to do in the case of the heavy rail network. The parties can give the arbiter narrow terms of reference and can agree to set aside his direction. It is almost as if, having invented the arbiter, they wish they hadn't. It is very different from the standard model. The model in terms of railways was established in our famous victory in the Court of Appeal in 2002, when the Lord Chief Justice said that the rail regulator is not constrained by the extremities of what the individual parties want, in a section 17 case concerning compulsory third party access to the network. He can have an agenda of his own and he can go well outside either extreme laid down by the parties. But *your* hands are a little bit more closely tied.

You said that it may be possible to achieve all your objectives through licences, and therefore why have a contract and not a licence? I was very interested in that point and I expect there will be some discussion of it. You said that the SRA buys from Network Rail. I don't agree with that. They *could*. The SRA has the power to enter into contracts with pretty much anybody (this presupposes that they have any money) but I don't agree that SRA specifies the infrastructure outputs. What it does is to specify the infrastructure outputs with *its* contractors, the train operators, and they in turn will want to buy certain outputs from Network Rail. And it most certainly doesn't specify outputs, therefore, as required for the whole network because there are open access operators, not many of them, but they do exist, as do freight operators, who are very concerned about these matters.

You stressed the need for clarity on who has the final say as to what is to be delivered, implying that on the heavy railway it is not present. There has been a great deal of obfuscation; Mr Bowker's predecessor was very concerned that he who pays the piper should call the tune: in other words the SRA should decide all the outputs and the regulator should be little more than a supermarket price checker, with the SRA being the chief buyer. Those notions have not entirely gone away but they are wrong because the SRA has now acknowledged that the regulator sets the size, quality and efficient cost of the network. It is very difficult to change that state of affairs once people have invested real money in it.

You mentioned the length of the contracts and the difference between very long contracts with review provisions and shorter contracts. I would say that long contracts didn't work for the long franchises, because all the franchisees suffered greatly from the incompetence of Railtrack. This culminated in the Hatfield accident and the complete disintegration of the network. I think they failed for that reason rather than because they were too long or didn't have a sufficient mechanism for review.

You mentioned the notional infraco and I entirely agree with you. This is very much how utility regulators have to approach things. We need to do this in the case of the heavy rail network. It is very difficult because there is only one infrastructure provider of real importance, and therefore we have to do internal benchmarking, external comparisons, international benchmarking; that's what we have done in the present access charges review.

You said it is often discussed, and it will probably be discussed forever, whether a licence is a regulatory contract. I never thought it was. Certainly you wouldn't take the licence if you didn't agree to what was in it; but it is much more, in my opinion. It is an authorization to operate rather than a contract. And it is not a contract because the licence cannot be enforced against the licensing authority unless the licensing authority misuses it by acting illegally, irrationally, improperly or disproportionately. There is a fundamental distinction here. The regulatory contract is meant much more in the economic sense rather than the legal sense: what have you agreed to? One of the things you do agree to with the licence (and this is much more flexible with licences than contracts) is a change mechanism. The change to the PPP contract, if I understood you correctly, is principally every seven-and-a-half years, when LUL respecifies what it wants, whereas the licence modification regime in the utility statutes can be used by the regulator at any time and repeatedly, and the scope of the changes you can make as regulator is probably very much larger, and is therefore a more powerful instrument. I have used the licence modification regime in section 12 of the Railways Act 1993 nine times in the last four-and-a-half years, mainly because the network licence granted to Railtrack was so inadequate and needed to be fixed.

You mentioned that you have a smaller number of customers and therefore the contractual model may be more appropriate. I think that it is simpler to go for the contract when you have one principal customer, the LUL, rather than millions of direct customers. You have millions of indirect customers of course. In railways we have a bunch of customers – train operator customers and Network Rail – then the funders, the passenger transport executives, and the Strategic Rail Authority, and whoever else wants to give money to this company.

Finally you mentioned the notion of the partnership director, this new non-executive director, a sort of spy on the board (as it seems to me) appointed by LUL to keep the conscience of the company clean. In other words, these people, having entered into this enormously long contract, specifying everything down to the tiniest detail, can't be trusted to act in accordance with the public interest and they need some kind of restraining influence. I think this is a complete nonsense. It was invented, as far as I know, by John Prescott in 2001 when the government first interfered (they have done it a few times since then, or tried to) in independent economic regulation in the heavy railway, when they decided to agree with Railtrack to bring forward a large sum of money from the Regulatory Asset Base established for 2006 into the current control period, because Railtrack was running short of money. One of the prices the government extracted for accelerating these funds, because I decided they would not be paid until 2006 through the RAB, into 2001, was the appointment of the public interest director on the board of Railtrack. I thought it was a wrong-headed notion and it certainly did not work. But it scared the market because it looked like political intervention in the affairs of a private sector company, which is exactly what it was. It also looked like political intervention in a regulatory settlement, and it didn't do any good at all. The Department of Transport spun it in such a way that Alistair Morton, the former Chairman of the SRA, was interviewing the directors of Railtrack and telling them which ones of them had jobs. Can you imagine anything more frightening to the capital markets, or indeed to almost anyone else? It wasn't true, but that's the way they wanted to present it. It seems that you have public interest directors but they have been brought about in a rather more sensible, lawful way. I still wonder whether or not they will make much of a difference; after all they have duties to act in the best interests of the company and they should not be taking orders from anybody else.

You did say that the arbiter is a very unusual animal: is he a regulator, is he an arbiter, an adjudicator, or what? I expect you will find out, but it is going to be a voyage of discovery to determine exactly where the boundaries of the jurisdiction are and what are the dynamics.

You asked 'Is it an impossible job?', as some have said. As I said to the Secretary of State for Transport, regulators can do wonders but they cannot do magic. I expect the same is true of arbiters.

8.   Commitment and control in regulation: the future of regulation in water*

Colin Mayer

1.   INTRODUCTION

Water has been one of the most successful UK privatizations. We started the 1990s with a water system that was antiquated, leaking and thoroughly unhealthy. We have begun this decade with one that is modern, renovated, leaking less and a little bit healthier.[1] Investment is up by more than 50 per cent and all of this has occurred in an industry which many said could never or must never be privatized. Access to water was a human right that should be made publicly available by public institutions. The public relations problem that the water companies now face is to persuade the affluent that taps are as chic as bottles.

The government, the industry and not least the regulator should take credit for this. Since we are a nation of self-deprecators, we are reluctant to recognize success and much prefer to mock failure. But there has been success and, on the regulatory front, Ian Byatt and Philip Fletcher and their teams together with the Competition Commission should take credit for that. It could have all been very different if we had not had a regulatory system that established a sound regime for measuring the cost of capital, valuing assets and undertaking comparative efficiency exercises. It took sound economic judgement to create a regulatory system from almost nothing.

Any subsequent analysis or criticism should therefore be considered in this context. As we will describe shortly, the way to characterize what has happened in water as in many other regulated industries is that phase one was focused on getting the companies off the government's books and encouraging investment at almost any price, phase two on operating efficiency and the current phase three on capital efficiency.

As the British corporate sector has known for two centuries, it is much easier to operate than invest, so too the regulator and regulated firms have found the achievement of operating efficiencies easier than capital efficiencies. It is not difficult to appreciate why: investment takes time and the time component of investment is the critical issue that the water and most regulated industries now face. It is particularly pertinent in water because, with operating efficiencies in large part attained, it is trail blazing in capital efficiency.

The water industry is currently undergoing fundamental changes. This paper will describe those changes and suggest that their underlying causes are rather different from those that have been suggested to date. Traditional theories only provide a partial explanation for what has happened and a fuller appreciation is important for understanding its consequences. The paper will argue that recent developments have been part of a regulatory cycle in which there is a shift in emphasis in the primary goals of regulation and companies have responded accordingly.

There have been good and bad consequences of this. Costs of running the business, especially their capital costs, have fallen but risks have risen and in particular we may be storing up problems for the future. One policy question that this raises is how the regulatory system should respond to the changing incentives and goals of firms. The reinterpretation of what has happened provides some useful insights in answering this question. But it also suggests that regulators should be seeking to influence as well as respond to the changes that are in process.

Section 2 of the paper describes what has happened. Section 3 discusses why it has happened. Section 4 will consider the consequences of what has happened and Section 5 will evaluate the appropriate policy responses to it. Finally Section 6 will conclude.

2.   WHAT HAS HAPPENED?

The early years of water privatization can be considered as the easy-money period. While British industry was going through a recession, water companies were having as much money as water and sewage poured into them to facilitate the privatization process and increase investment. Allowed rates of return were high and substantial investment programmes were approved. As profits and executive remuneration started to rise as fast as investment programmes, attention turned to reducing prices and encouraging efficiency. Allowed rates of return were reduced, projected expenditures were cut and models of operating efficiency were developed. As a consequence, allowed rates of return declined from over 12 per cent to around 9 per cent between the beginning and end of the 1990s. Companies routinely complained that they could not meet the targets and then promptly proceeded to beat them comfortably.

But it was the 1999 periodic review that really applied the pressure. Following years of price increases to fund the investment programmes, the 1999 review sought to bring average household bills down to their levels in the early years after privatization. Rates of return dropped from 9.3 per cent to 6.6 per cent in one year between 1999/2000 and 2000/2001 following an average cut of 12.3 per cent in P_0 (the initial price) and were projected to fall below that thereafter.

The subsequent turn of events was not perhaps what Ofwat anticipated. In short succession in 2001, Sutton and East Surrey, Mid-Kent and Glas Cymru announced leveraged buy-outs, recapitalizations and acquisitions with proposed leverage levels in excess of 75 per cent. They were in turn followed by Anglian Water, Dee Valley Water, Portsmouth Water, Northumbrian Water, Southern Water and South Staffordshire Water proposing recapitalizations and buy-outs with leverage levels between 70 and 90 per cent. In total some 35.7 per cent of the assets of the water industry are now in highly geared companies (with leverage in excess of Ofwat's assumed range of 45–55 per cent).

3.   WHY DID IT HAPPEN?

Why did this occur? There are two leading theories of the determinants of firms' capital structure (levels of leverage). The first is what is termed the pecking-order theory. This states that companies have a preference for using retained earnings over external finance and external debt in preference to new equity issues. This reflects the comparatively high cost of raising external finance in relation to internal finance and of raising new equity in relation to debt. The pecking-order theory suggests that there is no particular level at which one would expect to observe firms' leverage; instead, leverage changes in response to the financing needs of companies (their investment requirements) and their internal resources. When firms have large investment requirements in relation to their earnings, they turn to bonds and banks to meet their financial requirements. As a consequence, their leverage rises. Conversely, when earnings are high in relation to investment needs, then leverage declines.

This theory provides at least a partial explanation of developments in water. As previously noted, in the early days of privatization regulatory settlements allowed companies to fund their investment programmes and earn high rates of return on their capital employed. They were therefore able to maintain low levels of leverage through most of the 1990s. However, declining rates of return in the second half of the 1990s and in particular at the last review forced firms to the capital markets and, as predicted by the pecking-order theory, they did so nearly exclusively in the form of debt (with the notable exception of the recent United Utilities equity issue).

The pecking-order theory therefore provides a convincing description of the steady increase in the average levels of leverage in water from around 20 per cent at privatization to the 50 per cent central estimate assumed in the last review. However, it is a less plausible explanation for the discrete jumps that occurred in some but not all companies over the last few years. These look much more like conscious policy decisions than mechanical funding responses.

The theory that suggests that firms choose their capital structure is termed the trade-off theory. This argues that firms have optimal levels of leverage that trade off, for example, the corporate tax advantage of employing debt in preference to equity against the risks of financial distress and insolvency associated with high levels of leverage.

According to this theory, an increase in leverage in the water industry would be expected to be associated with a shift in the benefits of leverage over their costs. For example, an increase in the tax advantage of debt over equity or a reduction in the financial risks of the water industry could explain increasing leverage. There were some tax changes in this direction at the end of the 1990s, in particular the reduction in tax credits on dividends that may have contributed to the higher levels of leverage. But again this does not explain the leap in leverage over the last few years and, if anything, the tightening of the regulatory formula in the 1999 periodic review increased rather than diminished the financial risks of the industry. At first sight, the trade-off theory does not therefore look to be a very promising explanation of leverage in water.

But other developments occurred do go in the right direction. These were the structural changes that separated the utility parts of businesses from the remainder through ring fencing, separate legal vehicles and disposals. These changes have had the effect of carving out pure low-risk utilities that are protected from diversifications, asset transfers and dividend distributions in the remainder of the business. In essence their corporate governance has been tightened, constraining the discretion of management to pursue related and unrelated activities. Corresponding with the reductions in risk, the trade-off theory predicts the higher optimal levels of leverage that have been observed in these companies.

The trade-off theory is therefore consistent with what happened in water. In particular, both the pecking-order and the trade-off theory see the changes in leverage in water as being derivative rather than fundamental. In the case of the pecking-order theory, the higher levels of leverage derive from the difference between the investment requirements and internal resources of firms, and the trade-off theory views the increases in leverage as being a consequence of the governance changes. But even the trade-off theory does not explain why the restructurings have occurred all of a sudden in such a short space of time.

One view is that companies were driven to them. It is no longer possible for firms to operate the equity model with relatively loose governance arrangements and generous amounts of equity reserves. They now need to get the cost of running the core utilities down to an absolute minimum, consistent with the low rates of return assumed in the last regulatory review. This has involved stripping out equity and setting up governance arrangements that are suitable to debt financing.[2]

A second view is that it is a response to regulatory uncertainty. The last review demonstrated the exposure of companies to a tightening of the regulatory noose and they are using debt as an instrument to restrain the regulator. Any further tightening and the victim will be dead.

There is a more instructive way of describing both of these points. Debt gives shareholders a put option to exit – to put the firm in the hands of the creditors and receiver – if performance is sufficiently poor to trigger a default. However, under the terms of the licence, default also gives the regulator the right to exit – to put the firm in special administration and terminate the existing licence. High levels of leverage therefore reduce the commitment of both licensees to the licensed operations and of the regulator to the licensee. The higher the level of leverage, the greater the rights of both parties to exit.

It is only in the interests of firms to raise the stakes in this way if they gain more from increasing their right to exit than they are conferring on the regulator. This will occur if firms are exposed to greater downside losses from staying in the business. In that case the value of being able to exit increases and this is precisely what has happened. So long as governments and regulators wanted to privatize more industries or encourage more investment, the past (i.e. sunk) investments of firms were protected. But as priorities switched from privatizations and investment to increasing efficiency and productivity, in particular capital efficiency, these past investments became exposed.[3] And there was little that governments or regulators could do to avoid this. Companies therefore responded by enhancing their ability to exit and they chose higher levels of leverage to do this.

This provides a richer view of what has happened. Changes in governance and capital structure are both products of time – the privatization cycle. In the early stages, when investment is the predominant concern, rights to exit are of little value to firms. Leverage is low and governance structures are consistent with equity finance. In later stages, as new privatizations and the backlog of investment diminish, leverage increases and governance structures adjust accordingly from equity to debt models. As investment requirements increase again,[4] leverage levels can be expected to fall and corporate structures to adapt in tandem.

To summarize, both the pecking-order and trade-off theories provide at least partial explanations for what has happened in water. Leverage levels were initially low because earnings were high and tax advantages of debt were modest. They increased in response to tougher regulation, less favourable tax treatment of equity, and the introduction of tighter governance models. However, to understand why patterns of leverage have changed so rapidly over the last few years one has to put relations between regulator and firms in a time context of the privatization cycle. The tighter regulatory regime and the changing capital and corporate structures are all predictable outcomes of evolving priorities in the water privatization programme.

4.   WHAT ARE THE CONSEQUENCES?

If the corporate restructuring programmes achieve their goals, then they should have one clear outcome: they should reduce the capital costs of running water businesses. They reduce the exposure of utilities to wealth transfers from, for example, raising debt against their assets for other activities, and costly diversifications. The cost of capital of the ring-fenced or securitized water companies should be lower than those that remain an integral part of larger groups.

This is precisely what was found in a study by OXERA for Ofwat of the highly leveraged water companies.[5] Measuring the cost of capital is never as scientific an exercise as the textbooks suggest, primarily because of uncertainty about the equity cost of capital, both in relation to the overall market premium on equity over and above the riskless return on government securities, and the systematic risk of the firm concerned, that is, its beta coefficient. However, one of the attractive features of the highly leveraged companies, at least from the perspective of an academic concerned with measurement not consequences, is that their cost of capital can be estimated with an unusually high degree of precision. The reason is obvious: by definition, highly leveraged firms have little equity so that imprecision in its measurement is of little significance.

In its Ofwat study, OXERA concluded on the basis of a wide range of potential equity costs of capital that the pre-tax cost of capital of the leveraged firms was in the range 3.25 to 4.25 per cent. A recent update has confirmed that a narrower range of 3.5 to 4 per cent applies to the corporate restructurings that have occurred since the Ofwat report. This is appreciably below the cost of capital that Ofwat used in the last periodic review (4.25 to 5.25 per cent on a *post-tax* basis) and suggests that the restructurings have indeed been associated with significant reductions in the water companies' cost of capital. This does not violate the Modigliani and Miller principle that the cost of capital is unaffected by leverage since the reduction is driven by real reductions in the risks of the businesses either through corporate restructurings or through the strategic use of debt to reduce regulatory exposure.

In drawing this conclusion, the Ofwat report warned that the results might have been distorted by inappropriate pricing of the financial instruments. Investors may have underestimated the risks involved, they may have made incorrect assumptions about the underlying performance of the firms and they may have misunderstood the nature of the regulatory regime. In particular, they may have overestimated the likelihood of the regulator passing through higher refinancing costs in the future to customers. As the number of cases of restructurings increases, the likelihood of systematic mispricing of securities diminishes but the possibility that risks turn out to be significantly greater than those assumed by the market cannot be ruled out.

The more serious issue from a regulatory perspective is that there might be a divergence between private and social valuations of the restructurings. Even if the debt securities are correctly priced in the market, from a social perspective they may be overvalued. The reason for this is that investors do not take account of the wider social costs of water company failures, in particular the potential disruption to services arising from the termination of a licence. These costs are small provided that licences can be transferred seamlessly between failing firms and new owners. It should be possible to organize this in relation to the operations of a single firm; it may be somewhat more complex in regard to substantial capital programmes in the course of construction but it is where several firms fail simultaneously that the most serious problems are likely to be encountered. In other words social/private divergences are most serious where industry-wide failures can occur.

'Systemic risks' are less likely in water than in financial services and in particular in banking, where they are most frequently discussed. There is not the same degree of interconnectedness of water companies as there is between financial institutions. Nevertheless, water companies are exposed to common cost shocks in the form of operating and capital costs. Most significantly for highly leveraged companies, they are exposed to similar refinancing costs that in the event of an adverse change in market sentiment could move against the industry as a whole.

There are, of course, material adverse condition and shipwreck clauses that allow companies to apply for passthrough of such risks. In the case of financing charges, Ofwat has in the past allowed for embedded debt in setting charges. However, this may not apply in the future. In any event, these conditions go to the heart of an important issue raised by leveraged structures: to what extent will they effectively force regulators to allow automatic passthrough of cost increases to customers? We will return to this issue in the next section.

The final impact of the changing structures is on investment. One of the most widely discussed effects of leverage is on investment incentives and risk taking. Incentives are distorted at high levels of leverage by the fact that returns in the event of insolvency pass to creditors, not shareholders. Shareholders do not therefore take full account of the benefits of investment and may be prone to pursue excessively risky projects that generate high returns for shareholders if they do well and large losses for creditors if they do badly. In practice, markets attempt to contract round these problems by including covenants that restrict the ability of management to exploit creditors in this way. Restrictions on diversifications are a particularly pertinent case in point.

While the standard investment issues raised by highly leveraged structures may not be as serious as sometimes suggested, there is one that is particularly relevant to regulated utilities. Recall that high leverage raises the option value to exit. This option is especially valuable for firms that are able to extract value from the business to the benefit of investors by running down the capital stock to the cost of customers. In other words in highly leveraged companies there is an underinvestment problem created not by a divergence of interest between creditors and shareholders but between investors as a whole and customers. Unless regulators are able to monitor the quality of the capital stock with great accuracy, rising levels of leverage increase the risk of firms sweating assets, minimizing investment and leaving future generations of owners and customers to clean up the mess.

The primary motivation for privatizing industries in the form of licences rather than franchises was to minimize this short-termism problem: it is difficult to provide franchisees with adequate incentives to invest towards the end of the life of a franchise. The greater the levels of the leverage, the higher the probability that firms will prematurely exit a licence and the more relevant are the investment problems of franchises to licences.

In summary, there are three main consequences of the changing structures of water companies. First, the cost of capital of the water companies is reduced because of their reduced exposure to managerial and regulatory risks. Second, the private cost of capital incurred by investors may understate the social cost borne by customers, particularly in the event of industry-wide failures. Third, there is a potential underinvestment problem created by the possibility of failure resulting in withdrawal of the existing operator.

The central regulatory questions that highly leveraged structures raise are, therefore: how should regulators respond to the lower cost of financing; should they reduce the return that firms are allowed to earn correspondingly; how should they cope with risks of multiple firm failures and how should they ensure that water company investors do not prosper at the expense of future generations of customers? It is to these policy issues that we now turn.

5.   WHAT ARE THE APPROPRIATE POLICY RESPONSES?

On the cost of capital and the rate of return, there are three possible responses. The first is to leave allowed rates of return unchanged in line with essentially the equity model, and an assumed 50 per cent level of leverage. The second is to reduce rates of return on restructured firms to their lower cost of capital and keep the rates of return of other firms unchanged. Differential costs of capital are routinely employed in individual firm beta coefficients. The third approach is to reduce allowed rates of return on all companies to the lower cost of capital of restructured firms. Which of these or what combination is appropriate?

The answer to this question depends on the appropriate relationship between regulator and firms. As previously described, we have moved from a commitment to a control model. We started with commitment on the part of firms and regulators to promote investment and we have moved to a control model with regulators imposing tighter efficiency targets and firms raising their exiting options. A high cost of capital can only be justified by commitment on both sides and a low cost of capital requires both parties to be able to exercise effective control.

What are the characteristics of commitment and control? Let us start with commitment. On the side of the firm, commitment requires the employment of significant amounts of equity to provide adequate reserves. It requires regulators and firms to agree medium to long-term development plans for the businesses setting output and standards targets. Most significantly, it requires regulators to commit to price determinations that span more than one regulatory period. This does not imply fixing prices but it does involve reducing the degree of regulatory discretion.

There have already been significant moves in this direction through, for example, the rolling incentive allowance that permits companies to keep efficiency savings for fixed periods before they are passed through to customers in lower charges. The emergence of routine approaches to the determination of the cost of capital and regulatory asset values are other examples. But what emerged in the last review is that despite the implementation of these procedures, the regulator at the end of the day has considerable residual discretion.

The most sceptical observers view a regulatory review as being driven by a political bargain, with the components of the price determination being fixed to give the right answer. More sympathetic individuals recognize the impossibility of tying down all the components in a formulaic manner. In either case, commitment is difficult to achieve. I will discuss ways in which more can be done in this direction below.

The alternative control approach will require regulators to take a more active role in allocating and reallocating licences. There will be failures in the presence of small amounts of equity and regulators need to be prepared for them. They need to have in place quite precise procedures for how licences will be reallocated, what happens if appropriate new operators are not immediately forthcoming, how companies can if necessary be managed in an interregnum, how ongoing capital programmes can be sustained and so on. Special administration procedures do exist and no doubt a great deal of further thought has gone into how they will operate in practice, but this should be made transparent.

The question of who should bear the cost of these procedures also needs further consideration, namely whether it is the firms concerned, the industry through perhaps a risk-based levy, or the economy more widely through general taxation. On the principle that this is close to an insurance fund, the best allocation of costs may be achieved by the second of these, namely a risk-based industry levy.

The most serious management problems for regulators will arise in the case of multiple industry-wide failures. Regulators may be able to transfer one or two licences relatively effortlessly, but several simultaneous failures will create serious disruption. Railtrack is a salutary reminder of the costs of an industry failure that will in all probability be with us for years to come. The implication of this is that in the presence of high levels of leverage industry wide cost shocks will have to be passed through to customers. A move to a low cost of capital regulatory framework will therefore involve a greater absorption of industry-wide risks by customers.

In a previous lecture in this series,[6] I described how 'relative price regulation' (RPR) could achieve this automatic passthrough of industry-wide costs while maintaining firm incentives. The principle is that prices are adjusted to bring aggregate rates of return in the industry as a whole in line with the cost of capital while leaving rankings of rates of return of individual firms unchanged. It therefore preserves incentives by encouraging individual firms to beat the average. Strictly, the prices of a particular firm are adjusted downwards by the average excess return of all other firms (the 'n minus one' principle) so the firm in question cannot affect its own clawback. Aggregate industry risk is therefore borne by customers and firm-specific risks by investors. Investors can diversify the firm-specific risk, leaving them with a cost of capital equal to the riskless return.

While relative price regulation does not eliminate the risk of failure of individual firms, it reduces the risk of industry-wide failures and establishes a low cost of capital in line with that of highly leveraged companies. It therefore facilitates the control approach to regulation. In addition it can be used to substitute rule-based adjustment for regulatory discretion and therefore to enhance regulatory commitment as well.

A move to a control model of regulation will involve a greater degree of industry-wide cost passthrough. It also creates the potential for brinkmanship between regulator and firm. In principle, firms should only seek insolvency if their ongoing values from the licence are less than their liabilities. However, faced with a regulator who can affect valuations, there may be potential benefits from threatening strategic default at positive net present values. If the cost to the regulator of a company terminating its licence is greater than it is to the firm itself, the firm may be able to improve its regulatory settlement by threatening default.

Financial ratios and cash flows give a firm the opportunity of doing this. A breach of a debt covenant, relating for example to interest coverage, can trigger a default and therefore be used to affect a regulatory bargain.[7] Financial ratios therefore take on an importance that is independent of asset valuations. While regulators have always taken note of them, the requirement to ensure that firms are able to finance their functions has in general been interpreted as referring to asset valuations and the cost of capital, not a requirement to meet particular financial ratios. That may remain the case but the use of default as a threat means that financial ratios are likely to play a more significant role in the future.

A move to a high-leverage, low cost-of-capital control model therefore raises issues about cost passthrough and strategic games but at the end of the day the regulatory system will probably be able to cope with both of these. The more serious problem relates to the third consequence described above – investment. The water industry is a long-term asset business. Infrastructure can remain in place for decades. Returns to investment only accrue over an extended period. Incentives are simply not aligned if firms believe that there is a significant possibility that they might exit without being able to realize the full value of their investments.

It might be thought that this problem can be mitigated through monitoring and auditing firms' capital stock, that is, through control mechanisms. A great deal of important work is done on this. But at the end of the day it is almost impossible for regulators to ensure that current activities are not being run at the expense of future generations. A creeping deterioration in capital stocks may take years to become evident.

The only real solution is for companies to be committed to provide services over a long term and essentially into the indefinite future. For companies to be willing to make this commitment, they require equivalent commitments from regulators and governments not to exploit past, sunk investments. In other words there has to be balancing of commitments. For reasons that were previously discussed, it is difficult for regulators and governments to do this, and the nature of the regulatory process is such that current regulators cannot fetter the discretion of their successors. While the Competition Commission has done a great deal to establish continuity, it too cannot promise to abide by precedent.

Herein lies the heart of the time problem that afflicts privatizations and regulation around the world. There is an inherent mismatch between the commitment that the technology requires and that which regulators and governments can provide. There are alternatives, for example rate-of-return regulation and fixed-term franchises, but there are problems with each of these – incentive problems with rate-of-return regulation and investment problems with fixed-term franchises. In some respects, the ingenuity of the market in reacting to the commitment problem through highly leveraged transactions has been impressive. However, from a regulatory stability perspective these developments are worrying. They have raised the stakes of the regulatory game and in the absence of appropriate responses, they risk in time bringing the privatization programme into disrepute.

In answering the question about appropriate rates of return in water, the regulator should therefore view these as determining rather than being determined by organizational and capital structures. Firms are responding to what they perceive to be the nature of the regulatory contract. If, as is being suggested here, an equity model is more appropriate than a highly leveraged structure, then the regulator should ensure that costs of capital that are consistent with the equity model are used in the determination of allowed rates of return. Furthermore, if the regulator wishes to encourage more companies to retain or implement equity structures, then an element of conditionality could be introduced into price determinations; that is, higher rates of return could be offered to low rather than highly leveraged firms.

One way in which regulators could increase the credibility of their commitment to the equity model is to front-load returns.[8] Regulators may not be able to commit to particular returns in future reviews, but they can offer correspondingly higher returns on new investments in the short run. A higher return could be earned on new investments for a rolling five- or ten-year period, analogous to the treatment of efficiency gains, before expenditures are amalgamated in the regulatory asset base at a lower cost of capital. For example, if the cost of capital in an equity model is 5 per cent and in a leveraged model is 4 per cent, then new investments could earn a return, of say 6 per cent, for ten years, which together with a 4 per cent return thereafter yields an average 5 per cent rate of return over the life of the asset. While this proposal looks like a split rate of return between new and old assets, it is not. All assets on average earn the cost of capital over their lives. Returns are simply reprofiled to the early years of an investment when regulators are able to commit credibly to paying them.

Notice that the higher returns on new investments do not arise from higher risk. Fixed costs and options to defer may make the cost of capital on large new projects higher than on existing assets, Terminal 5 in BAA being a case in point. But even where these considerations do not apply, higher returns in the short run are justified by the below-cost-of-capital return that is earned in the longer term. Once the age and depreciation schedule of an asset is known, the appropriate premium on returns in the short run can be automatically determined in a mechanical fashion. In addition, the embedded debt problem could be eased by using the current interest rate to determine the cost of capital of new investments over their first five or ten years and a historic average of past yields for the cost of capital on assets in the regulatory asset base.

In summary, the changing structures necessitate some key responses from regulators, including the passthrough of a higher proportion of industry-wide costs to customers and the establishment of procedures for dealing with corporate failures. But regulators should seek to influence as well as respond to developments. They should attempt to mitigate problems of commitment by employing rules rather than discretion and they should use the cost of capital to encourage firms to employ equity as well as debt forms of finance.

6. CONCLUSIONS

The last few years have witnessed a radical shift in the organizational and capital structure of firms. From lowly leveraged firms at privatization, water companies have now become either averagely or in some cases highly leveraged. Some of these developments can be readily explained in terms of the financing requirements created by large investment programmes. The changing organizational structures have also contributed to the low-risk businesses required to create highly leveraged firms. However, the traditional theories of capital structure do not explain the marked changes that have occurred recently.

These are more clearly seen in the context of the control features of leverage and the privatization cycle. Highly leveraged firms restrict the ability of regulators to reduce their valuations before triggering default. In the early days of privatization, when there was greater concern about promoting investment than extracting efficiency gains, this was not an overriding consideration. But as the regulatory agenda changed, so too the exposure of firms' assets increased. The tightening of the regulatory contract at the last review encouraged firms to seek low-cost financing vehicles and mechanisms for restricting the potential for further downside adjustments.

This has significantly altered the nature of the regulatory relation. Some companies have now become pure ring-fenced water companies with appreciably lower costs of capital than previously. However, in the process of creating these low-cost vehicles, divergences between private and social costs of capital may have been increased. In pricing securities, investors will not take account of the impact of failure on customers and, in particular, will not factor in the possibility of sector-wide failures.

Still more seriously, the exit option granted to shareholders by high levels of leverage presents investment problems in an industry characterized by very long-lived assets. It creates short-termist difficulties that are not dissimilar to those associated with short-term franchises.

There are two routes forward: the commitment and the control approaches to regulation. The commitment route views the relation between regulator and firm as a long-term one in which firms plan investments over long horizons with substantial equity cushions to protect against adverse shocks. In return, regulators commit to sustain the value of capital employed over long periods. It is the latter requirement that is the most difficult since the regulatory structure does not allow regulators or governments to commit in this way.

The transition of corporate structures from commitment to control is therefore natural. The second route is then for the regulator to follow suit and establish better control systems. This includes preparing for the financial failures that high-leverage structures are likely to engender. Procedures for ensuring that licence transfers can occur at low cost need to be put in place.

Since effective control of industry-wide failures will be complex, it should be recognized that the changing structures have intensified the degree of passthrough of industry-wide cost shocks. There is a variety of provisions in place such as material adverse clauses that allow this to happen, but additional procedures, such as the use of a form of relative price regulation, should also be considered.

A move to more rule-based arrangements would also have the advantage of increasing the degree of regulatory commitment. This is important because, while best efforts can be made to have efficient control mechanisms in place, they are unlikely to be able to cope with the most serious consequence of a move in this direction: the potential for underinvestment. Monitoring and control regimes do not have the precision required to prevent abuses from occurring and at the end of the day only a system in which the commitments of regulators and firms are balanced can achieve this. A failure to commit inevitably takes its toll in the form of underinvestment in an industry with long-lived assets.

One of the implications of the reinterpretation in this paper of developments in water is that regulators should view allowed rates of return as being determinants of, not just determined by, firms' chosen capital and organizational structures. They should seek to influence the structures through setting rates of return that are appropriate to them. If, as is being suggested here, an equity model is in the long term a more suitable basis for firm–regulator relations than a highly leveraged one, then regulators should seek to sustain rates of return that are consistent with it. One way in which this might be done is to front-load returns on new investments sufficiently so that when they are combined with lower subsequent returns on the regulatory asset base, they yield average returns over their lives in line with the equity model.

The institutional changes required to solve the commitment problem are more extensive than those discussed here, and in the absence of such institutional innovations, regulators will only be able to do limited patchwork. But as described at the beginning, the performance of inevitably imperfect systems has to date been remarkably good. With a few more patches, then, the regulatory machine should be good enough to run for several more years.

NOTES

*   I am grateful to Colin Robinson and Leonard Waverman for the invitation to give the lecture on which this paper is based, and to Chris Bolt, Philip Fletcher, Dieter Helm, Andrew Meeney and Sylvia Wenyon for comments on an earlier draft. The views expressed here are those of the author and not those of any institution with which he is associated.
1. A total of 99.86 per cent of samples met drinking water standards in 2001 – a 92 per cent fall in the number failing compared with 1992.
2. This is essentially a free-cash-flow theory that leverage has increased to reduce slack and sweat the assets.
3. Annual capital expenditures in the water industry rose from between £1.5 and £2 billion in the first half of the 1980s to between £3 and £4 billion in the 1990s. In the last periodic review, they were projected to decline from around £3.8 billion at the beginning of the review period to under £3 billion by the end.

4. Ofwat's preliminary analysis of companies' draft business plans indicates that they anticipate £20 billion (i.e. an average of £4 billion per annum) of new investment over the coming review period (Ofwat PN 36/03, 16 October 2003).
5. *The Capital Structure of Water Companies: Final Report to OFWAT by OXERA*, 31 October 2002.
6. Colin Mayer, 'Water: the 1999 price review', in Colin Robinson (ed.), *Regulating Utilities: New Issues, New Solutions*, Cheltenham: Edward Elgar, 2001.
7. In several of the restructurings, defaults on interest payments on senior but not junior debt can trigger insolvency.
8. This is discussed in Dieter Helm's introductory article to *Water, Sustainability and Regulation*, OXERA, 2003.

CHAIRMAN'S COMMENTS

Philip Fletcher

The first point I want to make is obvious enough: real life tends always to conflate, mix up and become more complicated. So we could say we have seen the Stone Age of getting the companies off the government's books, the Bronze Age of concentrating on operating efficiency and the Iron Age in which we find ourselves concentrating on capital efficiency. We wait for whatever the IT Age will be in a few years' time. But in practice, in my perception at least, there is no such clear dividing line between these three epochs of regulation of the privatized water industry.

In particular, I would say that there is still a huge investment drive in this sector. The companies have been spending something over £3 billion per year ever since privatization. In many ways, not least for simplicity and the comfort of the regulator on financing issues, I wish that we could see an end in sight.

But there is no end in sight. The companies within the sector have been running on constant negative cash flow ever since 1990. There is every prospect, looking forward, that they will be required to continue to run a negative cash-flow position. This certainly presents some regulatory hurdles, as well as big challenges for the companies, and raises other concerns about long-term stability that, perhaps to a degree, overlap with Colin Mayer's concerns. I think those concerns can be overcome and are being overcome. I do not see them as in any way insuperable, but they are an important fact of life to be taken into account in an industry which is entirely dependent on the private sector, thank goodness, rather than on the taxpayer, for its resources and where the investor, the lender and the bond holder must see an adequate return for the risk that they perceive that they are incurring.

So we have first this continuing appetite for new investment. Professor Mayer's juxtaposition of the commitment and the control models, I found helpful. But I did not agree with all his consequent thoughts on it. It seems to me that there is a high level of commitment still involved in this; it is not a cosy commitment. There is a requirement on the regulator to enable companies to finance their functions taking account of all the factors that Colin Mayer has aired and others that the time available did not permit.

There is also the requirement on the companies to continue to deliver. In Ofwat we believe that delivering these various commitments is best served by as transparent, consistent and objective a regulatory regime as we can achieve, so long as we have the flexibility to respond to events. And it is this continuing commitment to a clear regime that gives investors confidence in assessing the risk to enable them to make the investment, without unduly high demands on the rate of return over the long term, and enables the companies to keep going.

I think we may part company on the extent to which a regulator can commit his successors. Of course the theory is absolutely right that a decision cannot be binding, but in practice the more that the regulator cements the way in which a regulator behaves, the more certain it is that the regulator's successor, like it or lump it, will be bound to follow a very similar course. This is probably more true of an individual regulator, still more of a regulatory board, than we would see with the Competition Commission, where a separate panel, even though it does have regard to precedents, is established for each case examined by that panel. The cement is the threat, very seldom the reality, among other things, of judicial review. The deliberate creation of reasonable expectations provides a company with ammunition which it can fire against the regulator, if the regulator in some sort of maverick and inconsistent way starts failing to deliver against those reasonable expectations.

There is a third area of development that is important in explaining the patterns that Colin Mayer has so succinctly conveyed to us. That is the City. We have seen in recent years debt available at a price which, in historic terms, has been low. None of us expects that to continue over time. I too accept, in general, the Modigliani and Miller approach. But for a period of time, if there is an advantage from raising money by debt, and if the City has developed its instruments so that small and large companies alike find it easier to access that debt, then we would expect – and we have seen – a move by this sector, whose profile lends itself to a significant role for debt to take advantage of that set of events.

Colin Mayer went on to say that high levels of gearing constrain the regulator. But we don't see ourselves as so constrained. I entirely accept that if the whole industry packed into a narrow frame, then the constraints would start to bite. That is why it is important that the industry should continue to have access to a variety of sources of funding, including equity. This doesn't mean that 50 per cent gearing is necessarily a perfect ratio. I can well see it moving up to reflect events. But a very high level of gearing carries within it seeds of possible instability that we need to watch carefully. Of course we have a mechanism, as he explained, in the term 'special administration'. We have never had to apply it; I hope we never shall. But it is very important that it is there. We do oil it and wheel it out from time to time and make sure that it is in working condition.

Far more important than 'special administration' is the normal operation of the market, and over the three years that I have been regulator we have seen huge turnover through mergers and acquisitions and consolidation and restructuring even irrespective of high gearing, although higher gearing has often gone with it. I welcome that as part of the normal operations, notwithstanding the special merger regime to which the industry from time to time objects, and which brings the Competition Commission to the fore when water companies want to merge with one another.

Would Colin Mayer's specific mechanism, which as far as I know has not been advanced before, of front-loading returns on capital investment, have the desired effect of further reducing turbulence and risk? Here I am not sure and would welcome others' contributions. Some of the questions that arise in my mind include, first of all, whether investors would be at all comfortable about accepting returns in later years. I can see it applying to private finance initiative projects focused on, say, one major investment where the investors are committed, at least initially, for the duration of the project – something like Terminal 5 at Heathrow, for example. But would it apply where the assets, as in the water companies' case, are mostly a mixture of investments, much of it in small packets? If returns are below the market cost of capital for a period, I would see this as encouraging companies to gear up. So one would just be deferring the problem further down the track. If shareholders can realize the capital value of the excess returns in the earlier years by leveraging early, then wouldn't they have every incentive to do so?

As a regulator I can also see some possible practical problems, notably complexity. If specific returns are attached to specific assets, they would have to have very long lives or we would start to find ourselves with a number of different rates of return attached to different assets, all being applied simultaneously. I could see investors becoming confused and worried about the loss of the transparency of a consistent single cost of capital, which they have at the moment. That would lose one of the key benefits of the current system.

The issue of defining or identifying the age and depreciation schedule for an asset is also fraught with practical difficulties. Thus we don't apply normal depreciation rules in respect of the below-ground assets. We assume an almost indefinite life. It is not just decades; as the industry constantly complains, it may be centuries. That does not mean that the assets are at risk of instant failure, but we need to take into account very long lives indeed and would face difficulties in estimating just how long those lives might be.

I would like to emphasize that incentives, as Colin Mayer has brought out, are a very important part of any system of economic regulation. We need to work hard at these. As an example of the point I was making earlier about committing successors, Ofwat has recently consulted on incentives that will only take effect after 2010, that is four years after the current regulator passes into history and is succeeded by a regulatory board under the Water Act, which received the Royal Assent in November 2003.

The final point I want to make is that I shall be giving the final price limits on 25 November 2004.[1] So it is a particularly apt time to get contributions to Ofwat's thinking as we enter into this last and, no doubt, most testing period of the current review.

NOTE

1. In the event, the price limits were announced on 2 December 2004.

9. Do we need European merger control?

Jacques Steenbergen and Leonard Waverman

1. INTRODUCTION: MERGER CONTROL IN COMPETITION LAW

1.1 Summary

Our general answer to the question posed in this paper is: while it may be exaggerated to claim that we *need* European merger control, it is a useful competition policy instrument. However, fewer mergers should be banned or interfered with via divestitures/settlements. More reliance should be placed on *ex post* abuse law. The mergers stopped by the Commission should only be those that cannot be adequately dealt with if actual abusive behaviour emerges *ex post*.

1.2 Outline

A certain degree of discomfort with merger control led in 2002 to (and was fuelled by) a wave of judgements of the Court of First Instance in Luxembourg that were critical of Commission decisions. After a brief discussion of these cases, there are three major issues to discuss:

1. How well does merger control work? Do competition agencies ban only potentially anticompetitive mergers and allow procompetitive mergers?
2. Should we rely totally, or at least more, on another leg of competition law – the prohibition of abuse of a dominant position? That rule does attack unilateral abusive behaviour or abuse of a jointly held dominant position. Why not allow mergers, and then end any abuse that does eventually follow?
3. What about subsidiarity? Do we need more or less EU merger control or can national governments alone or together handle cross-border EU or global mergers?

1.3   EU Competition Law

EU competition law rests, as in all Western economies where competition policy exists, on three legs: Leg One – laws which prevent anticompetitive agreements; Leg Two – laws which prevent abuse of a dominant position/ monopoly action; Leg Three – merger law. Leg Three is very different from the other two legs in fundamental ways.

A relatively recent development

First, antitrust law in the EU or the USA began with only the first two legs – merger review was added much later. At the EU level, Articles 81 (agreements which restrict competition) and 82 (abuse of a dominant position) were essential features of the 1957 Treaty of Rome. Merger review was added in 1989, over 30 years later. Similarly in the USA, the Sherman Act of 1890 attacked monopolization and agreements in restraint of trade; the Clayton Act of 1917 extended antitrust law to the review of mergers. Note that the EU in 1957 did not include the merger provisions of the Clayton Act, established 40 years earlier.

Why were mergers not included at the EU level in 1957 as potentially anticompetitive acts? The prevailing view was that firm size was too small to compete with larger American firms, and hence that mergers were probably procompetitive. This is perhaps a gentle way of describing European and national industrial policy – the desire to build national champions. The 1980s was a decade that started with an economic crisis and later saw a wave of mergers at a time when European markets integrated and industry achieved a more European scale. Debate began at the European level of the need to control cross-border mergers which were not helping competitiveness but were instead anticompetitive. This debate between advocates of industrial policy and advocates of free competition lasted a decade and the exact wording of the EU Merger Law reflected this tension.

Unlike cartels and abuses, concentrations are by nature not illicit

A more crucial difference between merger control and the other two legs of competition law is that mergers are not, by nature or design, anticompetitive or illicit. Mergers are largely procompetitive business actions designed to lower costs, improve efficiency, expand markets or require resources. Of the 2350 mergers notified at the EU level since 1989, over 90 per cent have been waved through. Agreements which restrict competition or abuse of a dominant position are not welfare-increasing acts in the slightest. While it is difficult to judge what is an agreement that is anticompetitive, or conduct that is abusive, we do not ask that all agreements or all business actions above a certain size be notified, as we do with mergers.

Difference between merger control and Articles 81 and 82

Merger control aims at the *ex ante* control of undesirable side effects of legitimate operations while Articles 81 and 82 sanction *ex post* established infringements. When we judge conduct as anticompetitive we are looking into the past; when we judge whether a merger will be anticompetitive we are looking into the future. Since judges, antitrust officials, lawyers and economists often disagree in assessing the anticompetitive nature of past behaviour, we must be especially judicious in the tests and rules we set in judging the future impact of something – a merger that has not yet taken place.

A major difference between control of dominance and merger review is as follows. If an agreement is anticompetitive – say a cartel that has fixed prices – there is no other law which can prevent harm. Similarly, if a dominant firm engages in predation to prevent rivals from entering, there is no substitute for banning the action today. However, mergers are different – we ban mergers which *could* create or increase dominance. There is another possibility and one we explore below – allow mergers *ex ante* but condemn abuse of dominance *ex post*, with substantial penalties such as sale of assets.

This view is buttressed when we examine economists' recent analyses of the performance of antitrust law in general and merger law in particular. These studies show a severe gap between the desires of merger law – to prevent only those mergers that could lead to market structures which are conducive to abuse and the actual regulatory outcome – the cases chosen and the decisions made. In particular the work of Duso et al.[1] calls into question our abilities, or at least the Merger Task Force's ability, to ban only those mergers that are anticompetitive. Crandall and Winston[2] show that in the USA, merger review has not increased consumer welfare, and has in some cases reduced it. Much more economic analysis is needed, but the available evidence is not supportive of antitrust Commissions doing a 'good' job in merger analyses. A question is whether it is indeed feasible *ex ante* to know which mergers will raise prices, hence our suggestion of more reliance on the *ex post* abuse leg of competition policy.

2. TOUGH TIMES FOR MERGER CONTROL: WHAT CAN WE LEARN FROM RECENT CASES?

2.1 The Cases

The Court of First Instance of the European Communities (CFI) annulled on 22 October 2002 the Commission decision whereby the concentration between Schneider Electric and Legrand was prohibited (case T-310/01),[3] and on 25 October 2002, it annulled the prohibition decision concerning the notified concentration between Tetra Laval and Sidel (case T-5/02).[4] These two judgments followed the earlier annulment on 6 June 2002 of the Airtours/First Choice decision (case T-342/99) (no fast-track procedure).[5] This unprecedented wave of annulments created an atmosphere of crisis that has somewhat obscured the impact of the judgments.

When we try to put these judgments into their proper perspective we can conclude as follows:

- The Schneider and Tetra Laval judgments were the first after a fast-track procedure[6] in merger control cases. A judgment was given after eight to nine months (it took the Court between 33 and 41 months to give judgment in the earlier cases).
- The Court's analysis is as thorough as in the standard procedure. The Court is as willing as in other procedures to look at the substance of the case. It could, in the Schneider case, have used the procedural argument based on the discrepancies between the statement of objections and the decisions for the markets outside France as well as for the French market to annul the decision without any need to look into any of the other arguments.
- The Court begins with the Commission logic and checks whether the Commission applied its logic consistently, and whether its conclusions are supported by the evidence referred to in the decision or available to the Commission.
- These judgments are not critical of the Commission's analytical framework, but it was judged in each case that the Commission reached its conclusions without sufficient evidence, if not in contradiction with this evidence. This is especially true for the assessment of leverage and of the future effects of a concentration. In the Schneider case the CFI rules that the Commission was entitled to ask for the mass information that was required from the parties. We are nevertheless convinced that the annulled decision was not sufficiently supported by factual evidence because the Commission had insufficient data. The problem was that the Commission asked for too much information of limited relevance, and lacked the file management capacity to manage the intake and the use of what came in.
- The fast-track procedure can accelerate further and can perhaps be compressed to approximately five months, but it will never be quick enough to offer an effective remedy for most merger control cases. The impact of the Court will primarily be indirect, by setting benchmarks in the relatively few cases that are likely to go to court.

2.2 A Change in Climate

For the first time several merger control cases came before the Court in the same semester. This can partly be explained by a relative increase of the percentage of notified public bids (in which case the parties are more likely to appeal a decision because they already hold the shares). It should be added that there are also rather more prohibition decisions. This can partly be explained by the following factors:

- Industries are more concentrated after years of intensive M&A activity, it is therefore logical that a higher percentage of cases raise serious doubt about the meaning of Article 6 of the Merger Regulation.
- There is increased concern at the Commission about the negative impact of transactions because there is also increased scepticism in respect of their positive contribution. The impression exists that transactions might often be more in the interests of top management and advisers than in the interest of the companies and of society. Regulators (especially on the Continent) tend to be unconcerned by shareholder value if not suspicious of the 'short-termism' that is often associated with the maximization of shareholder value (they are most concerned by the liability that may result from a destruction of shareholder value). This significant divergence between the value systems of merging parties and officials, and some negative experiences of officials (e.g. with the circumvention of divestment obligations) have led to a less constructive and less pro-business attitude of many officials, especially among younger officials at DG-Competition.

This has led to:

- lower thresholds for dominance (the warnings are at a 40 per cent market share);
- more need for data in notifications, especially on non-affected markets, and during the procedure in response to ever longer questionnaires (in the Schneider case hundreds of thousands of data were asked for and transmitted);
- more emphasis on oligopolistic dominance, portfolio theory, leverage and an even more prospective analysis of the impact of concentrations;
- a more sceptical analysis of the remedies offered by the parties.

One of the key concerns raised by these cases is what happens after an annulment. The Commission interprets Article 10(5) of the Merger

Regulation as meaning that the parties should renotify the transaction and that the Commission restarts a Phase I procedure. The CFI's Schneider judgment suggested that the Commission should only focus on issues that remained open after the judgment. A restart from zero is a most frustrating experience for the parties and greatly limits the effectiveness of the legal remedies. It means, for example, that there is no effective sanction in case the Commission does not produce adequate evidence. It is to be regretted that the review of the Merger Regulation has not remedied this problem. The new text of Article 10(5) explicitly confirms the Commission's interpretation. We would prefer that the CFI decide the case or decide what issues can be re-examined by the Commission.

3.   DOES MERGER CONTROL WORK? THE EVIDENCE ON THE EFFICIENCY OF MERGER CONTROL

3.1   The Economists' Perspective

Economists have been exploring the impacts of mergers for decades. Earlier work concentrated on whether acquiring or acquired firms benefited more from the merger. That work shows that the acquiring firm generally receives little of the stock market gains, and that the shareholders in the acquired firm receive a premium. More recent analyses indicate that, together, the two merging firms earn little additional profits – on average 1 per cent, and that these increased profits are generally due to increased efficiency.[7, 8] In the mid-1990s, economists began to investigate not only what drove mergers and who gained, but also whether the policing of antitrust policy on mergers was successful. A paper by Bob Crandall and Cliff Winston examines price–cost margins in US industries following merger review.[9] Two recent papers (Atkas et al.;[10] Duso et al.[11]) examine EU merger decisions: both these papers use stock market data to assess the efficacy of mergers.

Crandall and Winston examine merger reviews of the Federal Trade Commission (FTC) in the 1984–2001 period – nine merger reviews that were settled at the court level, 88 settled by a consent decree, and 368 second requests for information. They group these by the 20 two-digit SIC industries (they are left with 260 observations). They determine whether and how merger reviews, mergers blocked, and second requests affect industry price costs margins. Table 9.1 provides the results.

Mergers successfully blocked by the FTC are associated with *lower* price–cost margins but the results are not statistically significant. An

Table 9.1 Price–cost margin parameter estimates in US antitrust cases (robust standard errors in parentheses)

Variable	Coefficient
Court-based outcomes	
Mergers successfully blocked by the FTC or DOJ (2-year lag)	−0.040
	(0.032)
Mergers unsuccessfully challenged by FTC or DOJ (2-year lag)	−0.038[*]
	(0.011)
Consent decrees (2-year lag)	0.017[*]
	(0.004)
Other outcomes	
Second request for information made by FTC or DOJ (2-year lag)	−0.001
	(0.002)
Industry characteristics	
Import–sales ratio	−0.071[*]
	(0.020)
Log of the growth of the number of firms (5-year lag)	−0.721[*]
	(0.188)
Capital–sales ratio	−0.105[*]
	(0.008)
Constant	0.518[*]
	(0.018)
R^2	0.45
Number of observations	260

[*] Statistically significant at the 1% level.

Notes: As for Table 2.2.

Source: R. Crandall and C. Winston, 'Does Antitrust Policy Improve Consumer Welfare? Assessing the Evidence', *Journal of Economic Perspectives*, **17** (Fall 2003), pp. 3–26. See also this volume, Table 2.2.

unsuccessful challenge – that is, the merger goes through – is also associated with *lower* price–cost margins. But this is the opposite result of what merger authorities claim – the merger was attacked because it was thought to be anticompetitive; thus if it is allowed, price–cost margins should *rise*, not fall. Hence the authors conclude that mergers successfully challenged by the FTC are probably efficiency-enhancing.

Consent decrees are associated with statistically significantly *higher* price–cost margins. This suggests that either the FTC did not demand enough *or* that the constraints imposed saddled the firms with inefficiencies. Crandall and Winston conclude that 'efforts by antitrust authorities to block particular mergers or affect a merger's outcome by allowing it only if certain conditions are met under a consent decree have not been found to increase consumer welfare in any systematic way, and in some instances the intervention may even have reduced consumer welfare' (p. 20).

Atkas et al. (see note 10) examine the stock market response to merger announcements. They find that the stock market is indeed a good judge of the EU's approval process. The announcements of mergers which are ultimately prohibited by the Commission have *smaller* stock market reactions than do announcements of mergers that sail through. Stock market data demonstrate that, contrary to folklore, non-European firms are *not* treated differently from European firms. Finally, they show that conditional approvals are correlated with the initial market reaction. They interpret this as meaning that the parties to the merger are willing to bargain most and provide concessions to the Commission when the gains are high. They analyse the stock market responses in 60 per cent of the 1210 mergers notified in the 1990 to 1999 period. The authors find certain asymmetries in decisions, notably size: larger firms are more likely to go into Phase II, but are also more likely to have mergers approved than smaller firms. These results are interesting but do not address the question as to whether the Merger Task Force (MTF) and the Commission are increasing economic welfare by preventing anticompetitive mergers while permitting only procompetitive mergers. It is this crucial area where Duso et al. tread. Below we also provide some preliminary results analysing several UK Competition Commission decisions in the same way as Duso et al. analyse MTF decisions.

Duso et al. (2003) also utilize stock market data but include the responses of the stock market prices of competitors. Economic theory (see Vives and Burguet[12]) shows that the impacts of mergers on consumers can be derived from the mergers' impacts on competitors. Basically, an anticompetitive merger will benefit competitors and harm consumers. A merger whose effect is to raise product or service prices will be met by stock market appreciation in the shares of firms competing with the merging entities. In this scenario, consumers are likely to lose.

However, where a merger is mainly efficiency-enhancing, competitors' market valuations will fall. Consumers are expected to benefit when efficiencies occur. Hence, one can evaluate the consumer welfare effect of a merger: it has the opposite sign of the market reactions in the share prices of competitors to merging parties. Duso et al. add changes in the market value of competitors' share prices to those of the merging parties in the Atkas et al. analysis. This analysis measures the 'abnormal' returns in share prices relative to general market indexes in 'windows' around the merger announcement. As information may spill before the actual press announcement and the stock market may take time to adjust to the news, a window of three to five or more days is normally taken around the actual announcement of the merger.

Duso et al. go much further than measuring the impacts of share prices on merging parties and their competitors. One can measure the efficacy of EU merger control. Since the social value of a merger is identical to the sign of the price change in the share prices of competitors, consumer welfare *rises* if the merger lowers competitors' share prices and *vice versa*. How 'correct' are MTF/EU decisions relative to competitors' share prices changes? Three types of errors are possible –banning procompetitive mergers (type I errors); imposing remedies on procompetitive mergers (weak type I errors) and allowing anticompetitive mergers (type II errors). Duso et al. analyse 73 Phase II decisions (completed by end 2001), and match this with 91 randomly chosen Phase I decisions.

Their results given in Table 9.2 are chilling. Including weak Type II errors, the Commission erred in 51 per cent of the cases. These errors are both ways and split quite equally between type I and type II errors. Of the 14 prohibited cases, four should not have been prohibited under the Duso et all methodology – two of the three successful appeals to the CFI in 2002 (Airtours; Tetrapack/Sidel) as well as GE/Honeywell.

Table 9.2   Measuring the efficacy of EU merger control

	Phase I		Phase II			
	6.1.b	6.1.b with remedies	8.1.	8.2.	8.3.	
Negative gains (procompetitive)	28	20	9	23	4	84
Positive gains (anticompetitive)	27	16	7	20	10	80
	55	36	16	43	14	164

Source: T. Duso, D. Neven and L.-H. Roeller, 'The Political Economy of European Merger Control: Evidence Using Stock Market Data', CEPR Discussion Paper DP3880, January 2003.

If half the decisions in this sample are wrong, is the Commission effectively flipping a coin? The answer is no. The Commission is not simply making random errors, systematic biases exist. These biases are of five types:

1. There is a large persistent error in blocking procompetitive mergers or imposing remedies on pro-competitive mergers.

2. If at least one firm is headquartered in one of the EU's five large countries, there is a 21 per cent lower probability of getting a procompetitive deal blocked; other things equal, there is a 57 per cent probability of this type I error.
3. There is also a large probability of type II errors – an anticompetitive merger being cleared – 40 per cent.
4. The probability of an anticompetitive merger being cleared falls when national rather than EU markets are defined. This is, however, not a 'good' bias, since the Commission errs in banning mergers or imposing remedies when unwarranted. Thus the probability of being found to be anticompetitive rises with national, that is, narrow market definitions.
5. Firms in the transport, storage and communications sector did worse than other industrial sectors in the sense that there is a significantly higher probability of getting a procompetitive deal killed than in other industrial sectors.

We have undertaken a small sample study of UK Competition Commission decisions taken since 2000. We follow similar procedures to Duso et al. We gathered data on the stock market performance of firms involved in cases referred to the Competition Commission, as well as share price data for their competitors. Note that we do not here look at the announcement of the merger itself, instead we concentrate on the date the merger is referred to the Competition Commission, the date the Competition Commission makes a decision, and the date of the public decision. The studies by Atkas et al. and Duso et al. infer that merger announcements forecast well the decisions by competition authorities. Indeed, Atkas et al. find some support for this long-term efficient market analysis. We feel that analysing share price movements of merging parties and their competitors at the time of major antitrust decisions gives a clearer picture of how markets felt competition and hence consumers would be affected. Following Vives and Burguet and the reasoning of Duso et al., if a merger is blocked, the share prices of the merging parties should fall. However, when would share prices of rivals also fall and when would they increase? There is correlation in the share price movements across an entire industry sector. Perhaps the merger signals other consolidations, all firms are in 'play'; hence if the merger is banned and competitor's share prices fall, then there is no further 'play'. Distinguishing between this and consumer welfare gains is difficult.[13]

We look to see if competitors' share prices rise or fall on referral and decision dates. Seven cases are shown in Table 9.3 but in only four of these can we find publicly listed competitors. There were in fact 38 merger referrals to the Competition Commission in this four-year period, but many of the cases shown in Table 9.3 did not involve two parties whose shares were traded

Table 9.3 Competition Commission announcements' effects on abnormal returns: event analysis results

	Relevant dates (referral, completion, publication)	Firms involved: **Merging Firms** Competing firms	Merger allowed?	3-day abnormal returns (% change in share price – % change in relevant index)					11-day abnormal returns (% change in share price – % change in relevant index)				
Case 1	12/11/99 n/a 18/4/00	**Vivendi SA BSkyB** Carlton Comms Granada Chrysalis	Yes		Viv	BSkyB	CC	G	Ch	Viv	BSkyB	CC	G	Ch
				R	−2.1	−1.5	9.0	5.9	2.5	−1.1	3.1	12.0	3.5	27.1
				C	n/a	n/a	n/a	n/a	n/a	n/a	n/a	n/a	n/a	n/a
				P	4.2	4.9	5.2	0.8	−7.2	−2.5	4.0	7.9	−5.1	−23.1
Case 2	23/2/01 12/6/01 10/7/01	**Lloyds TSB, Abbey National** Barclays Alliance & Leicester	No		Llo	AN	Bar	A&L		Llo	AN	Bar	A&L	
				R	−0.6	−2.0	−2.8	1.6		−0.8	−0.6	−3.5	−1.0	
				C	−0.5	0.7	1.5	0.5		−0.9	0.8	4.3	9.2	
				P	0.1	1.4	1.2	3.3		−2.4	2.1	−3.4	2.8	
Case 3	26/11/01 22/2/02 3/5/02	**Johnston Press, Trinity Mirror** Daily Mail News Corp.	50/50		JP	TM	DM	NC		JP	TM	DM	NC	
				R	−0.1	1.7	0.5	0.5		2.8	2.1	3.3	−4.6	
				C	−0.5	−0.7	−3.5	−1.7		6.0	8.5	−2.7	3.1	
				P	−1.4	−0.2	−0.6	−2.9		8.0	−5.0	−0.8	−3.8	
Case 4	10/1/02 24/4/02 23/5/02	**Neopost, Ascom Holding**	Yes		Ne	As				Ne	As			
				R	6.3	−7.1				7.3	−22.1			
				C	4.8	−1.3				9.8	0.7			
				P	1.2	−0.4				0.8	−15.4			
Case 5	14/1/02 13/5/02 14/6/02	**Coloplast, SSL International**	No		Co	SSL				Co	SSL			
				R	2.1	−2.3				1.2	−0.7			
				C	0.6	−1.4				−3.0	−3.3			
				P	−1.1	−3.6				−1.8	−3.9			
Case 6	9/5/02 27/9/02 22/10/02	**Group 4 Falck, Wackenhut Corp.**	Yes		G4F	WC				G4F	WC			
				R	0.5	−0.2				6.1	−3.3			
				C	0.9	8.2				−8.3	9.0			
				P	2.4	5.5				2.0	5.2			
Case 7	11/3/02 19/5/03 7/10/03	**Carlton Comms, Granada** BSkyB Chrysalis	Yes, with conditions		CC	BSkyB	G	Ch		CC	BSkyB	G	Ch	
				R	−4.4	−3.7	−6.5	−0.3		12.2	−5.3	12.1	−9.5	
				C	5.9	1.0	6.6	−0.5		25.3	−2.8	19.1	−4.9	
				P	18.1	−3.7	13.4	0.5		24.1	−3.1	16.3	−4.7	

Source: Author's calculations on stock market data.

on public markets. Three of the seven cases involve the media/newspaper sector and one involves banks.

The Lloyds–Abbey National proposed merger was referred to the Competition Commission on 23 February 2001. We begin with a three-day window. There was little abnormal movement in share prices on referral as the decision to refer was widely expected. The market did not expect the merger to proceed.

Nor was there any movement in either Lloyds' or Abbey National's share prices on the date the minister announced that the merger was banned. Competitors' share prices, however, did increase that day – consistent with an 'incorrect' decision; that is, these data are consistent with consumer welfare falling. However, all bank share prices appear to rise. The 11-day window shows different results. The referral lowers share prices for competitors – Barclays and Alliance and Leicester – much more than Lloyds and Abbey National. In the Duso et al. framework this suggests the market initially sees the potential for competitors to be worse off (and thus consumers to be better off) if the merger is approved. The date of the case completion but not public decision (6 June 2001) sees substantial positive abnormal returns for competitors – perhaps signalling that the banning of the merger would reduce market pressure on competitors. The public announcement sees mixed results – positive and negative abnormal returns. In summary, we see little consistent stock price indications here.

The referral of Vivendi–BSkyB's proposed venture sees strong positive abnormal gains for competitors in the three-day as well as the 11-day windows. Note that both Vivendi and BSkyB have negative abnormal returns in the three-day window, which turn positive in the 11-day window. On the date the venture is allowed, Carlton's share price rises significantly; Granada's is unchanged in the three-day window and falls significantly in the eleven-day window, while Chrysalis's stock price is down a substantial amount. This data are consistent with the market viewing the approved venture as somewhat procompetitive.

When the Carlton–Granada proposed merger is cleared in October 2003, the two merging parties' share prices rise appreciably and competitors' share prices fall in the 11-day but not the three-day window. The Duso et al. methodology suggests, then, that the merger is procompetitive and in consumers interests.

The proposed newspaper merger of Johnston Press and Trinity Mirror is allowed in part and banned in part. Stock market reaction is mixed. However, the actual decision lowers share prices of competitors, signalling either efficiencies or tough decisions on future newspaper mergers.

For three other cases we have not been able to identify publicly traded competitors who compete in the UK.

This analysis on the UK decisions is rudimentary, and we look at individual cases, not averages, across all cases. These spotty data indicate that the UK's Competition Commission's merger decisions are generally procompetitive.

3.2 The Lawyers' Perspective

The legal profession did not lose much time when they saw the opportunities offered by merger control. Lawyers inevitably applied their own thinking to policies and concepts. These concepts gradually acquired a meaning 'in law', somewhat disconnected from their initial source of inspiration and 'natural habitat'. The lawyer puts to (his own) music what politicians made of the ideas of the economists. After this multi-layered translation, the underlying ideas may well have become unrecognizable to economists. The lawyer must recognize that the usefulness of his construction depends primarily on the validity of the initial (competition policy) choices. The economists' analyses in the previous section shows that it was the time to check whether the train was still on track.

This being said, 'the law' also introduces into competition policy concepts that are vital for an acceptable enforcement. They must impact on the shaping of competition policy in general and merger control in particular. These concepts do, however, create their own challenges: legal certainty v. pragmatic flexibility, equal treatment and the risk of an excessively mechanical assessment of clauses the principle of proportionality, and so on. We must regularly examine whether the impact of these legal concerns does or does not alter the impact merger control can and should have.

However, even when a lawyer admits that the legal concepts may not become the main driver of merger control (or any other aspect of competition policy), he may not be willing to concede that all is well if individual economists have their way. There is bound to be a distinction between 'good' economics and 'bad' economics. But one cannot reduce all differences of opinion between economists to the choice between a correct and an erroneous application of economic theory. So: who makes the choice? Many welcome the greater impact economists now have on merger control and competition policy in general, but bringing the economist to the table is only part of the answer. Although lawyers and economists tend to agree that politics should not invade the daily running of competition policy, we need political consensus on the main options, and perhaps even more on how to choose between options, say between those formulated by economists holding different views. Consensus and acceptance do not usually come without debate. It is not good politics or governance to make too many significant choices implicitly, if not by coincidence, because they happen to be dictated by the views of the team in charge if the views of that team were never debated and the team only answers to itself. The courts only judge whether the Commission could reasonably arrive at a conclusion. They cannot be expected to rule (and should not rule) on the merits of specific economic approaches. One solution can be that the views of the chief economist are discussed before his appointment. The choice between schools and views is not even scrutinized *ex post* by the courts.

In order to avoid the traps of a competition policy driven by short-term political concerns, the political debate requires a degree of restraint that is not a common characteristic of politicians. Competition policy requires a stable environment in which the key options are not frequently put into question. This has several implications.

First, merger control, like any part of competition policy, will fail to have any positive effect if it lacks acceptance ('legitimacy'). In a world where culture continuously changes and where anti-globalists are not the only ones to question the values of the 1990s, acceptance cannot be taken for granted. The political platform must be cultivated. This is even more the case for merger control than for other chapters of competition policy. Mergers are boardroom issues. Their impact is analysed by the unions. Merger control has a much higher visibility than other chapters of competition law. Competition law is often judged by the efficiency of merger control.

The debate should strengthen the trust that, notwithstanding the lack of any tangible short-term benefits (except in respect of the fight against abuse of dominance), competition law helps to safeguard competition. And that competition in turn contributes to the system of 'pulls and pushes' that is still the best we know to bring the people a reasonable blend of goods, services and income.

Second, the debate should do so by fine-tuning policy making, rather than by a continued questioning of the fundamentals, which is likely to result in utter confusion. The debate should be about sound economic propositions. It should not open the door for a discussion about any short-term political concern dressed up as a competition policy option.

4.   RELY ON DOMINANCE (ANTI-ABUSE PROVISIONS)

4.1   What can Anti-abuse Provisions Contribute to Merger Control?

Economists' evidence, which is still underdeveloped, suggests that antitrust policy in general, and merger review in particular, is fraught with errors. The work of Duso et al. shows that if movements in competitors' share prices

Do we need European merger control? 217

are the standard, EU merger review bans many procompetitive mergers as well as allowing a number of anticompetitive mergers to pass through. Duso et al. survey this evidence and suggest a policy change to remove type II errors – mergers which are allowed but which may be anticompetitive. They suggest increasing the time period for Phase I merger review as the short period is likely causing the Commission to permit too many mergers.

We are not so worried about type II errors as we are about type I errors. After all, we do have Articles 81 and 82 that attack collusion and abuse of dominance. Errors which permit some mergers with anticompetitive potential can be rectified – we can catch anticompetitive behaviour later. Thus type II errors may not be too serious if actual anticompetitive behaviour resulting from mergers is tackled later on. We discuss the merits of *ex post* and *ex ante* remedies below.

Type I errors – the prohibition of procompetitive mergers or the imposition of unnecessary remedies – are real costs to society. There is no back-up as for type II errors. Once a procompetitive merger is banned, society loses. Hence our concern is on preventing type I errors. In addition, adding regulatory hurdles – increasing surveillance, extending Phase I deadlines – will increase, not reduce type II errors.

Our major point in this paper is that merger review, being a forecast of probable effects, is necessarily error-prone. The CFI in Tetra Laval v. Sidal stresses the inability of *ex ante* review to properly target potential future abusive conduct.

> The Commission had alleged that Tetra Laval would engage in a variety of leveraging practices, many of which the Commission conceded would also constitute an abuse of a dominant position under Article 82. The Court held that the Commission could not merely presume that Tetra Laval would engage in illegal conduct. While the Commission was entitled to take into account in its assessment of incentives to engage in anticompetitive practices, it also had to assess the likelihood of the rules being respected despite Tetra Laval's knowledge that such practices would be illegal, despite the likely financial penalties and despite the behavioural undertaking that Tetra Laval had offered.
>
> As the Commission had not carried out such an assessment, the Court therefore held that in its analysis of whether the Commission had demonstrated sufficiently convincing evidence of the likelihood and the consequences of leveraging, it could only take account of conduct which would (at least probably) not be illegal. The Court found that the merged entity's possibility for leveraging was 'quite limited' – non-forced bundling, objectively justified loyalty rebates, and non-predatory price reductions.

A basic question, then, is why are we attempting to ban mergers because they may lead to an abuse of dominance? Why not wait until dominance is abused?

The traditional arguments for preferring *ex ante* merger review as compared to *ex post* penalties are that merged entities cannot be split up; and we need to prevent anticompetitive industry structures from arising.

In our view, these supposed 'defects' of *ex post* control of behaviour must be compared to the defects of *ex ante* merger control. Too often, the comparison is made between the difficulties of unscrambling eggs, *ex post*, versus the ease of preventing anticompetitive omelettes *ex ante*. However, the growing evidence of the inability of merger authorities to identify anticompetitive mergers *ex ante* must be added to the debate. The evidence not only of academic economists but also of the CFI is that merger review is fraught with difficulties precisely because it is a forecast of the future. It therefore appears to us to give greater weight to judicious merger review in the first instance, allowing most mergers except those where most neutral observers would suggest that accretion of market power was the main object and outcome of the merger.

It is also not obvious to us why mergers cannot be undone. Mergers which do become anticompetitive could be subject to divestiture of large shares of assets. It is true that it is difficult to determine the set of assets to be sold off as well as the potential purchasers. However, the MTF now does this in Phase I and Phase II remedy negotiations. Therefore, doing this for mergers found to be anticompetitive down the road is not infeasible.

How would we identify the set of mergers that the MTF should consider as *ex ante* anticompetitive? Here much more research is needed. There is little analysis of mergers that are allowed – Duso et al. identify a set of mergers which, according to their methodology, could be anticompetitive. Have they been? Have prices risen, quality fallen; has consumer choice been reduced or innovation curtailed? As for mergers, where remedies have been imposed, have the remedies been successful in preventing abuse? We simply do not know how mergers do, in fact, alter industry behaviour. Much more concrete evidence is needed. The FTC in the USA in autumn 2002 announced more review of decisions, beginning by examining concentration in the industry before and after merger reviews. This is a beginning.

Therefore, we recommend that the Commission only prohibit mergers where *ex post* remedies would be ineffective if actual abusive behaviour showed up. That is, the DG-Competition should not excessively rely on theories such as collective dominance or portfolio effects to condemn mergers as potentially leading to or increasing dominance. Instead, they should wait for an actual *ex post* abuse to be identified. At this point, the merged entity is attacked. Since we have little evidence as to the *ex post* impacts of different types of mergers on consumer welfare, we should wait for actual evidence of consumers' welfare losses.

4.2 What Should Merger Control not do to the Fight against Abuse of Dominance?

A key concern of the Commission in recent years is that anticompetitive concentrations might not be caught by the Merger Regulation. As a result the Commission uses an ever-broader interpretation of the concept of dominance. We fear that this might seriously pollute the economics and the logic of the EU rules of competition in general and of the policy in respect of abuse of dominance in particular. The present Commission practice in merger control tends to assume dominance when parties have a 40 per cent market share on any relevant market. This raises questions with regard to the interpretation of the concept of abuse (of a dominant position) under Article 82 EC. Indeed, behaviour that is anticompetitive when parties have, for example, a 60 per cent market share may still be a healthy commercial practice for companies having a market share of 40 per cent (e.g. normally aggressive discount policies).

It is our impression that competition policy can be more balanced and effective if merger control is less directly linked with antitrust policy directed towards undertakings with a dominant position. The rewording of the substantive test is therefore to be welcomed, but the impact of the new wording on the evolution of merger control and the enforcement of Article 82 EC will require careful monitoring.

5. THE EU AND THE MEMBER STATES: WHAT ABOUT SUBSIDIARITY?

The proliferation of national merger control rules after the implementation of Regulation 4064/89 (the Merger Regulation) has confronted industry in Europe with the complications of multiple filings of transactions that do not have a 'European dimension' in the meaning of the Merger Regulation. For such transactions the parties can not benefit from the 'one-stop-shop' rule.[14] Multiple filings are particularly irritating and hardly ever produce any added value. The EU Commission's policy of decentralization of the enforcement of competition law,[15] and the member states' interpretation of subsidiarity mean that a fully integrated merger control policy is unlikely. What we need is at least damage control. In this contribution we can only point to some examples and suggestions. At the same time, this very limited evidence we have of UK merger decisions suggests more consistent decisions than at the EU level.

5.1   Focus on Genuine Competition Concerns

In the Green Paper the Commission proposed to address the issue of multiple filings by an automatic community competence in case a notification is required in at least three member states. In the recast Merger Regulation, the Commission relies on a system of reference by national authorities to the Commission or to each other. However, neither of these two approaches looks into reasons why there is a need to file in several jurisdictions. A significant percentage of multiple filings are caused by the fact that some member states can have jurisdiction without sufficient jurisdictional nexus. This may be due to particularly low thresholds, or to unilateral thresholds that do not take into account the position of at least two of the undertakings concerned on the market of that member state. A comparison of national thresholds shows that Finland defines jurisdiction in view of worldwide turnover without really appreciating the impact of the transaction on their national market, and Germany and Italy can have jurisdiction if only one of the two parties has a significant position on their national market.

The problem of multiple filings is therefore to some extent the consequence of inefficiencies in the competition laws of member states. Automatic community competence in cases of multiple filing requirements (as suggested in the Green Paper) risked importing these inefficiencies into the EU merger control regime. This additional burden on the Commission (and on the parties because the EU merger control rules have more burdensome notification requirements than some of the member states involved) is partly avoided by the system of references. There are nevertheless still good reasons to limit the need to notify in member states to cases that are really likely to affect their market significantly.

5.2   Transparent Rules on Jurisdiction

A system of references (like a rule granting automatic community jurisdiction in case a transaction needs to be notified in three or more member states) requires that the parties and the competition authorities can determine easily and with sufficient legal certainty whether a transaction exceeds the national thresholds for merger control. This requires in practice that national thresholds are easily verifiable. At least, the national merger control rules imposing a mandatory notification of concentrations should use readily identifiable and clear tests based upon turnover and not market share or local asset values. This is currently not the case in a significant number of EU jurisdictions.

Five of the national regimes in the EU with mandatory notification requirements have thresholds that are not conducive to a legally certain outcome with regard to establishing jurisdiction. Greece, Portugal and Spain have merger control rules with mandatory notifications and thresholds expressed in market share. In Ireland the notification of a transaction is required based upon very low asset or turnover thresholds and, as the geographical scope is unclear, the authorities often grant 'no jurisdiction' letters to remedy this ambiguity in the law. In Finland, the worldwide turnover thresholds are tempered by an imprecise requirement that the target have a 'physical presence' in Finland.

5.3 Harmonized Notification Procedures

The burden of multiple filings can also be reduced significantly by a harmonization of notification forms and time limits for notification. The German and Dutch notification forms for transactions that can be cleared in a Phase I procedure (not even a simplified procedure) illustrate how much more simple a form can be.

Perhaps even more important, a harmonization of notification requirements will enable undertakings to organize their internal databases in view of future notifications. Databases that are tailored to notification requirements will reduce the burden of notifications and improve the quality and comparability of data. Such harmonization is therefore not only relevant in case of multiple filings requirements. The benefits of such harmonization will survive a solution of the problem of multiple filing requirements.

NOTES

1. T. Duso, D. Neven and L.-H. Roeller, 'The Political Economy of European Merger Control: Evidence Using Stock Market Data', CEPR Discussion Paper DP 3880, January 2003.
2. R.W. Crandall and C. Winston, 'Does Antitrust Policy Improve Consumer Welfare? Assessing the Evidence', *Journal of Economic Perspectives*, 2003, pp. 3–26; reproduced here as Chapter 2.
3. The Schneider case was concerned with the markets for electrical equipment in buildings downstream from the medium voltage network (e.g. switchboards and terminal equipment). Some of the key issues were:
   - The geographic market for all product markets except the market for terminal equipment: while the parties agreed that the markets for terminal equipment were national, they argued in the administrative procedure that, as the Commission had decided in the Lexel decision (decision of 3 June 1999, case IV/M.1434), the markets for the other products were European. In the appeal procedure the parties dropped this argument but argued that if the markets were national, the Commission should have analysed each of the markets in the light of their specific characteristics.
   - The question whether the sales of manufacturers with vertically integrated distribution networks were in direct competition with manufacturers selling to independent wholesalers.

- The question whether the new entity would have a privileged access to distribution channels because of the quality and spread of their combined product range.
- The question whether their undisputed strength (if not dominance) on the French market resulted in a dominant position on the markets in other member states.
- Discrepancies between the statement of objections and the decision.
- Various legal issues concerning remedies and especially the question to what extent remedies must be assessed in the light of the abilities and resources of the purchaser.
- The authors were legal counsel and economic expert respectively to Schneider Electric.

4. The Tetra Laval case was concerned with the liquid food packaging sector. Some of the key issues were:

- The question to what extent PET bottles and carton drink boxes are part of the same market.
- The question to what extent the dominant position of Tetra Laval on the market for carton boxes would give the new entity leverage to make the customers of carton boxes switch to Sidel PET bottles.
- The assessment of the likely impact of the remedies proposed by the parties.

5. Earlier, the Court of Justice annulled in 1997 the Kali und Salz decision (cases C-68/94 and C-30/95) on an appeal by France. Other appeals were rejected: see the Gencor/Lonhro, Kesko/Tuko, and RTL/Veronica/Endemol cases. Worldcom/Sprint and GE Honeywell are still pending at the time of writing.
6. In a fast-track procedure the parties must limit the number of arguments and there is only one exchange of written observations.
7. G. Andrade, M. Mitchell and E. Stafford, 'New Evidence and Perspectives on Mergers', *Journal of Economic Perspectives*, **15**, Spring 2001, 103–20.
8. In the 1990s, economists began to examine empirically the reasons for authority decisions. M.B. Coate and F.S. McChesney, 'Empirical Evidence on FTC Enforcement of the Merger Guidelines', *Economic Inquiry*, **30**(2), 1992, 277–93. R.S. Khemani and D.M. Shapiro, 'An Empirical Analysis of Canadian Merger Policy', *The Journal of Industrial Economics*, **41**(2) (1993), 161–77.
9. Crandall and Winston, 'Does Antitrust Policy Improve Consumer Welfare?', (Chapter 2, this volume).
10. N. Aktas, E. de Bodt and R. Roll, 'Market Response to European Regulation of Business Combinations', working paper, 2003.
11. Duso et al., 'The Political Economy of European Merger Control'.
12. X. Vives and R. Burguet, 'Social Learning and Costly Information Acquisition', *Economic Theory*, **15**(1), 2000, 185–205.
13. Duso et al., p. 10.
14. Concentrations have according to Article 1 of Reg. 4064/89 a 'Community Dimension' where:

(i)   the aggregate world-wide turnover of all the undertakings concerned is more than ECU 5 billion; and

(ii)   the aggregate community-wide turnover of each of at least two of the undertakings concerned is more than ECU 250 million;

(iii)   *unless* each of the undertakings concerned achieves more than two-thirds of its aggregate community-wide turnover within one and the same Member State.

(iv)   the aggregate world-wide turnover of all the undertakings concerned is more than ECU 2.5 billion; and

(v)   the aggregate turnover of the undertakings concerned in each of at least 3 Member States is more than ECU 100 million; and

(vi)   in each of the Member States mentioned sub (v) at least two of the undertakings concerned have individually a turnover of more than ECU 25 million; and

(vii)   the aggregate community-wide turnover of each of at least two of the undertakings concerned is more than ECU 100 million;

(viii)   *unless* each of the undertakings concerned achieves more than two-thirds of its aggregate community-wide turnover within one and the same Member State.

15. Implemented in respect of Article 81 EC by Regulation 1/2003.

CHAIRMAN'S COMMENTS

Derek Morris

I would like to touch on two major points in the context of what the authors have presented and one desideratum on the UK.

The first point is this: the authors ask 'Why not leave any potential problems arising from a merger to be dealt with *ex post* through Article 82?' In other words, only deal with problems if they actually do emerge. That means you can get round the problem which they have identified empirically; that is, it seems as if many of these merger decisions are systematically biased in the wrong direction.

There is an alternative, perhaps slightly subtler, version of their proposition, which is simply to say that type II errors, that is, allowing anticompetitive mergers to go through, are much less serious than type I errors, that is blocking a procompetitive one, because if the authorities commit a type II error they have got another chance; they can subsequently use Article 82 to deal with the problem. But if they block a procompetitive merger, that creates a real and lasting detriment. So the implication would be that, if there is a merger regime, it should err heavily on the side of allowing mergers through.

So I would like to suggest an alternative answer. Clearly if Article 82 can deal with or encompass all the harm that a merger may generate, then the answer to their question 'Why not leave well alone?' is 'Why not indeed?' Why not leave well alone and pick matters up later? Or at least only block mergers where, to quote from their paper, 'almost any neutral observer would identify potential harm', in other words 'no-brainers'. (I think a 'neutral observer' is a mental construct: in 13 years at the Commission, I have never come across a neutral observer, but one understands what they mean here.)

The alternative proposition is, to put it at its boldest, that most of the potential dangers of a merger if they emerged *ex post* would never, and indeed could never, be addressed by Article 82. What is the case for that? Let me try it out on you. Competition is a process of rivalry, I know that is true because it says so in our guidance. It says it in the Office of Fair Trading's guidance as well. But it underlies a type of economic pluralism: there are different firms, different decision takers, different sources of choice and diversity and innovation, all of which competition fosters. Competition is also, of course, a spur to efficiency, to the bringing on of new techniques. It brings about excellence in all sorts of ways: effective working practices; knowing, meeting and indeed anticipating customer wants. Some mergers may dampen all of that and as a result generate less intense competition, changing the trade-off facing firms between the potential gains on the one hand of more intense competition, versus, on the other, a more 'live and let live' approach – 'I'll focus on this area, you focus on that area'. All this can engender serious welfare losses.

Now I hope that is a reasonably straightforward picture, but not one of the drawbacks that I have just mentioned could, in my view, be the basis of an Article 82 case. Try to think it through. Could you be fined for not being sufficiently rivalrous? For providing insufficient alternatives or choices? Or insufficient innovative thinking or new ideas or new products? Could you be fined, would it be against the law, or in breach of a prohibition, to be inefficient and your costs too high? Or for not doing enough to find out about your customers? You haven't attacked somebody else's niche in the marketplace and so on. I think that would be unlikely. I know I exaggerate here, but look at the terrible state of the East German economy before the Berlin Wall came down. When people went to look they didn't say 'Good heavens! These people have been carrying out all sorts of abuses, which in Western Europe would be prohibited by Article 82 – excessive prices or predation or exclusionary tactics or the like. What they had not been doing was competing, being rivalrous, finding new alternatives, new opportunities, new products and so on. There was a total lack of competition and that was what was so detrimental to consumer welfare.

Now I am tempted, purely for the purposes of discussion, to go one step further, and say that the whole point of Article 82 is to prohibit specific anticompetitive practices, of predation and exclusion, bundling and so on. But the proposition I put to you is that a robust merger regime is, to use almost universal best practice terminology here, to stop a substantial lessening of competition, *however* it might occur. That I think is why there has been such a problem with the ECMR, in that its origin had its beginnings in a read across from Article 82. I think that read across was flawed and that is why it has to be changed. Apparently, we are moving to a test of 'substantial impediment to effective competition, in particular dominance'. That very wording explains clearly that impediments to effective competition must be broader than dominance. Dominance is a subset in the new wording. So when the authors mention the advantages of keeping mergers and dominance separate, I tend to agree. I am not aware of any case under the UK merger regime where the Competition Commission has recommended that a merger be blocked because it anticipated illegal behaviour, that is, behaviour that would have been prohibited under Article 82 or would now be prohibited under Chapter 2 of domestic law. In fact there is a very interesting legal point. Could you ever, apart from where a company has committed a serial set of illegal activities, *expect* as a result of a merger that firms would conduct themselves illegally? I imagine if we ever based a case on that we would find ourselves up for judicial review quite rapidly. We would need to have some very strong evidence to anticipate illegal behaviour.

Take the Lloyds–Abbey National case that has been referred to. Essentially, that was about blocking an incumbent from acquiring a new entrant. If it had acquired the new entrant, and let's suppose there had been a series of similar acquisitions of other new entrants around at the time, there would have been fewer new ideas coming into the market, fewer sources of diversity and so on. Perhaps fewer ideas that threatened the incumbent because they came from different backgrounds, different marketing expertise and the like. But what abuse would there have been subsequently under Article 82? I find this difficult to answer.

So my first point is the proposition that there is a critical role for merger policy, irrespective of Article 82. There is also a practical point: if the authorities are dealing with a company in a merger, the company will want the merger to go through so it will assist the authorities. If you identify problems you will get companies' cooperation to find ways of dealing with the concerns that the Competition Authority has – maybe divestment, maybe a behavioural remedy, and so on. If you let the merger go through and then *ex post* tackle the company under Article 82, typically and for obvious reasons this will be bitterly opposed every step of the way.

My second point is on the evidential side – evidence that perhaps half of the cases looked at in Europe that were in the sample may have been the wrong decision. Two approaches were mentioned. I am not very impressed with the first type of study. There has for many years been and still remains a rather critical, methodological problem, which can be summed up in the phrase 'the defensive merger'. If companies perceive that they are operating in a sector where profits are falling, and the sector is under a profitability pressure; that can be (and this is not an extreme or eccentric case) a very strong reason why firms want to merge. They feel that it will give them some advantages that can deal with the deteriorating situation. If the merger goes through, that may mean the profit decline experienced by the firm is less that it would otherwise have been.

From the competitive point of view, the merger may be a good one that should have been let through, or it maybe an anticompetitive merger that shouldn't have been let through. But in either case, *ex hypothesis*, the profitability of the sector will go down. That is why the merger occurred, and therefore to suggest that the causality is the other way round is simply a methodological error. There is no way of telling whether the merger decision was correct or not by looking at the post-merger evidence on profitability. There are similar types of argument that can be applied, for example, to the consent decree data referred to.

The second type of study, for example the work by Duso et al., is in an entirely different category. Looking at the share price movement of *competitors* is potentially a much more powerful and methodologically sound approach. Just a few points on that.

First, as a preamble, I believe it was Lexecon who put forward this type of argument in the Airtours case, on behalf of Airtours, and the European Commission rejected the argument. They said that this sort of evidence is indirect, that a lot of noise surrounds it and that what is needed is a model that explains all the share price movements that are going on, not to try to pick off just particular price movements and claim to know why that happened. There were also problems about the impact of announcements by competitors and so on.

This area of analysis was not part of the appeal, and you might well conclude that maybe Airtours did not think it was robust, but I don't think we can infer that. Because it was not part of the appeal the CFI couldn't look at it but they certainly had some adverse criticism of the European Commission on the grounds of not having adequate reason to reject some other types of data, for example on market share volatility and they might have said the same thing here.

So maybe the European Commission has got 50 per cent of this case wrong, I don't know. Let me just make three points.

First, as the paper points out, other factors might influence what is going on, and two in particular. The first is this: the moment a merger is cleared, it is likely to mean that other players in the industry 'come into play'. If the authorities allow one takeover maybe they will allow others. It is quite rational to see competitors' share prices rise because of that factor. As the paper explained, the rule is simple on the basic model. If share prices of competitors fall, whatever the competition authorities' decision (block or clear), it was a sound one. But if share prices of competitors rise, then, on the basic model, the competition authorities' decision was the wrong one. But if bringing other people into play, in the wake of a cleared merger, pushes up competitors' share prices, there will be a systematic bias in this sort of analysis, telling you that the competition authorities got the decisions wrong.

To my mind there is a worse problem. One of the fundamental things we know about share prices and the stock market is that investors hate uncertainty. Time and again you find that once there is clarity, or more certainty, share prices bound upwards. If there is such an effect, then whenever a competition authority makes a decision and matters become clear, uncertainty is reduced, and share prices rise. As we have seen, a rising share price of competitors always tells you the competition authorities got it wrong, and so again there is a significant systematic bias towards saying this. They may have got it wrong, but we don't know this from the analysis, which is quite worrying.

Finally, on the UK figures, as has been brought out, interpretation is difficult. In one of the four cases looked at, the Competition Commission *partly* cleared the merger, and so it is extremely difficult to know what was going on, but what about the others? There is the problem that, sometimes, one competitor's share price goes up and another's goes down, so what do you infer? I also note that the evidence of the three-day window and the 11-day window can differ, so what happens there? What I think you get, consistent with what the authors said, is that two of the three decisions where you can get some clear answer appear to be correct, which is very gratifying. There are the Vivendi/BSkyB one and the Carlton/Granada one.

What about the Lloyds TSB decision? Well, if you look at the Barclays share price, it went down and so that decision was right as well. If you look at Alliance & Leicester, its share price shot up and so you'd say the decision was a wrong one. So was the Commission right in two-and-a-half out of three cases? Should I settle for that? The answer is 'no' because the Alliance & Leicester result is very significant. Let's ask what was going on there. Lloyds TSB, an incumbent firm, sought to take over Abbey National, a new entrant into SME banking. Alliance & Leicester was another new entrant. It seems to me extremely likely (though this is entirely speculative) that if Lloyds TSB had acquired one of these new entrants, perhaps with new ideas, new strategies, and so on, in the shape of Abbey National, they would have been in a very strong position to trounce any new initiatives by Alliance & Leicester. I think almost anyone looking at that situation would say that if the merger, as happened, was blocked and Lloyds couldn't get its hands on Abbey National, and couldn't get that advantage, then Alliance & Leicester's competitive position would be stronger. And what happened? Its share price went up. So here is a situation where a competitor's share price went up but the merger was procompetitive. The share price movement recognized that blocking the merger really did give chances not just for Abbey National but for Alliance & Leicester and maybe others coming along, to bring in new ideas and really threaten the position of the incumbents.

So the merger preserved scope for Alliance & Leicester to compete effectively and its share price went up. The point of that is not to boast that we got all three right. Rather the point is that while this sort of analysis can be used, as I have already said, this sort of example shows how incredibly careful you have to be in understanding what is going on at the time. There is also the practical point that the really important empirical data only come out when the decision of the authority is announced. That is precisely the point where the decision is made. The very data that could be useful, in this case the movement of Barclays, or Alliance & Leicester share prices, don't emerge until the decision is made.

What I would conclude from these two points is two propositions: first, that there are reasons to keep a powerful merger policy quite separate from the use of, and indeed the wording of, Article 82. Second, there is a case for the authorities trying to use financial data of the sort that have been presented in the paper, and I think that they can be useful but I would urge caution. You need to be very careful how you use them, where you can actually access them.

Index